RAJ RHAPSODIES: TOURISM, HERITAGE AND THE SEDUCTION OF HISTORY

New Directions in Tourism Analysis

Series Editor: Dimitri Ioannides, Missouri State University

Although tourism is becoming increasingly popular as both a taught subject and an area for empirical investigation, the theoretical underpinnings of many approaches have tended to be eclectic and somewhat underdeveloped. However, recent developments indicate that the field of tourism studies is beginning to develop in a more theoretically informed manner, but this has not yet been matched by current publications.

The aim of this series is to fill this gap with high quality monographs or edited collections that seek to develop tourism analysis at both theoretical and substantive levels using approaches which are broadly derived from allied social science disciplines such as Sociology, Social Anthropology, Human and Social Geography, and Cultural Studies. As tourism studies covers a wide range of activities and sub fields, certain areas such as Hospitality Management and Business, which are already well provided for, would be excluded. The series will therefore fill a gap in the current overall pattern of publication.

Suggested themes to be covered by the series, either singly or in combination, include – consumption; cultural change; development; gender; globalisation; political economy; social theory; sustainability.

Also in the series

Tourism and Borders
Contemporary Issues, Policies and International Research
Helmut Wachowiak
ISBN 0 7546 4775 7

Christian Tourism in the Holy Land
Pilgrimage during Security Crisis
Noga Collins-Kreiner, Nurit Kliot, Yoel Mansfeld and Keren Sagi
ISBN 0 7546 4703 X

Urban Tourism and Development in the Socialist State
Havana during the 'Special Period'
Andrea Colantonio and Robert B. Potter
ISBN 0 7546 4739 0

Raj Rhapsodies:
Tourism, Heritage and the
Seduction of History

Edited by

CAROL E. HENDERSON
Rutgers University-Newark, The State University of New Jersey, USA

MAXINE WEISGRAU
Barnard College, Columbia University, USA

ASHGATE

Published by
Ashgate Publishing Limited
Gower House
Croft Road
Aldershot
Hampshire GU11 3HR
England

Ashgate Publishing Company
Suite 420
101 Cherry Street
Burlington, VT 05401-4405
USA

Ashgate website: http://www.ashgate.com

British Library Cataloguing in Publication Data
Raj rhapsodies: tourism, heritage and the seduction of
history. - (New directions in tourism analysis)
     1. Heritage tourism - India - Rajasthan 2. Rajasthan
     (India) - Civilization
     I. Henderson, Carol E. II. Weisgrau, Maxine K.
     338.4'791544

Library of Congress Cataloging-in-Publication Data
Raj rhapsodies : tourism, heritage, and the seduction of history / edited by Carol E. Henderson and Maxine Weisgrau.
        p. cm. -- (New directions in tourism analysis)
     Includes bibliographical references and index.
     ISBN 978-0-7546-7067-4 (alk. paper)
     1. Heritage tourism--India--Rajasthan. 2. Heritage tourism--Social aspects--India--Rajasthan.
3. Rajasthan (India)--Description and travel. 4. Rajasthan (India)--History. I. Henderson, Carol E.
II. Weisgrau, Maxine K.

     G155.I4R356 2007
     338.4'791544--dc22

                                                                        2006039299

ISBN 13: 978-0-7546-7067-4

Printed and bound in Great Britain by Antony Rowe Ltd, Chippenham, Wiltshire.

Contents

Dedicated to the memory of Padmashri Komal Kothari, affectionately known to generations of scholars he inspired as 'Komalda'

List of Illustrations

Notes on Contributors

Nicolas Bautès (PhD, Geography, Paris 7-Denis Diderot University) is affiliated with UMR Société et Territoires UPPA (France) and the Institute for Social Service, Federal University of Rio de Janeiro (Brazil). He has done extensive fieldwork in India (Rajasthan, Gujarat) and Brazil (Rio de Janeiro) and is currently engaged in comparative research on urban revitalization in Rio de Janeiro and Mumbai.

John E. Cort (PhD, Study of Religion, Harvard) is Professor of Asian and Comparative Religions at Denison University. His research focuses on the Jains of western India, where he has conducted fieldwork regularly for two decades. He is the author of *Jains in the World: Religious Values and Ideology in India* (2001), and editor of *Open Boundaries: Jain Communities and Cultures in Indian History* (1998). He is the co-author, with Lawrence A. Babb and Michael W. Meister, of the forthcoming *Desert Temples: Sacred Centers of Rajasthan in Historical, Art Historical and Social Contexts*.

Tim Edensor (PhD, Sociology, Lancaster University) is Reader in Cultural Geography at Manchester Metropolitan University, John Dalton Building. His research interests include spatial analysis of tourism destinations, national identities, and industrial ruins in Great Britain. He is the author of *Industrial Ruins: Space, Aesthetics and Materiality* (2005), *National Identity, Popular Culture and Everyday Life* (2002), and *Tourists at the Taj* (1998).

Jason Freitag (PhD, Middle East Languages and Cultures, Columbia University) is Assistant Professor of History at Ithaca College. His research focuses on nineteenth century European constructions of histories of India, with emphasis on the work of James Tod. He is the author of 'Tod's Annals as Archive and History' in the forthcoming volume *Tod's Rajasthan*, Giles Tilltoson, ed.

Anne Hardgrove (PhD, Anthropology and History, University of Michigan) is Assistant Professor of History at the University of Texas at San Antonio. Her interdisciplinary scholarship focuses on history and identities in South Asia. She is the author of *Community and Public Culture: The Marwaris in Calcutta c. 1897–1997* (2002). Her current research project, 'The Global Erotic: Translating the *Kamasutra*' addresses issues about the global construction of sexuality, in light of the transnational circulation and flow of erotic texts and ideas.

Carol E. Henderson (PhD, Anthropology, Columbia University) is Faculty Associate and Research Associate in the Department of Sociology and Anthropology at Rutgers University, Newark. She is currently studying how the spaces associated with violent mass death in the Indian War of 1857 became sacred in memorial landscapes. She has conducted research on famines and environmental impacts on rural community interactions in the Thar desert, in Rajasthan. She is author of *Culture and Customs of India* (2002).

Christina A. Joseph (PhD, Anthropology, University of Rochester) is Part-Time Assistant Professor, Departments of Anthropology and Lifelong Education, Administration and Policy, University of Georgia, Athens, GA and a consultant to the Centers for Disease Control (CDC) in Atlanta, GA. She has conducted fieldwork in India and the United States on sacred space, pilgrimage, tourism and the Diasporic South Asian community. Her current research projects focus on journalist and author Katherine Mayo, and on the construction of national identity among second-generation Indian college students through cultural performances.

Jayasinhji Jhala (PhD, Anthropology, Harvard University), is Associate Professor of Anthropology at Temple University. He is the author of numerous articles on art and anthropology, nomadism, religious worship, indigenous interpretations of local culture, and ethnographic filmmaking. He has produced, directed and edited several ethnographic films that illustrate his interests in the cultures of India, Hindu marriage, and Rajput ideology and politics, while speaking to various issues in cultural representation and visual anthropology.

Elena Karatchkova (PhD, South Asian Studies, Moscow State University) is Senior Research Scholar, Institute of Oriental Studies, Russian Academy of Sciences in Moscow. She has conducted extensive research in Rajasthan on the ethnohistory of Princely States. Her current project includes research into both historic and contemporary constructions of Jaipur and Amber through travel writing and oral tradition discourses.

Usha Sanyal (PhD, History, Columbia University) is Visiting Assistant Professor at Wingate University, and part-time instructor at Queens University of Charlotte. Her research has focused on the Ahl-e Sunnat wa Jama'at (or 'Barelwi') movement in British India. She is currently working on madrasa education and reform, and textbook controversies in South Asia. She is the author of *Devotional Islam and Politics in British India* (1999) and *Ahmad Riza Khan Barelwi* (2005), and numerous articles on Islam in India.

Jeffrey G. Snodgrass (PhD, Anthropology, University of California, San Diego) is Associate Professor of Anthropology at Colorado State University. He is currently examining how the mental health and healing practices of Tribal (Adivasi) communities in western and central India are being impacted by deforestation. His book, *Casting Kings: Bards and Indian Modernity* (2006), and numerous articles, explore story, puppet theatre and tourism in Rajasthan from the perspective of Bhat participants, as mechanisms that reformulate and subvert caste relations. The recipient of numerous research grants, he has conducted extensive fieldwork in Rajasthan.

Maxine Weisgrau (PhD, Anthropology, Columbia University) is Associate Term Professor of Anthropology at Barnard College and Associate Adjunct Professor, School of International and Political Affairs, Columbia University. She has conducted fieldwork and research on non-government organizations and rural community interactions in Rajasthan for several years. Current research projects focus on the constructions of race in colonial India and Bhil ritual and identity. She is the author of *Interpreting Development: Local Histories, Local Strategies* (1997); co-editor with Morton Klass of *Across the Boundaries of Belief: Readings in the Anthropology of Religion* (1999); and author of the forthcoming *Experiencing Life and Death Before Birth: Global Anthropologies of the Unborn.*

Foreword

Tim Edensor

Until quite recently, academic writing about tourism was confined to a realm untouched by the flow of theoretical ideas from outside the area, suggesting that tourism was a discrete practice, unaffected by other social and cultural processes and hence a suitable subject upon which to construct distinct theories and typologies. Accordingly, theories paradoxically became both over-specific and over-general in identifying tourist motivations, kinds of tourists and tourist space. This hermetic situation has been thoroughly dispelled by recent attempts to incorporate studies of tourism within broader theoretical frameworks so that contemporary ideas about postmodernity, identity, globalisation and political economy may be exemplified in tourist contexts. Notions about performativity, embodiment, materiality and the non-visual experience of place are some of the more recent attempts to extend conceptions of tourism (see Baerenholdt et al., 2004; Crouch, 1999; Edensor, 2001, 2006; Franklin and Crang, 2001; Franklin, 2003; Obrador Pons, 2003; Saldanha, 2002).

This absorption of ideas from other disciplines has also been imperative because touristic impulses and tendencies now saturate many areas of everyday life, from the taking of virtual journeys to fantastic and exotic realms to the place-marketing, heritage production and consumption-oriented spectacles that suffuse so many areas, encouraging locals to gaze at the spectacular within their own neighbourhoods. It is becoming increasingly difficult to identify any destination that is not manufactured or sold as a desirable sphere within which tourists can investigate the novel and the familiar.

This huge, global expansion of tourism also reveals the extraordinarily ethnocentric conceptions that typified studies of the 'tourist' recent times. My own work, *Tourists at the Taj* (1998), which explores the varied tourist practices and understandings of place at Taj Mahal, in the city of Agra, located in Rajasthan's neighbouring state, Uttar Pradesh, where domestic tourists make up 80–90 per cent of the average annual total of visitors, was one of the very first accounts to explore how non-western visitors might practice tourism and understand symbolic sites. At this time, the generic tourist was typically understood to be a white, Euro-American, middle-class, implicitly male traveller in search of exotic sights and spectacles in an 'authentic' domain in which he wished to escape his over-controlled, inauthentic life but was doomed merely to experience 'staged authenticity' (MacCannell, 1976). Alternatively, according to more dystopian versions, he might be duped by 'pseudo-events' and false spectacles in his quest for 'otherness' (Boorstin, 1964). While such accounts endlessly recycled a rather sneering conception of the tourists, they also entirely ignored the tourisms of numerous others. This also became particularly clear to me in a Rajasthani context, when in search of a brief respite from my fieldwork at the Taj Mahal, I spent a few days in Mount Abu. Amongst the tourists wandering around this picturesque location, I was rather conscious of being the sole Western visitor, for Mount Abu is not on the typical western tourist itinerary but is a hugely popular spot for domestic honeymooners, celebrants and sightseers. This volume adds to recent attempts to right this imbalance, with its consideration of both Indian and Western tourists to Rajasthan.

Again, escaping the over-general conceptions of tourism, recent work on tourism has insisted upon the specificity of tourist sites in accounting for the forms of tourism which occur. The chapters in *Raj Rhapsodies* collectively highlight how there is an enduring need for researchers to explore the situated and the local, and avoid making sweeping depictions of the tourist. What is particularly evident in the cases studied here are the ways in which expansive global processes and flows are adapted, ignored, and expropriated and can be overwhelming in specific cultural contexts. This has the virtue of refuting certain assertions that globalisation is producing a bland cultural mulch, serial homogeneity and a victimised east – in tourism, as in other spheres – by showing how locals continually (re)negotiate their identities and economic strategies in response to the opportunities, cultural impacts, economic distortions and politics of tourism in unique and improvisational fashion. These chapters then reveal that tourism is situated, multiple, dynamic and lacks any essential or overarching quality. It changes continually and is a site of contestation, generating a host of competing discourses and practices about place, identity and culture.

Besides providing individual contexts which rebut over-general assertions about tourism, the volume also constitutes an impressive portrayal of the complexities of tourism in one geographical area, highlighting what is a rich and varied tourist scenario. The interdisciplinary approach, combining geographical, sociological and historical approaches, is able to bring out the multiplicity of tourisms and the value of different theoretical and disciplinary approaches in unearthing this complexity. Yet the book also brings out several important, interrelated themes that address issues about the broader effects of global tourism. I briefly discuss two such themes below.

The first key theme is that tourism relies on and continually manufactures representations of space and culture. Travel agencies, tourist brochures, websites, travel programmes and other promotional devices (re)produce an endless stream of images and textual descriptions of destinations which inform notions of place at a distance that are not mediated by what lies outside the photographic frame and may be apprehended by other senses *in situ*. And in addition, these same images may be reproduced in hotels, gift shops and tourist bureaux at the destination, and further 'captured' in the photography of tourists themselves, and the 'sound bites' and potted accounts may be textually replicated in the narratives of tour guides. At the Taj Mahal, the stories and descriptions of the mausoleum offered by guides who conveyed tourists around the estate and the narratives found in contemporary guidebooks remarkably mirrored the accounts of nineteenth century British colonial travellers. There was a recycling of the mythic foci grounded in these earlier accounts which evoked an 'Orientalist' imaginary of India, replete with moral judgements about the superiority of western 'civilisation', mixed with the desires evident in fantasies about romance, decadence, sensuality, cruelty, sex and the unfathomable.

It is clear that the tourist production of Rajasthan is similarly reliant on Orientalist narrative tropes and fantastic images and they sustain the ways in which tourism attractions are presented and selected. In fact, Rajasthan appears as a distillation of Indian-ness in which visions of an unchanging culture, sweeping sand dunes, elephants, bejewelled tribal women, elaborate royal palaces and notions of decadent luxury persist. The key focus of Rajasthani tourism, the royalty supposedly embodied by the romantic Rajputs, obscures the multiple other groups, sites, cultures and identities to be found in the state as tourists continue to tour the palaces of maharajas, go on camel safaris and buy specific craft artefacts. There is little reference to the present, the urban, the industrial, the intellectual, contemporary art and literature, the lower classes and castes, current politics and poverty, social inequalities and gender inequities, and the important histories of nationalist, subaltern and colonial processes. Strikingly, these themes are so powerful that those that do not fit are either neglected or squeezed into the frame. These exclusionary images and narratives constitute something of a spatial and temporal fixing in their neglect of other potential attractions and histories, somewhat akin to the way in which the tourist 'Golden Triangle' of New Delhi, Agra and Jaipur conjures up a series of interrelated spaces and times that foreground Muslim, princely, architectural and medieval themes which neglect the present and other historical eras, lower class groups, and non-religious and royal architecture.

We must be wary of condemning strategies to attract tourists to particular attractions, cities and regions because tourism is a hugely competitive industry at a global level; a key objective must be to produce an instantly recognisable place-image amidst the welter of tourist representations. In the selling of tourist representations on the world tourist market there is no room for multi-faceted images of place. What counts is the slogan, the immediately recognisable image, the reference to renowned historical places and characters and the trading upon established myths – which like all successful myths are available for widespread and varied interpretation. It seems clear that the stereotypical representations of Rajasthan continue to be peddled on the global market, including those which circulate on the Internet to produce a 'cyberorientalism.' Yet while such imperatives lead to the erasure of depth and complexity in representations of place, we should beware of drawing too many pessimistic conclusions from this recycling. For instance, the Internet is a vast, changing, complex space in which information is continually supplemented and erased, and because of its very structure which foregrounds a continuous linking to other websites, searches may often lead to the unexpected, the disturbing and the incomprehensible, and to other visions and stories that disrupt the romantic visions of tourists. In the cybersphere, information is less subject to official control and the orthodox may be supplemented by proliferating dissonance and excess.

Moreover, despite their seeming fixity, representations must be placed in their historical context. Longstanding travel depictions of Amber have been rife with romantic colonialist fantasies of the mystical, cruel and uncanny, and yet these have been posited in contradistinction to the mooted modernity of Jaipur. Ironically, with the advent of contemporary tourism, these distinctions have been erased and both cities now serve the desire to experience the archaic and royal. Whereas colonialism sought signs of modernity that reflected the 'enlightened' views of British colonialism to complement the fears and desires of confronting otherness, today's Western tourist tends to seek only an archaic otherness, traditional and wholly different.

Crucially, all representations are saturated with ambivalence, contradiction and contestation and so despite the tendencies to fix meaning, fixed meanings cannot hold at local levels. This volume powerfully reveals the contestations over meanings both those amongst locals, and those between local groups and western tourists. The painted havelis of Marwaris are certainly represented as part and parcel of Rajasthan's romantic heritage though as smaller, less splendid residences than the Rajput palaces, and yet by locals they are understood as emblems of an over-ambitious, status conscious group that has become too self-important. The meanings and practices associated with the shrine devoted to Sufi saint Mu'in al-Din Chisti in Ajmer have continually mutated and been contested by diverse groups, including many non-Muslims. It is presently being more intensively commercialised, which has led to further complaints from Muslims within the context of a globally contested Islam, and has been subject to the vicissitudes of the pared down, 'fundamentalist' Hinduism of the BJP and its associates who would deny the site its cultural and religious significance as part of the wider exclusive project to mark out others, notably Christians and Muslims, who are branded less-than-Indian. Likewise the temple complex at Osian is similarly multiply interpreted and used differently by Jains, Hindus and non-pilgrim tourists, exacerbated by their complex spatiality embodied in various gods, associated shrines and temples, where, for instance, certain deities may extend their influence across space whereas others are more specific to locale.

This struggle for meaning also applies to the vexed position of Brahmans in Pushkar, holy men caught between the economic need to attract tourists and maintain religious and cultural integrity, who must continually deal with western tourists desirous of exotic spirituality as well as the 'outsider' Rajputs who have entered the tourist economy and are thought to violate Pushkar's sanctity. A resolution of sorts is found in the ways in which the abjection of Hindu values to accommodate tourist desires is slotted into Hindu belief systems. This is to be expected in a degraded age of *kalyuga*, the last stage of a cycle of decay, a conception which allows criticism of policies conducive to tourist expansion whilst justifying the economic need to involve oneself in this distasteful business.

The second theme that emerges in *Raj Rhapsodies* is that the influence of tourism has the power to reconfigure local power struggles, often resulting in ongoing battles between different groups, and the attempts to maximise opportunities for gaining political and economic influence. There are, quite clearly, winners and losers in the global tourist industry. At the Taj Mahal, an imbalanced power struggle was evident between small and big traders, hoteliers and tour operators. When my initial research was carried out in 1993–94, a small bazaar area adjacent to the Taj, Taj Ganj, catered to backpackers and other poorer, younger tourists, providing cheap hotels, craft shops, and restaurants. Taj Ganj was an area where wandering traders might apprehend passing tourists in attempting to sell their wares. At that time, the larger hotel groups, restaurant owners and craft emporia sited in the old European quarter, a more spacious, green, well-kempt and regulated realm, were, in alliance with the local state, attempting to maximise their profit and control more informal tourist businesses by clamping down on itinerant peddlers and so-called shabby exteriors in the bazaar area. In addition, they were exerting a tighter control on the movements of large package tourist groups visiting the Taj who rarely strayed away from the large emporia, restaurants and official guides and into Taj Ganj which, however, remained lively with backpackers and traders. When I returned to the area in 2003, the hotels, cafes, shops and traders were in an advanced state of impoverishment as the large traders and local politicians had extended their control. More damaging than these strategies of powerful rivals however, was the decision of the Archaeological Survey of India, administrators of the Taj complex, to raise the admission charge into the Taj by 700 per cent, making a visit beyond the financial scope of western backpackers, the majority of these have since avoided Agra, dealing a devastating blow to these small traders and rendering the area quiet and depressed.

These battles between big and little tourist concerns, between 'official', preferred products and the unofficial, is part of broader regulatory and bureaucratic tendencies to close down tourist practices and experiences and confine the meaning of place so as to produce a more reliable, predictable, product (Ritzer and Liska, 1997). Such processes produce what I have termed 'homogeneous' tourist space in contradistinction to the 'heterogeneous' realms of bazaars and more informal tourist areas (Edensor 1998). The designation of specific areas in Udaipur as 'official' tourist spaces similarly marginalises those who might benefit from a less partial, more encompassing definition of tourism and its participants.

Raj Rhapsodies similarly charts the shifting ways in which actors use tourism to (re)present themselves, wield political influence, acquire status, make money and shape tourist space. Jodhpur's Maharaja Gaj Singh II, who has positioned himself as an emblematic symbol of Rajasthan for all the above purposes, is a multifaceted beneficiary of touristic theatre within which he is able to represent himself as both traditional and cosmopolitan. Likewise, the Bhats of Udaipur have attempted to use their folk art 'traditions' of puppetry and puppet-making, exploiting the desires of tourists in search of 'traditional' culture as a springboard to higher social mobility and status, primarily through the staging of extensive funeral feasts for dead fathers. Additionally, through the construction of modern houses and the display of prestigious commodities, they simultaneously re-present themselves as those who maintain 'traditions'. Moreover, through puppet dramas they attempt to reconfigure inter-caste relations to re-invent relationships with nobles which had never existed previously.

These power relations are also manifest in the relations between 'hosts' and 'guests' where stereotypes – of the overwhelmingly powerful western tourist and the helpless third world local or the sexually voracious male as threat to Euro-American female tourist – are grossly simplistic, for such relations are often contradictory, nuanced and shifting. The normative depictions in travel literature and cyber accounts of naïve and inappropriately dressed western women tourists subject to the oppressive 'eve-teasing' tactics of predatory men, chime with colonial fantasies of the dangers of western women in the face of uncontrolled sexualities of the colonised. However, instead, there are varied, shifting positionalities, forms of sexual encounter and relationship narratives through which such affairs are negotiated. Indeed, women tourists may often initiate such affairs and certain narratives partly reclaim power by suggesting that Indian male sexual potency fills the gap vacated by enfeebled, white, Euro-American males, so that opportunities are available for younger Indian men to consort with older western female tourists.

The above comments highlight broad issues that are part of the acceleration and proliferation of global flows and networks which centre upon places. These dynamic processes continually bring into question the character of place and culture, at once suggesting new forms of essentialism which emerge out of boiled down global tourist marketing strategies *and* increasing complexity, contestation and ambiguity. The complex foldings of tourist space with other places and times, the dense social networks that emerge, and the multiple connections with elsewhere foreground the processual nature of place. Places have never been singular and unchanging but global tourism has brought contests over place into sharper focus, for even as place becomes packaged for the tourist, its exclusions for tourists and locals alike emerge. Places and people are marginalised on tour itineraries and guided routes become tighter, excluding potential beneficiaries from the tourist economy and purifying tourist understanding of place. Yet new attractions, interpretations and tourist desires continually emerge in the quest for the novel and the peculiar, and economic strategies of marginalised groups to gain a share of the tourist pie emerge. Local people involved in the industry must act as cultural brokers, shifting between interpreting host cultures and learning about guests' cultures and transmitting this information back to their local peers. In consequence, they produce hybrid and changing cultural forms and practices, a syncretic process that is richly addressed in the chapters which follow.

References

Baerenholdt, J., Haldrup, M., Larsen, J. and Urry, J. (2004), *Performing Tourist Places* (Aldershot: Ashgate).

Boorstin, D. (1964), *The Image: A Guide to Pseudo-Events in America* (New York: Harper & Row).

Crouch, D. (1999), 'Introduction: encounters in leisure/tourism', in D. Crouch (ed.) *Leisure/Tourism Geographies: Practices and Geographical Knowledge* (London: Routledge).

Edensor, T. (1998), *Tourists at the Taj* (London: Routledge).

—— (2001), 'Performing tourism, staging tourism: (re)producing tourist space and practice', *Tourist Studies*, 1: 59–82.

—— (2006), 'Sensing tourism', in C. Minca and T. Oakes (eds.) *Travels in Paradox: Remapping Tourism* (Boulder, Colorado: Rowman and Littlefield).

Franklin, A. and Crang, M. (2001), 'The trouble with tourism and travel theory?', in *Tourist Studies* 1(1): 5 22.

Franklin, A. (2003), *Tourism: An Introduction* (Sage, London).

MacCannell, D. (1976), *The Tourist* (London: Macmillan).

Obrador Pons, P. (2003), 'Being-on-holiday: tourist dwelling, bodies and place', in *Tourist Studies*, 3(1): 47–66.

Ritzer, G. and Liska, A. (1997), '"McDisneyization" and 'post-tourism': complementary perspectives on contemporary tourism', in C. Rojek and J. Urry (eds) *Touring Cultures: Transformations of Travel and Theory* (London: Routledge).

Saldanha, A. (2002), 'Music tourism and factions of bodies in Goa', in *Tourist Studies*, 2(1): 43–62.

Acknowledgements

This book is the culmination of individual scholarship, fieldwork, collaboration, formal and informal conversations, and the enormous support and cooperation of scores of people, and institutions, in the United States and in India. We must begin however by thanking our contributors, including those whose works could not be included in the final volume. By all of you sharing your insights, research, and scholarship with us, we benefited greatly from the varied and multiple perspectives reflected in all the works that we read in preparation for this publication.

We particularly want to thank the many participants in the Rajasthan Studies Group. David Magier has been particularly helpful in his capacity both as 'list master' to the RSG and Director, Area Studies at Columbia University. Owen Lynch, Charles F. Noyes Professor of Urban Anthropology at New York University, contributed many suggestions for us to follow up in developing ideas for this project. Frances Taft, President of the Rajasthan Studies Group, was instrumental in the early stages of this project by suggesting contributors, organizing a session on this topic at the Fifth Annual Conference on Rajasthan Studies in Jaipur in 2001, and participating in a round table Discussion on tourism in Rajasthan at the South Asia Annual Meetings in Madison, Wisconsin in 2002. We would like to thank her and especially, the Rajasthan Conference organizers, Surjit Singh and Varsha Joshi of the Institute for Development Studies and of the Institute of Rajasthan Studies, in Jaipur, for initiating discussion of this topic. Those discussions with all the participants and audience members in these various conference sessions were invaluable in the evolution of the vision of this publication.

We both want to acknowledge the tremendous support and inspiration of two of our mentors at Columbia University: Ainslee T. Embree continues to amaze us with his encyclopedic knowledge of South Asian history, as well as his ability to zero in on the absolutely perfect question that pushes inquiry forward. The late Morton Klass, Professor Emeritus of Anthropology at Barnard College and Columbia University was, before his untimely death, a continuous source of inspiration and commitment to the practice of fieldwork in all its permutations and transformations.

Our respective fieldwork sites and the people who so generously opened their homes, minds, and hearts to us in Rajasthan are foundational to this work. Maxine Weisgrau therefore gratefully acknowledges the unending hospitality of people in and around Udaipur, Gogunda, Bagadunda and Solaria; the members of Ubeshwar Vikas Mandal and Sewa Mandir continue to inspire my present and future study. And to Roma and B. N. Bhatia a special thanks for your continuing friendship. Carol Henderson owes a tremendous debt to the families of Surani and Borunda villages in

Jodhpur district, whose warm hearts and generosity, over two decades, have inspired my work to explore new directions, long before I began to think about tourism. None of my visits to this district could have been possible without the friendship and support of the family and friends of Komal Kothari in Jodhpur, Jaipur, and Udaipur. In New Delhi, I am indebted to the ongoing friendship of the P. Singh family.

The editors, readers, and coordinators of this project at Ashgate Publishing have been invaluable in their professionalism, enthusiasm, and attention to detail. Dimitri Ioannides, editor for Ashgate's *New Directions in Tourism Analysis* series, gave us particularly careful and insightful comments, as did the anonymous reviewer of our project proposal.

Ariana Barth has been an invaluable right hand in the final editing and production of the manuscript, and we thank her for her care and devotion to this phase of the project. We also wish to acknowledge with appreciation Russell Povel's timely creation of the maps used with this volume and helpful assistance with the images used in this book.

Our respective spouses, Scott Horton and Ron Palazzo, are gratefully acknowledged for supporting our endless weekend and holiday editing and writing sessions spent with this project.

Introduction

Raj Rhapsodies, Tourism and Heritage in India

Carol E. Henderson and Maxine Weisgrau

In the late 1980s this book's editors took a field trip together to India's major cities of Jodhpur, Jaipur and Udaipur, and stayed for one night at a five-star luxury hotel in one of the converted royal palaces. This region was in the grip of a devastating drought, the result of a monsoon failure. As field anthropologists working in rural communities, we both had first-hand knowledge of the toll on human beings and livestock of the recurrent droughts in communities underserved by state and national infrastructure. We were therefore stunned to see, in the bathrooms of this hotel catering to well heeled foreign and domestic tourists, signs explaining that to get comfortably hot bath water, just open the tap and let water run down the drain for about ten minutes. Even to anthropologists reluctant to study what was then perceived as a frivolous topic like tourism (see Crick 1989; Nash and Smith 1991; Wilson 1993), this disregard for local needs, contrasted with the perceived requirements of the luxury tourist, could not be ignored.

Increasingly, Rajasthan has been marketed as the most heritage-laden, traditional, and authentic of India's states. A trip to Rajasthan becomes a trip to the 'real' India. In one sense, this vision of Rajasthan is ennobling, because it highlights moments designated as culturally pride worthy. But this vision also demeans, for it deletes, omits, and obscures salient features of Rajasthani life. This book demonstrates that many of the 'authentic traditions' dear to tourist guidebooks have their roots in colonial encounters, as reified in Anglophone traditions through the writings of nineteenth- and early twentieth-century observers. We argue instead for the contingent nature of tourism representations. We view tourism through the lens of shifting and negotiated power relations and demonstrate how tourism narratives obscure or remove from view the economic and social fracture lines in contemporary society, such as in Rajasthan, the power struggle by peasants and members of other subaltern groups against feudal overlords in the twentieth-century and the successful achievement of democracy in former regimes. These forms of resistance contrast with the enthusiasm for royalty exhibited by tourism guidebooks.

In the past two decades, Rajasthan state (population 50 million) began its emergence as one of India's top tourism destinations. Our trip coincided with efforts by state and local actors to improve tourism infrastructure and to make Rajasthan into an appealing destination for travellers. Tourism had not been on our respective

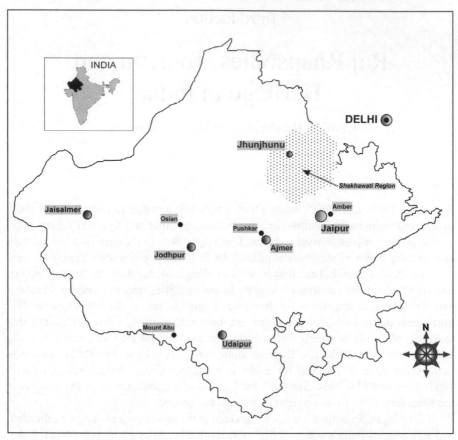

Map I.1   Map of Rajasthan: Sites discussed in this book

research agendas. Maxine Weisgrau was engaged in a study of nongovernmental organizations (NGOs) and women's issues in central Rajasthan. Carol Henderson, following research on droughts, had initiated a study of sheep flock management, wool production, and woollen textiles development in the western Thar desert (see Weisgrau 1993, 1997; Henderson 1989, 1998, 2002). We would subsequently discover that issues of tourism development intertwined with our work.

In a sense, this book was inspired by that sign in a room in a luxury hotel, for it prompted this inquiry into the political economy and cultural politics of tourism, with all their complexities, potentials, and inequities. It made us aware of the multiple and competing discourses on 'tourists' as opposed to 'non-tourists;' of local *versus* global actors, and of the domestic and international constituencies which would observe, comment on, and participate in tourism activities. It became increasingly necessary to us as long-term observers of Rajasthan to regard tourism seriously as an instrument of political economy, as well as an obvious force in the social and economic transformations linking India to a global economy of consumption and multiple forms of representation. Tourism income, in a growing state economy, is a precious commodity, and like each drop of water in a drought-prone environment, has many players battling over its control. This is a scenario enacted across the globe, as developing economies seek to exploit their tourism potential (Britton 1982; Wood 1993).

Throughout the book, each of our contributors asks a series of questions: What different messages are sent through the medium of tourism encounters? How do these messages confirm dominant images of India, and in what ways do they mute or render invisible alternative visions? What is the role of history, colonial domination, and Orientalist discourse on the figuring of contemporary tourism? How does the allocation of spaces for tourism represent local conflicts and struggle over resources? How do existing forms of identity, hierarchy and domination play out in the newer struggles over tourism resources?

Today, at least one third of all international tourists to India come here, and Rajasthan accounts for almost one-third of the nation's tourism earnings. Ironically, despite this significance there have been few studies – outside feasibility and planning documents oriented to servicing this industry – of how tourism intersects with travellers, entrepreneurs, and residents of tourism destinations in India. The academic literature has rarely documented how Indian groups conceive of tourism, exploit it, or make it their own. Although the issue of heritage tourism looms large in European and North American tourism discourse, it has hardly been touched in the study of tourism in India, and less so for Rajasthan.

As plans for this volume evolved, we realized the necessity of an interdisciplinary approach. The characteristic that unites all our contributors is fieldwork. Each of us has spent extended periods of time in Rajasthan, and continues to conduct research in various parts of the state. Some of our contributors have carried out research since Rajasthan began its tourism boom, while others have matured as scholars along with it. We have all thus experienced elements of the tourism industry in tandem with our research, and in ways that often challenged our perspectives.

Our contributors have converged on areas of interest, and have brought together the tools of multiple disciplines in a comparative framework. In the study of tourism, the interdisciplinary stance calls for an epistemology of knowledge that allows us to approximate the processes and perceptions of tourism's elites and subalterns. Whether as producers or as consumers of tourism services and products, the actors in this complex landscape create a historically and politically situated moment in the ongoing processes that create and constitute tourism.

The contributions to this collection address how 'heritage' images have become the familiar icons of travel in India. We are particularly interested in the potency and uses of the concept of 'heritage' – with its presumed imprimatur of historicity – as a marketable commodity in the tourism industry, how it enters into the mobilization of social capital among local actors, and its links to ongoing societal transformation. But the use of history in the tourism encounter requires the editing out of much of its realities; battles are heroic but in the historic imagination bloodless. Subalterns are ready to die for their leaders; and women are nonexistent in the representation of these struggles, except occasionally as willing suicides on the funeral pyres of their husbands (Edensor and Kothari 1994; Erdman 1994).

Rajasthan's emergence as India's 'heritage' state is the imaginary counterpoint to the India of the high tech enclaves such as Bangalore, India's Silicon Valley, or the exploding urban centres of Delhi, Mumbai and Calcutta. Rajasthan epitomizes the 'real' India, where – tourism marketing says – the cultures and lifestyles of the past have been transmitted intact, unchanged, and available to the tourist gaze (Urry 1990).

Inventing Heritage

Recent critical approaches examine the impact of Orientalist and Western perceptions of India in tourism discourse (Mills 1991; Bhattacharyya 1997; Mohanty 2003). The familiar images of sand dunes, palaces, forts, and elephants, all associated with Rajasthan, have become tourism icons of travel in India, rivaling the Taj Mahal as the global image of India (see Edensor 1998; Ramusack 1995). These images are so prevalent that they are used even in airline and tourism advertising for destinations not including Rajasthan.

During the past two decades, the concept of heritage has become a major point in both the production and the consumption of tourism destinations worldwide. Heritage, as Chhabra, Healey and Sills state, '...is representative of many contemporary visitors' desire...to directly experience and consume diverse past and present cultural landscapes, performances, foods, handicrafts, and participatory activities' (2003:703). Social scientists conceive of heritage as a continuously recapitulated and reformulated story that people tell about themselves, others, and the past. Tourists flock to sites such as Colonial Williamsburg in Virginia, the Ghanaian slave castle of Elmina, and Britain's Stirling Castle to relive what each of these destinations represents as a historic reality, but is in fact at most a partial or contested perspective – if a historic reality at all (Handler and Linnekin 1984; Gable et al. 1992; Bruner and Kirshenblatt-Gimblett 1994; Bruner 1996; Edensor and Kothari 1994).

Some scholars have interpreted this desire on the part of travellers to consume the past as a response to modernity, a search for tradition and authenticity in the musty byways of one's own and others' cultures (MacCannell 1979; Breckenridge 1995), even when the traditions in question have to be invented (Hobsbawm and Ranger 1983). Other scholars more recently regard the emphasis by tourists on heritage as a post-modern performative bricolage, which morally situates the tourist, at least momentarily, with respect to the claims and stories told by others (Kirshenblatt-Gimblett 1995; Bruner 2001).

Scholarly definitions diverge from the tourist and conventional popular wisdom that situates heritage as an inherent, stable, or relatively unchanging attribute of a society, a people, or even, an individual. Essentializing claims about history and related forms of identities are common in tourist discourses (Echtner and Prasad

Figure I.1 **Downtown Jaipur after 'Operation Pink' unified storefront appearances. Many of the signs are English words transliterated into *deva nagari* script.** *Photo courtesy of Elena Karatchkova.*
All rights reserved.

2003). The representation of heritage as something that is static and timeless, derived since time immemorial from a distant past, is attractive to tourists, in part because of its reassuring familiarity. They want to believe these claims are true and if not, to be able to suspend disbelief sufficiently as to enjoy the illusion of truth. These claims are readily apparent in the tourism discourses on India in general and Rajasthan in particular, which rhapsodize these entities as traditional, 'timeless' and 'unchanging.' These claims are scrutinized throughout this volume, for they too have histories.

Heritage itself, as this volume explores, is a prized cultural commodity in the making of tourism destinations. Although tourism marketers energetically attempt to define the boundaries of the destination (Chambers 2000), tourists bring their prior motivations, knowledge, and ideas to sites and participate in the construction of its meaning (Bhattacharyya 1997, Chronis 2005). Power relationships inherent in such representations were explored by Valene Smith and contributors in the pioneering edited volume *Hosts and Guests* (1978; 1989), as systems of binary oppositions: developers against locals; elites against non-elites; 'experts' against non-experts; and even, scholarly investigations into popular claims, as against the claims themselves. More recently, scholars have discarded this binary framework in order to focus on multiple forms of power and competing claims.

One of this volume's editors (Henderson) recalls on her first fieldwork in Rajasthan in the early 1980s, the near-universal silence by villagers on 'what life was like before Independence, under rule by the Maharaja', when many rural seniors were then young women and men. 'We used to run and hide', was the laconic comment of one distinguished elder gentleman, when asked how he and others dealt with the then-Maharaja's agents. Ann Gold and Bhoju Ram Gujar, who take up this issue in a recent work (Gold and Gujar 2002), also found villagers were reluctant to speak of the 'bad old days.' The stories they collected of this era comprise a disheartening list of exploitation, oppression, sexual harassment, and suffering. However, Weisgrau's Bhil informants occasionally wistfully recalled what they claimed was direct access to local rulers, as opposed to today's impenetrable bureaucracy. Clearly, none of these story-tellers is engaging in 'feudal nostalgia.' No matter how much tourism discourse trumpets the 'old days', local subalterns recall the 'heritage period' as one of exploitation and oppression.

Tourism discourse transforms Rajasthan from the poverty-stricken state lagging in most socioeconomic indicators in economic development reporting, into a colourful panorama of ancient customs, romantic history, peoples, and monuments. The state's economic and social progress, such as new industries, urban development, and entrepreneurship, are edited out of the tourist encounter, as is the rural reality. What is valued is the imagined 'old.' That which was once locally and proudly heralded as 'modern' is now bulldozed to create an imagined vision of the past, as occurred in Rajasthan's state capital of Jaipur in 2000, with the destruction of retail stalls in the city centre to restore it to its 'old' look (see Chapter 3).

Growth in India's economy, particularly rapid following the economic reforms of the early 1990s, enhanced India's appetite for domestic tourism. India's middle-class (usually referred to as the top 10 percent of its population) represents a group that is elite by Indian standards. They, too, experience India's monuments; enjoy a Himalayan vacation or honeymoon; have a seaside experience; and as urbanites with limited contact with rural life ways, through tourism experience the 'real' or 'authentic' India. Parents want their children to visit important sites associated with Indian and family history. Retired persons often dream about a pilgrimage tour or retreat. Farmers and others who live in rural areas similarly find ways to travel, combining a religious duty, such as a trip to Varanasi, Braj, or Rishikesh, where important funeral rituals may be completed for deceased family members or personal pilgrimages be carried out, with sightseeing and other activities that any tourist recognizes (Gold 1988). Non-resident Indians (NRIs), Indians with legal residence and/or citizenship outside India, who return to India regularly are also a major market for travel and tourism.

Each of these groups comprises somewhat separate constituencies of tourism, with different motivations, desires, needs, and perspectives. Each group further breaks down, by gender, by age, by socioeconomic status, by religious affiliation and personal life-goals. Each may have distinct understandings of 'heritage.'

Studying heritage tourism (also called 'cultural tourism') illuminates the collusion and competition among issues within the intersection of gazes. In this collection, therefore, tourism is theorized as an intersection of gazes, of multiple and conflicting narratives. Each chapter's exploration of tourism destinations and the peoples, objects, and events encountered show shifting political and economic trends, historical contingency, cultural understandings, and a changing construction of how meaning may be embedded in the practices and identities of tourism.

Contextualizing Tourism in Rajasthan

Tourism is India's third highest foreign exchange earner, behind information technology and textiles, and accounts for 5.6 percent of GDP, according to the government of India's Central Statistical Organization (Federation of Indian Chambers of Commerce and Industry n.d.). According to Indian government statistics about 3.9 million foreign tourists visited India in each year between 1998 and 2005. Domestic tourism dwarfs this figure, with over 160 million visits annually according to the Planning Commission of India (n.d.; see also Department of Tourism, Govt. of Rajasthan 2002). Geographic distance from European, Japanese, Australian and North American consumers also tends to position India as a destination for upscale leisure travellers. Each foreign tourist in India represents considerable income potential because of duration of stay as well as daily expenditures (Thadami 1999).

India received great publicity in western countries through the highly-publicized visits of Russian Premier Nikita Khruschev in the mid-1950s, that of the Queen of England in 1961 – the first by a British monarch since Indian independence in 1947, and by U.S. President Dwight D. Eisenhower in 1959. The intense publicity in the United States generated by the goodwill visit to India by U.S. First Lady Jacqueline Kennedy and her sister Lee Radziwill in 1962 put not simply India, but Rajasthan on the tourist map for Americans. Mrs. Kennedy visited Jaipur and Udaipur, where the Lake Palace hotel had just begun to open its doors to guests. The 1968 visit by the Beatles is credited with stimulating youth interest in India travel.

Despite its tourism income, Rajasthan continually falls in the bottom third of India's national statistics on household income and standard of living. One night's stay at a five-star luxury palace hotel exceeds the annual income of a typical Rajasthani family. This situation has led to a dual economy effect. There is the tourism economy, and there is the local economy. In the local economy, public relief works geared to extreme poverty levels presuppose that a person can live on the equivalent of U.S. $1.00 a day (around 50 rupees). Even a backpacker or budget tourist far outspends the weekly wage in the local economy.

Rajasthan emerged as a significant tourism destination in the 1990s. Throughout this decade, domestic and foreign tourism arrivals in the state expanded, on average between five and seven percent per year (investrajasthan.com, n.d.). This greatly changed opportunities in Rajasthan. Prior to the 1990s, deficient transportation infrastructure, hotels, electricity, communications and water supplies made tourism difficult, outside a few urban centres such as Jaipur or Udaipur. The lack of electricity for air conditioning limited the tourist season for all but the most intrepid or affluent traveller to the two or three winter months. The 1990s' considerable road, rail, electrical and water infrastructure development did much to bring Rajasthan's tourism potential up to par with other parts of India. Opportunities for tourism improved with privatization of air travel and banking. Eased restraints on access to foreign capital by corporations and individuals further promoted investment in tourism, primarily benefiting India's upper and middle classes.

These processes fuelled the domestic demand for leisure travel. The top Rajasthan destinations for domestic tourists in 2001 were Mount Abu (1.28 million); Ajmer (1.27 million); Pushkar (865,000); Udaipur (663,000); Jaipur (656,000); Jodhpur (383,000) and Nathdwara (319,000). International destinations show a different pattern of visitation. The top destinations for foreign tourists in order are: Jaipur (173,000); Jodhpur (70,000); Udaipur (57,000); Ajmer (54,000) and Jaisalmer (47,000) and Pushkar (46,000) (Indiastat.com 2006).

In the late 1980s and 1990s, a fashion for what was called 'ethnic' or 'tribal' chic contributed to interest in western India – Gujarat, Rajasthan, and parts of Maharashtra. Rajasthan – in part because of poverty, lack of purchasing power by residents and lack of penetration of rural markets by manufactured goods – retained active communities of craft producers, whose work soon adorned New Delhi and Mumbai drawing rooms. It was a short step from purchasing these in 'ethnic arts' emporia in urban centres to penetrating Rajasthan in search of fine artisanal goods.

Greater investment in education infrastructure by the government, and the omnipresence of NGOs, have increased rural awareness of the feasibility of tourism entrepreneurship. During this period, many Rajasthan-based NGOs developed outlets for crafts and other tourist-related enterprises. One concept exploited by many NGOs is to create marketing units for local products that otherwise would find no buyers, and thereby to support indigenous crafts and arts industries. A variety of NGOs are now partnering in various aspects of the tourism industry, providing modest opportunities thus far for participation in the tourist economy in ways that claim to be less exploitative than in other segments of the industry, through 'fair price' policies or profit-sharing mechanisms.

Rajasthan's tourism industry highlights the considerable stock of what are termed heritage properties. These are castles, palaces, and large residences being assimilated to the discourse of heritage, and refurbished to meet tourist needs. Control of these built heritage sites is unequally distributed among the population. In many smaller destinations, and in a few large ones, a single family controls the heritage site. Quasi-monopolistic control over these sites affects entrepreneurial investment by others, and often depresses the bargaining position of locals, who suffer from a depressed wage economy.

Overall, the lack of income potential in the surrounding rural economy contrasts dramatically with the tourism economy. In rural areas there are large underemployed or unemployed populations, particularly in the off season for agriculture which in the non-irrigated agricultural zones coincides with peak periods of tourism. This seasonality and underemployment in agricultural work provides a continuous flow of unskilled labour to tourism employers. During drought years, which occur much more frequently than rural people would like, this labour base expands dramatically and so does the struggle to capture segments of the tourism market.

Package tour operators and owners of the large resort-like properties attempt to limit others' access to 'their' tourists: gates, guards, and guides, separate transportation networks and facilities, create a moving 'bubble' within which the tourist may selectively experience Rajasthan. Those who move outside this infrastructure, such as budget or backpacker tourists, often complain about the seemingly endless stream of people offering various services and products. What these independent budget tourists do not perceive is that the same processes that produce the – to them – delightfully inexpensive meals, travel and accommodations, about which they frequently boast in their Internet travel blogs, also impel large numbers of Rajasthanis toward tourism entrepreneurship, where one good day (with such a tourist) can make up for days or weeks of rejection elsewhere.

Heritage and the Reconstitutions of Colonial History

Seen in historical perspective, the earliest travel writing on Rajasthan in the Euro-American tradition appeared during the colonial period and is coloured by its authors' experiences, as filtered through the lens of Orientalism (Said 1978; Mohanty 2003). Although what is now Rajasthan was a congeries of independent princely states (then called Rajputana), British political agents, administrators and military personnel shaped governance, administration, fiscal management, and especially visibly, the built environment (Banerjee 1980). Many of the heritage destinations in Rajasthan, for example, clearly bear the imprint of Victorian and Edwardian aesthetics, reflecting their purpose in accommodating the European presence.

Most of Rajasthan was not officially part of the British Raj. Every eighteenth and nineteenth-century European visitor encountered the border controls exerted by the princely rulers and occasionally, tribal groups, throughout western India. This factor contributes to the British imagining of these states as a periphery occupied by unpredictable, wild peoples. The British tendency was to identify with the local ruling elite, such as James Tod 'the man who loved the Rajputs'(Kipling 1899:17), and to demonize the tribal and peasant communities whose voices are largely absent from these early travel narratives.

The history of Jaipur, today Rajasthan's capital with a population of around two million, encapsulates many of the themes and ironies of tourism discourse in Rajasthan.

At the end of the nineteenth-century, British travel writing touted Jaipur as the height of modernity, a theme that appears to have originated around 1820 (Jaipur was founded in 1728). The late nineteenth-century administrator Thomas Hendley suppressed Rajasthanis' role in producing a modern city in order to highlight the British role in Jaipur. By Independence (1947), guidebooks marketed Jaipur as an exemplary traditional city.

Figure I.2   Ubiquitous visualization of royalty begins at the entrance to tourist destinations with attendants in festive version of formal noble dress at the City Palace, Jaipur. *Photo courtesy of Maxine Weisgrau.*

Tourism discourse underplays nationalism, anti-British fervour, and resistance to colonial and feudal rule in Rajasthan In 1949, Rajasthan's framers had to persuade the princes to agree to become part of India, and to create a coherent identity for the new state's residents as Rajasthanis, rather than as Mewaris, Marwaris, Shekhawatis, to name just a few of the sociolinguistic groups in the 20-plus independent states that merged into Rajasthan. Each princely state had its own history of triumphs against its neighbours and valorized itself above others. The new Rajasthan's process of sub-national development drew in part on the heritage discourse promulgated during the colonial period. The sites, battlegrounds, and heroes of the new state of Rajasthan were praised for their resistance to Mughal, and later British rule. Many of the locations in Rajasthan's cities were renamed for local nationalist politicians and leaders.

The colonial-era cultural infrastructure, including the tradition of collections and museums – founded on or organized in line with European conventions – were simply adapted to the new Rajasthani identity (Breckrenridge 1989; Ramusack 1995). The norms of representation and material practices associated with the public's access to these collections reconfigured the concept of Rajasthani history and identity around royal heritage. It emphasized written sources over oral traditions that, at this time, had not been documented to any great extent, thus silencing many forms of rural, peasant, and subaltern movements.

The image of Rajasthani history is 'frozen' as Rajput, royal, and urban (see Edensor and Kothari 1994). This image is a male, elite, and Hindu vision of history and citizenship that excludes others. This vision of Rajasthani history and citizenship has multiple implications for Rajasthan's other groups, for example, the many Muslims who, when British India divided into the new states of Pakistan and India, opted to remain in Rajasthan, rather than move to Pakistan, a decision attested to by many family narratives (Das 1996; Henderson 1989). It is only within the last decade or so that subaltern groups have begun to recover their voices, in part within touristic encounters (see Bharucha 2003).

Tourism Narratives of Heritage Across Space and Time

The creation and legacy of tourism representations frames the chapters in the second section of this book.[1] Each of the chapters looks at an aspect of the historical development of ideas about Rajasthan, two as seen in colonial period travel writing, and two as seen in contemporary perspectives. Each of the four chapters explores

---

1   Historically there are many ways to transliterate Indian words into Roman script. The chapters in this book use terms derived from a variety of Indian languages: Gujarati, Hindi, Marwari, Mewari, Shekhawati, Sanskrit and Urdu, to name just a few. We have retained all cited authors' original spellings in direct quotes placed in the text. For other terms, we have used contemporary recognized spellings of place names (i.e. Jaipur) and the generally accepted, recognizable versions of Indian terms found in English language literature (i.e. sari). Hindi terms are indicated in italics, followed by English gloss, for example, *chapatti* (bread).

in some detail the processes through which different contested narratives become historical 'truth' through repetition. This is the arena where colonial nostalgia looms largest.

In 'Shifting Terrains of Heritage: the Painted Towns of Shekhawati', by Anne Hardgrove (Chapter 2), the author documents the rise of diaspora communities of industrialists from Rajasthan during the early modern period as a response to new opportunities for the development of finance capital. The Marwaris, as they became known across India (though actually members of different Hindu, Muslim, and Jain traditional commercial groups from Rajasthan), created, in some sense, hybrid societies that reflected their engagement across cultural divides (Timberg 1978; Hardgrove 2004). From the 1850s to 1930s, wealthy émigré Rajasthani business families, members of colonial India's emergent capitalist class, built palatial courtyard mansions in the small towns of Shekhawati.

Hardgrove notes that the mansions clearly were status displays of their owners' rise to prominence, as potential sites for holiday-making, and as retreats outside British India, because of their location within princely states. These houses are material productions of a capitalist social group and accordingly, embody very different sociopolitical relationships than the built environments of Rajasthan's ruling groups or its traditional landed gentry. Indeed, it appears that local residents do not embrace the heritage associated with these aspects of the havelis. To tourists, however, the Shekhawati mansions are objects of touristic visual consumption read on a par with royal palaces.

The migration of 'heritage' from palaces to merchant havelis appears to have its own history. Hardgrove shows how current consumption of the mansions as visual objects is largely detached from the historical, political, and economic contexts of the mansions' original construction. As the mansions have become associated with heritage, this constructed image of the mansions selectively capitalizes on the romantic, Orientalist, and princely stereotypes of Rajasthan as an exotic land of deserts, forts, and painted mansions.

In 'Ghost Towns and Bustling Cities: Constructing a Master Narrative in Nineteenth-Century Jaipur', Elena Karatchkova (Chapter 3) examines how European travellers over time produced a master narrative of Jaipur. European writers, from the Anglican Bishop Ronald Heber (visited ca. 1825), the Frenchman Victor Jacquemont (visited ca. 1832), Russian Prince Aleksei Soltykoff (visited ca. 1845), Thomas Hendley (lived in Jaipur from the 1870s to ca. 1900), Rudyard Kipling (visited Jaipur early 1880s), to Edwin Arnold (visited Jaipur in 1885–86) viewed Amber's Fort-Palace complex as a romantic, abandoned site. These authors regarded Jaipur as 'modern', a contrast that deepened in each subsequent narrative. The chapter explores how the process of interpretation and reinterpretation led to the construction of a master narrative that reified Amber by 1900 as the embodiment of a 'superstitious' old India, and Jaipur as the vanguard city of a technological new India. It is possible in this to see the development, over time, of one of the key motifs of the Orientalist perspective on India, that of antiquity. This motif continues to serve in some form as a benchmark in contemporary tourism writing.

At about the same time as the first of the authors discussed by Karatchkova was writing, Lt.-Col. James Tod (1782–1835), political agent to the western Rajput states from 1818–1822, authored the first extensive historical account of this area, the *Annals and Antiquities of Rajast'han* published in two volumes in 1829 and 1832. Tod's words are frequently quoted in tourism writing about Rajasthan. This work seminally constructed many of the motifs associated with Rajasthan: fierce desert rulers, chivalric codes, and centuries-old traditions of independence from, and resistance to, outside overlords.

In 'Travel, History and Politics in Rajasthan: James Tod's Personal Narrative', Jason Freitag (Chapter 4) outlines how Tod's travel narrative in the *Annals* selectively constructed images and events. Tod's agenda, stated in the introduction of the work which was published in London after Tod left India, was to support his political argument regarding the British relationship with the Rajput states, that they were a people of, and with history, and that they therefore should be independent of British intervention. Ironically, Tod was the arm of the East India Company that created the treaties of subordination of the princely states to the EIC in areas of external affairs, i.e., their relationships with any other princely states. Tod's implementation of treaty provisions with the princes set precedents for more comprehensive British control over domestic, internal control than mandated by treaty provisions. Tod's call for independence of the princely states in the published book (1829–1832), after his separation from colonial service should be read in contrast to his actual record of increasing British intervention into domestic affairs in Mewar, among the several states where Tod's influence was felt. As many of our authors demonstrate in their chapters, Tod's work is often cited by those who would suggest that Rajput heritage is an unchanged 'fact' from the past, to render Rajasthan in tourism discourse as a place whose history is frozen in Tod's time.

The explosion of Internet use in the past decade has provided a new medium for the creation and dissemination of images of India. In 'Virtual Rajasthan as Tourism Destination: Marketing Cyberorientalism?' Carol Henderson (Chapter 5) looks at the explosion of websites marketing India tourism and their reliance on images of Rajasthan as the exemplar of India's cultural heritage, imagined as untouched by global processes. This image often contrasts with how other states of India market themselves as tourism destinations. Henderson's analysis of Internet images of Rajasthan, in turn, shows that these are selective and rest on implicit alterities between Rajasthan, as 'oriental' embodiment, and the 'modern' world, while distorting, reinterpreting, or obscuring characteristics of the state. In other discourses these qualities may signify quite different issues to contemporary Rajasthanis.

Key themes in tourism discourse construct Rajasthan as a timeless place and outside the conventions of everyday life. These Internet images of Rajasthan, mostly produced within India to appeal to an international market, show a lineage of descent from colonial era guidebooks, and are consistent with contemporary print marketing of Rajasthan in North America and Europe. The chapter considers the relationship between these images and Orientalist discourse that is central to the performance and meaning of tourism in India.

Tourism, Transgression, and the Shifting Uses of Social Capital

Heritage may become a cultural resource in local debates, including formulating a definition of the tourism destination; determining what group has most claims to the destination; and distributing its benefits and costs. These chapters explore how the internal dynamics of participation in the tourism economy, through local practice, institutions, and patterns of interaction, help to provide the basis for contesting heritage. Here, the cultural politics of heritage formulation loom largest: given the imaging of Rajasthan heritage, the question arises as to how colonial nostalgia and the prefiguring of India as a sacred place or as a land of kings intersect with contemporary multiple discourses, within settings of power differences. Sometimes, what is produced seems to reinforce narratives of static tradition; at other points, this is transgressed (though rarely marked as such) and reformulated to meet the evolving discourse on heritage.

Access to heritage drives a series of issues germane to the spatial distribution of tourism products and services as described in Udaipur by Nicolas Bautès. 'Exclusion and Election in Udaipur Urban Space: Implications of Tourism Development' (Chapter 6) describes how monopoly control over cultural heritage properties in Udaipur (population around 465,000) has a negative impact on that city's overall urban development. Bautès argues that the political, social and economic relationship between tourism and territory, in particular the impact of tourism on the city's urban layout, produces uneven economic development. The existence of one powerful heritage actor in this setting, who significantly controls most of Udaipur's identified cultural heritage, affects the ability of other actors to produce alternative tourism narratives. At dispute is the socially constructed nature of 'tourist space' in the city and political and economic control over that space. One effect of the unequal distribution of tourist spaces in the city has been effective dismemberment of the non-tourism zone urban area from the tourism zone, and the resulting inequitable distribution of tourism benefits and costs to the local population's entrepreneurs not focusing on tourists as primary customers.

After 1947, princely and aristocratic patrons curtailed their support to performers and others, the result of the downturn in their incomes after reform (Kothari 1990). Those who had been obligated under corvée labour systems to work for the aristocrats in menial tasks such as cleaning out the elephant stables (elephants being important symbols of royalty), abandoned this work as soon as they were free to do so. In most areas, cash payments largely replaced the mutual exchange of goods and services on a customary basis, or *jajmani* system (see Fuller 1989). Most remaining customary exchange relationships were those focused on ritual services.

Some groups, such as the Bhats, moved into abandoned occupations. In 'Names, but not Homes, of Stone', Jeffrey Snodgrass (Chapter 7) recounts how the Bhats moved into the tourism industry and subsequent developments: what happens after the tourists leave, and the performance artists go home for the night? In the first phase of the tourism boom, Bhats invested in social display through ritual funeral feasts within their community. They also asserted a new public identity as the traditional puppeteers to the kings of Rajasthan (which they never were before), and thus as the curators of heritage and the old ways. This presentation of self, however, allows the Bhats to reap advantages in the tourist industry and to exploit the possibilities of new patrons, such as international arts festival organizers, hotels, restaurants, museums, and tourists who view their performances and purchase souvenir puppets. More recently, the focus of tourism income has shifted to social displays that favour investment in stone houses, durable consumer goods, and education for their children. In this setting, claims of modernity and heritage become vested with novel meanings and understandings.

In 'Sickly Men and Voracious Women: Erotic Constructions of Tourist Identity in India', Maxine Weisgrau (Chapter 8) explores sexuality in contemporary tourism discourse. Stories and advice abound. Tourist guidebooks, websites, and cultural experts routinely advise Western women travelling in India to avoid certain forms of dress and behaviour, on the grounds that these challenge local standards and may invite unwanted sexual advances by Indian men. Weisgrau finds four visions of sexuality: that of Rajasthani men, who produce and sustain a contemporary, or urban, legend regarding Indian and Western men, and Western women; that of Rajasthani women, whose male kin are involved in the tourism industry, and who tell their own stories about these events and their meanings; that of Western women, who recount personal narratives of sexual encounters with Indian men: and that of the English-language guidebooks.

Emergent from this consideration of multiple gazes is a complex process of an Indian construction of the erotic Euro-American tourist, of masculinity and of femininity. These four sets of tales each incorporates a moral evaluation of sexuality that differs according to the intention, prior cultural framework, and position in an unequal power relation. Analysis of these stories suggests the connections between tourism interactions and global media with the construction of an eroticized Euro-American 'Other' and raises questions about the intersection between gender and heritage.

In 'From Privy Purse to Global Purse: Maharaja Gaj Singhji's Role in the Marketing of Heritage and Philanthropy', author Jayasinhji Jhala (Chapter 9), documents how the princely states' rulers also found both shifting opportunities and dangers in the periods before and after 1947. Post–1947 reforms of governance reduced the assets held by the ruler of Jodhpur and other aristocrats, and they experienced a considerable diminution in their standard of living (see for example Carstairs 1957; Gold and Gujar 2002).

Princely rule in pre-Independence India has often been termed 'feudal', a terminology that derives from the nineteenth-century use of European historical models to account for Indian political systems. In this model, 'feudalism' refers to a typology of political institutions focused on a paramount ruler and landed aristocracy, where the ruler's power rested on his ability to negotiate and manipulate competing claims through the grant or withdrawal of revenue-producing lands, taxes, and other charges such as labour corvées, which could be levied on non-elites (Rudolph and Rudolph 1967; Rudolph 1968; Sharma 1979: 121–133).

By the end of the nineteenth-century, and in keeping with these ideas, diverse Anglo-Rajput hybrid honorific forms had developed. Coats of arms, official gun salutes, and other ritual paraphernalia refracted the practices of the British monarchy onto the court ritual of Rajput rulers (Cohn 1983; Haynes 2002a and b; Robbins 1999). Many of these forms are now dearly held and firmly embedded in princely displays, sometimes reinterpreted as reworkings of earlier courtly practice. In contradistinction to this, tourism discourse presents these state institutions and courtly displays as products of changeless tradition, even though they clearly are historically situated.

Jhala notes that the rulers were able to sustain some courtly functions during the early post-Independence period. Later, the growth of tourism, and the earnings associated with it, provided the context within which the former ruling families repositioned many practices related to their courts, and adapted themselves to the new circumstances. Today in Jodhpur region (formerly Marwar), the Maharaja and his family have created distinctive forms of hospitality tourism that simultaneously engage diverse constituencies and meanings based on concepts of heritage.

Jhala argues that, with tourism, the ex-royals reconstitute royalty and tradition simultaneously as touristic spectacle and as symbolic capital for the enactment of political rituals involving kin, courtly, honorific, and 'host-guest' relationships. The deployment of vehicles, seating arrangements, sex segregation, the use of costumes, physical sites and ritual and speech acts during the birthday celebration of the Maharaja Gaj Singh II of Jodhpur express multiple meanings to an audience at once local, regional and global. These meanings in turn energize particular sections of the audience to participate in the spectacle in certain prescribed ways that serves a tourism advocacy agenda, and to underscore and to reify tourism's ongoing focus on royalty as key to Rajasthani heritage.

Tourism and Spiritual Spaces

Spiritual spaces, religious belief, and practices associated with the sacred often appear to be the most intimately linked with notions of heritage as static, rather than as a contingent product of multiple voices and diverse discourses. These final three chapters suggest that, in the arena of religion, there is a robust and ongoing dialogue. Of Rajasthan's numerous religious (and some quite well known to tourists) sites, we take up three cases, one Hindu, one Muslim, and one that is favored by Jains and Hindus. It is likely that the processes these authors uncover in their analyses might be identified at other places, too. Thus, these chapters challenge the prevailing tourist literature idea that 'religion' is the least alterable element of social practice and the constitution of heritage.

'Pilgrimage Shrines and Tourism in Rajasthan: Family, Place, and Adoration' by John Cort (Chapter 10) analyses the multiple constituencies of the Jain and Hindu temple complexes of Osian, a small town north of Jodhpur. Osian's dozen temples date from roughly the late seventh through the twelfth centuries. Two of these temples, one dedicated to a Hindu goddess and the other to the Jain religion's founder Mahavir, have been in nearly continuous use since the mid eighth century. Contemporary pilgrims and tourists mingle at these sites with local people drawn to these shrines by diverse motivations. One important group of temple patrons includes Jains who trace their families to nearby Shekhawati, and who appear to have superseded the shrine's Rajput patrons.

Cort notes that the same deity serves multiple functions: as family deity; as deity and guardian of the place that is Osian; and as a personal deity. Different identities of the deity are addressed by each type of visitor. Diverse visions of the destination cluster around these different groups' motivations, experiences of the aesthetic and spiritual impact of these deities. Who a deity is, whose a temple is, who worships a particular deity, and why that worship is performed – these are all questions that rarely if ever admit of single answers.

The intersection of multiple constituencies plays out somewhat differently in the case of Ajmer (and India's) most important Muslim shrine. In 'Tourists, Pilgrims and Saints: The Shrine of Mu`in al-Din Chishti of Ajmer' (Chapter 11) Usha Sanyal notes that many non-Muslims are attracted by the saint's ability to grant boons and his ecumenical message. Ajmer receives 1 to 1.5 million visitors annually (Indiastat. com.), numbers that dwarf visitors at nearby sites in Rajasthan.

The shrine grew with imperial Mughal patronage. The late nineteenth-century pressures that supported commercial growth and educational movements in Rajasthan also resonated among some Muslims in India. Debate over how best to encounter modernity figured prominently among reformist discourses (Lelyveld 1978). Sanyal documents how reformers focused on 'idolatry', 'bell-ringing', and other activities at the shrine, which they associated with Hindu religious practice. As with the Rajput royals described by Jhala, post-Independence state reforms cost the shrine income-producing lands. The family that had managed the shrine's affairs moved to Pakistan. In the 1980s, the rise of Hindu fundamentalist-inspired movements in the 1990s, culminating in a series of violent Hindu-Muslim confrontations – most signally the storming and destruction of the Babri Masjid, a mosque in Ayodhya in 1992, threatened to destabilize the accommodation between the shrine and its non-Muslim constituency, and between the shrine and its Muslim supporters.

The shrine is immensely significant not only to the economy of Ajmer, but also to that of nearby Pushkar, with its very sacred sites for Hindus. Visitors to one place go to the other: perhaps as tourists at one, and as pilgrims, supplicants, or worshippers, to the other. Rhetoric that affects the one shrine will reverberate with respect to the interests of the other.

The shrine management – and state government – emphasize that the site is a peaceful destination that welcomes visitors of all faiths. Recent strategies, employing the Internet and web blogs, appear to speak to an international audience by talking about personal fulfilment and self-realization in a nonsectarian fashion. Thus, heritage finds a place in electronic media to communicate the message of history uninterrupted.

In 'Hindu Nationalism, Community Rhetoric and the Impact of Tourism: The case of Pushkar, Rajasthan', Christina A. Joseph (Chapter 12) examines recent forms of conflict in the tourism environment. New tourism entrepreneurs are moving in on the local industry, formerly largely monopolized by a single group of traditional pilgrim priests. These Brahmans find themselves caught in disturbing and ambivalent circumstances. The most lucrative variety of tourism serves international visitors, not necessarily Hindu, who often blatantly 'break the rules'.

Pushkar's citizens agree that the biggest rule-violators are one distinctive and very small group of residents, its foreign 'hippies.' These are low-budget European-American travellers. They are drawn to India by its cheapness (it will fit a student budget) and image as a place to find spiritual regeneration and self-knowledge (currently the thrust of a Government of India marketing campaign for tourism).

Joseph documents the ways in which the Brahmans interpret tourism as a threat to tradition and religion. However, tourism's income potential is ignored by no one. This ambivalence is resolved through exclusionary, political and religious rhetorics, which permit Pushkar's service providers to condemn tourism collectively, while individually participating in and benefiting from it . Exclusionary rhetoric demonizes all outsiders equally, including hippies, foreigners, Christians, and Muslims – even as ways are found to meet these travellers' tourism and spiritual needs. Political rhetoric adapts the ideology of Hindu religious fundamentalism and normalizes it as part of civic discourse on tourism. By targeting Pushkar's very small group of Euro-American hippies, the Brahmans define tourism as an issue of religion and 'otherness.' This case provides insight into a local struggle over the control over should be meant by religious heritage and accommodating what Pushkar's Brahmans understand to be the mixed blessings of tourism.

Conclusion

This book does not presume that there is any fundamental or underlying essence of Rajasthani-ness, outside of how people construct this quality and its meanings. We do suggest that the tourism discourse that is produced about Rajasthan can be explored in terms of history, media, power relations, and a particular set of ideas. Ten to twenty years from now, these ideas may be different. The contingency of these ideas in time, space, and imagination suggests that there is no inherent reason why such tropes as 'royalty' stand in for Rajasthan. Perhaps in a decade, Rajasthan will no longer be an exotic tourism destination. Economic development may sweep away the elements that most potently attract and sustain certain forms of tourism discourse and tourism practices. Perhaps, in that time, tourism in Rajasthan will emphasize very different characteristics and practices.

This analysis also suggests the dangers of a high degree of dependency on tourism earnings, particularly in view of its distorting impacts on economic development, its tendency to produce dual economy effects that promote social inequities, and the potentially demeaning content required by some performances and products.

Unbalanced economic development renders local economies vulnerable to sudden downshifts, as may occur in the wake of a natural disaster or global political insecurities.

As the site for the enactment and construction of important cultural meanings and encounters, tourism in Rajasthan has appropriated the physical infrastructure of largely intact forts, palaces, gardens and late nineteenth-century mansions, along with its cultural infrastructure of vigorous performance traditions, arts, and crafts. Tourism discourse at present combines them in a seamless and highly orientalized version of culture and history. This is how tourists conceive of Rajasthan's out of the ordinary qualities and the accounts they give of their experiences resonate with these exoticized and scripted encounters. Equally scripted is the presentation by Rajasthani tourism providers of their vision of Rajasthan, coupled with their vision of tourists. Both nationalist as well as local concerns figure in these scripts.

The cultural politics of tourism in Rajasthan, as elsewhere in the world, focus on the concept of heritage. Throughout this volume our authors make the clear distinction between a single historic narrative, and the multiple constructions of the past that enter into heritage discourse. We are less interested in debunking popular accounts of local histories than in exploring the multiple meanings and interconnections of politics, power, and history, embedded in these accounts. This discussion clearly reverberates beyond Rajasthan and beyond India.

References

Banerjee, A.C. (1980), *The Rajput States and British Paramountcy* (New Delhi: Rajesh Publications).

Bharucha, R. (2003), *Rajasthan An Oral History: Conversations with Komal Kothari* (New Delhi: Penguin Publishing).

Bhattacharyya, D.P. (1997), 'Mediating India: An Analysis of a Guidebook', *Annals of Tourism Research* 24:2, 371–389.

Breckenridge, C.A. (ed.) (1995), *Consuming Modernity: Public Culture in a South Asian World* (Minneapolis: University of Minnesota Press).

Breckenridge, C. (1989), 'The Aesthetics and Politics of Colonial Collecting: India at World Fairs', *Comparative Studies in Society and History* 31:2, 195–216.

Britton, S. (1982), 'The Political Economy of Tourism in the Third World', *Annals of Tourism Research*, 9.

Bruner, E. (1996), 'Tourism in Ghana: The Representation of Slavery and the Return of the Black Diaspora', *American Anthropologist* 98:2, 290–304.

—— (2001), 'The Maasai and the Lion King: Authenticity, Nationalism, and Globalization in African Tourism', *American Ethnologist* 28:4, 881–908 .

Bruner, E. and B. Kirshenblatt-Gimblett (1994), 'Maasai on the Lawn: Tourist Realism in East Africa', *Cultural Anthropology* 9:4, 435–470.

Carstairs, G.M. (1957), *The Twice-Born: A Study of a Community of High-Caste Hindus* (London: Hogarth Press).

Chambers, E. (2000), *Native Tours: The Anthropology of Travel and Tourism* (Prospect Heights, IL: Waveland Press).

Chhabra, D., R. Healy and E. Sills (2003), 'Staged Authenticity and Heritage Tourism', *Annuals of Tourism Research* 30:5, 702–719.

Chronis, A. (2005), 'Co-constructing Heritage at the Gettysburg Storyscape', *Annals of Tourism Research* 32:2, 386–406.

Cohn, B.S. (1983), 'Representing Authority in Victorian India', in E. Hobsbawm and T. Ranger, T. (eds.), *The Invention of Tradition* (Cambridge: Cambridge University Press, 165–209).

Crick, M. (1989), 'Representations of International Tourism in the Social Sciences: Sun, Sex, Sights, Savings and Servility', *Annual Review of Anthropology* 18, 307–344.

Das, V. (1996), Critical Events: An Anthropological Perspective on Contemporary India (New Delhi. Oxford University Press).

Echtner, C.M. and P. Prasad (2003), 'The Context of Third World Tourism Marketing', *Annals of Tourism Research* 30:3, 660–682.

Edensor, T. (1998), *Tourists at the Taj* (New York: Routledge).

Edensor T. and U. Kothari (1994), 'The Masculinisation of Stirling's Heritage', in V. Kinnaird and D. Hall (eds.) *Tourism: A Gender Analysis* (New York: John Wiley & Sons, 164–187).

Erdman, J. (1994), 'Becoming Rajasthani: Pluralism and the Production of *Dharti Dhoran Ri*', in K. Schomer, J.L. Erdman, D.O. Lodrock, and L.I. Rudolph (eds.), *The Idea of Rajasthan: Explorations in Regional Identity*, vol. I, Constructions (New Delhi: South Asia Publications, 45–79).

Federation of India Chambers of Commerce and Industry (2002), 'India Profile', http://www.ficci.com/indiaprofile. Last accessed March 2002.

Fuller, C. J. (1989), 'Misconceiving the Grain Heap: A Critique of the Indian Jajmani System, in J. Parry and M. Bloch (eds.), *Money and the Morality of Exchange* (Cambridge: Cambridge University Press, 33–63).

Gable, E. et al (1992), 'On the Uses of Relativism: Fact, Conjecture and Black and White Histories at Colonial Williamsburg', *American Ethnologist* 19:4, 791–805.

Gold, A.G (1988), *Fruitful Journeys: The Ways of Rajasthani Pilgrims* (Berkeley: University of California Press.

Gold, A.G. and B.R. Gujar (2002), *In the Time of Trees and Sorrow: Nature, Power and Memory in Rajasthan* (Durham, NC: Duke University Press).

Hardgrove, A. (2004), *Community and Public Culture: The Marwaris in Calcutta* (New York: Oxford University Press).

Handler, R. and J. Linnekin (1984), 'Tradition, Genuine or Spurious', *The Journal of American Folklore* 97:385, 273–290.

Haynes, E.S. (2002a), 'Wearing Honour: the Introduction of Tangible Representations of Honour into the Rajputana States', in V. Joshi (ed.), *Culture, Communities, and Change* (Jaipur: Rawat Publications, 35–58).

—— (2002b), 'Lineage, State and Symbolism of Rule in Late-Nineteenth-Century Eastern Rajputana', in R.B. Barnett (ed.), *Rethinking Early Modern India* (New Delhi: Manohar, 33–83).

Henderson, C. (2002), *Culture and Customs of India* (Westport, Ct.: Greenwood Press).

—— (1998), 'The Great Cow Explosion in Rajasthan, India: Institutions, Landscape and Livestock in Historical Ecology Perspective', in W. Balée (ed.), *Advances in Historical Ecology* (New York: Columbia University Press, 349–375).

—— (1989), 'Life in the Land of Death: Famine and Drought in Arid Western Rajasthan', Ph.D. Thesis, Columbia University.

Hobsbawm, E. and Ranger, T. (eds.) (1983), *The Invention of Tradition* (Cambridge: Cambridge University Press).

Indiastat.com (2006), 'Tables on Domestic and International Tourist Arrivals in Rajasthan, Statistical Information on India', http://www.indiastat.com.osiyou. cc.columbia.edu. Last accessed 24 September 2006.

InvestRajasthan.com (n.d.), 'Advantages of Rajasthan Tourism', http://www. investrajasthan.com/advra/tou/18400. Last accessed 24 September 2006.

Kipling, R. (1899), *Letters of Marque* (Cleveland: International Fiction Library).

Kirshenblatt-Gimblett, B. (1995), 'Theorizing Heritage', *Ethnomusicology* 39:3, 367–380.

Kothari, K. (1990), 'Introduction: A View on Castes of Marwar', in Singh, M.H., *The Castes of Marwar (Census Report of 1891)* (Jodhpur: Books Treasure).

Lelyveld, D. (1978), *Aligarh's First Generation: Muslim Solidarity in British India* (Princeton: Princeton University Press).

MacCannell, D. (1979), 'Staged Authenticity: Arrangements of Social Space in Visitor Settings', *American Journal of Sociology* 79:3, 589–603.

Mills, S. (1991), *Discourses of Difference: An Analysis of Women's Travel Writing and Colonialism* (London: Routledge).

Mohanty, S. (ed.) (2003), *Travel Writing and the Empire* (New Delhi: Katha).

Nash, D. and V. Smith (1991), 'Anthropology and Tourism', *Annals of Tourism Research,* vol. 18.

Planning Commission of India (n.d.), 'Tourism', http://planningcommission.nic.in/ plans/mta-9702-ch23.pdf. Last accessed March, 2002.

Ramusack, B. (1995), 'The Indian Princes as Fantasy: Palace Hotels, Palace Museums, and Palace on Wheels', in C.A. Breckenridge (ed.) (1995), *Consuming Modernity: Public Culture in a South Asian World.* Minneapolis: University of Minnesota Press.

Robbins, K.X. (1999), 'The Honor of the Maharanas and Mewar's Relationship with Central Powers', *Journal of the Indian Military History Society* 16, 153.

Rudolph, L.I. (1968), *The Political Modernization of an Indian Feudal Order: an analysis of Rajput adaptation in Rajasthan* (Chicago: University of Chicago, Committee on Southern Asian Studies).

Rudolph, L.I. and S.H. Rudolph (1967), *The Modernity of Tradition: Political Development in India* (Chicago: University of Chicago Press).

Said, E.W. (1978) *Orientalism* (New York: Vintage Books).

Sharma, G.C. (1979), *Administrative System of the Rajputs* (New Delhi: Rajeesh Publications).

Smith, V.L. (ed.) (1978), *Hosts and Guests: The Anthropology of Tourism* (Oxford: Blackwell).

—— (1989) *Hosts and Guests: The Anthropology of Tourism* 2nd Edition (Philadelphia: University of Pennsylvania Press).

Thadami, M. (1999), 'The HVS International Hotels in India – Trends and Opportunities, HVS. http://www.hvsinternational.com.

Timberg, T. (1978), *The Marwaris: From Traders to Industrialists* (New Delhi: Vikas).

Urry, J. (1990), *The Tourist Gaze: Leisure and Travel in Contemporary Societies* (London: Sage).

Weisgrau, M. (1993), 'Social and Political Relations of Development: NGOs and Adivasi Bhils in Rural Rajasthan', PhD. dissertation, Department of Anthropology, Columbia University.

—— (1997) *Interpreting Development: Local Histories, Local Strategies* (Lanham, MD: University Press of America).

Wilson, D. (1993), 'Time and Tides in the Anthropology of Tourism', in M. Hitchcock et al (eds.), *Tourism in South East Asia* (New York: Routledge).

Wood, R.E. (1993), 'Tourism, Culture and the Sociology of Development', in M. Hitchcock et al (eds.), *Tourism in Southeast Asia*. (New York: Routledge).

Part 1
Creating Tourism Narratives of Heritage Across Space and Time

Introduction to Part 1

Carol E. Henderson and Maxine Weisgrau

There is a certain irony that the tourism practice of representing heritage as inherent, immutable, and linked to the far distant past, collapses so readily into invention, selective representation and, in perhaps more than a few cases, sheer expediency. These chapters track these permutations across space, time, and social relationships to elucidate the multiple voices, media, and interests that produce heritage narratives.

Why tourists – and in particular the Western tourists whose voices predominate in the narratives described in this section of the book – seek a sense of connection to the past, in this case, decidedly 'someone else's past' – reverses European American heritage tourism's preoccupation with its own past. Scholars suggest that the vision of the 'past' embodied in how Westerners talk about non-Westerners is ultimately a way of talking about oneself. Said's original vision of Orientalism (1978) emphasized relatively stable Western concepts of non-Western cultures; these chapters demonstrate that this stability itself may be a product of diverse processes, including changes in the relationship between those who are the objects of the tourists' interest, and the tourists themselves.

Guidebooks written for non-Indian tourists reiterate master narratives that mediate the vision of India. In these narratives Rajasthan is forever associated with royalty, as demonstrated by the discussions of varied forms of tourism texts in these chapters. As Hardgrove discusses, this association creates a vision of the painted houses of Shekhawati as homologous to the Rajput palaces. Never mind, as Hardgrove makes clear, that at the time of their construction Shekhawati's painted mansions were monuments to modernity, tributes to their owners' success in finance and industry, and in businesses such as coal mines, steel mills, ship yards, and textile factories.

The Western tourists and tourism mediators discussed by Hardgrove instead interpret these painted houses as products of pre-modern social, economic, and political relationships, with three major implications. First, these narratives strategically distance the houses from their creators and owners. As the guidebooks and travel books inevitably point out, the houses' owners have 'abandoned' them, even though these same sources point out how these houses have watchmen, are rented to tenants, and are currently being converted into museums and, more lately, into tourist attractions by their owners. Second, these travel accounts focus on the domestic elements of life in the painted images, rather than on the very modern public lives of their makers. Thus these accounts often focus on women's roles, as presumably the least changed and thus most distanced from modernity – without reference to how women residing within actually lived their lives. Third, the western authors and interpreters of the Shekhawati painted mansions obsessively refer to the putative 'misreadings' of modernity embodied in such paintings as of aeroplanes and railways. The outsiders' eye reads these as examples of a naïve style of visual representation in contrast to how the actual painters and those who commissioned the paintings regarded them.

Shekhawati's painted houses are understood locally to be status markers of capitalist success as are their contemporary counterparts, the Gilded Age mansions of Newport, Rhode Island. Shekhawati's mansions, Hardgrove shows, lost significant markers of their past as they entered tourism discourse. Simultaneously, the heritage discourse – largely focused until recently on palaces, as the chapters by Karatchkova, Freitag, and Henderson all demonstrate – has expanded. 'Heritage' now includes capitalist merchants' houses, the everyday practices of villagers ('living museums') and arts and crafts production, commoditized as tourist souvenirs.

Karatchkova identifies the reiteration in nineteenth and early twentieth century tourism discourse on Jaipur and Amber of an idea of a premodern India that is 'old,' 'savage,' and 'irrational.' Its obverse is the modern: that which is 'new,' 'civilized,' and 'rational.' For example, she cites a nineteenth century description of a goat sacrifice in the Kali temple in Amber which reminds the reader with historical precision that sixty years previously, was a human sacrifice. This moving target of 'sixty years' suggests that something more than a scrupulous historical accuracy is the author's intent. Just as contemporary urban legends typically gather a semblance of authenticity by inserting seemingly precise details, so too the reference to 'sixty years' suspiciously suggests the conscious insertion of the imprimatur of historicity.

Invariably, this temple sacrifice and its attendant bloody images contrast with the description of Jaipur's wide streets that meet at right angles. This draws, to the Victorian (and later) reader, a contrast between 'new' and 'old,' between 'civilized' and 'savage,' and between 'rational' and 'irrational.' Heber's late twenty-first-century readers are surprised by his observations of Jaipur's modernity, but he wrote his descriptions of Jaipur at the time when European town planning was attempting to incorporate these attitudes in the reconstruction of urban spaces. Wide streets, grid-patterns, and the harmonious blending of work and living spaces – all features of Heber's Jaipur – guided the design of urban spaces in Europe and the United States. Heber may well be holding up Jaipur as an ideal and a challenge to his European readership. By the end of the nineteenth century however, Jaipur has become simply a 'new' place that contrasts with Amber as an 'old place.' Today, this distinction is lost, as both Jaipur and Amber read, to tourists, guided by contemporary travel narratives and reiterated locally in tourism-oriented urban planning as 'old.'

Freitag's chapter unpacks the origins of the palace motif in Colonel James Tod's romantic vision of Rajputs as hardy baronial Europeans. Tod is important in understanding the roots of the tourist's vision of Rajasthan, for generations of authors uncritically and unself-consciously adopted Tod's stance. Tod's references to popular Western European Romantic movement artists appealed to his contemporary readers' nostalgic sensibilities, and linked Rajasthan's history to the valorizing of the European medieval and Gothic periods, then a motive for European tourism. For 'Rajasthan,' Tod asked his readers to imagine the Scotland of William Wallace, of Rob Roy, of Sir Walter Scott and the descriptive prose of Mrs. Ann Radcliffe. Freitag argues that Tod wrote the Rajputs into history, as peoples with a history, and therefore suitably understood as fully realized political actors on a par with the British. Alas, Tod's followers have read 'his' Rajasthan in quite a different fashion: as a place decidedly frozen in time.

Henderson examines the content of tourism marketing websites, and finds that this medium largely replicates the images of guidebooks and late Victorian travel writing on Rajasthan. The processes of simplification, reification and reiteration of certain key motifs (such as the palace), are joined by new content that clearly reflects globalizing pressures in the mass market for tourism.

The politics of these representations intersect with how heritage is constructed and portrayed in Rajasthan by local actors. At the start of the nineteenth century, Rajput kings were fully realized political actors competing with other powerful actors, in complex societies. The erosion of their political functions under the British Residency system included, by the end of the nineteenth century, British glorification of ceremonial functions. The meaning of royalty thus shifted from that of the early nineteenth century, when in Rajasthan (and in much of Europe, to be sure), kings were powerful political players, to settings where the work of politics was entrusted to parliamentary bodies of various types and kings largely performed ceremonial functions. Likewise, the painted mansions clearly held political functions in Shekhawati as places where their builders embodied great wealth in socially and politically meaningful fashion.

Today, Rajasthani website designers and tourism entrepreneurs – in large measure as do tourist guidebook authors – compile descriptions culled from these earlier sources, recognizing that the mass market demands images, brevity, and motifs that rapidly convey accepted messages about Rajasthan as a destination. Here, the success of these efforts may be directly measured through the consumption of these entrepreneurs' services. Heritage in the tourism context is therefore explicitly a commodity: great care is taken in these Internet texts to suggest that, above all, Rajasthan offers tourists its unchanged nature from the far distant past. This is guaranteed as part of the package deal.

Reference

Said, E. (1978), *Orientalism* (New York: Vintage Books).

Chapter 1

Shifting Terrains of Heritage: The Painted Towns of Shekhawati

Anne Hardgrove[1]

The ideas of Rajasthan and of heritage are nearly synonymous for many tourists to India. Rajput palaces emerging from desert sands lure visitors, who come to experience the pleasures of royal life in these former princely states. Such emphases of tourism stem, in part, from the practices of tourists who now have access to the public areas of castles and royal palaces in Europe.[2] The word 'heritage' suggests that the attraction of these sites is that the tourist participates – or seems to participate, however temporarily – in the legacy of the regal past, a heritage traditionally accessible only by birthright.

The so-called 'painted towns' of the Shekhawati region of Rajasthan (see Map I.1) are a case study of how tourism entrepreneurship creates new forms of heritage, and the willingness of tourists to participate in their consumption. In the past twenty-five years, Shekhawati's elaborately painted mansions have become the latest European American discovery in the burgeoning heritage industry of Rajasthan. The wall paintings cover both exteriors and interiors, and their subject matter includes an eclectic mix of religious imagery along with such elements as trains, cars, and depictions of Europeans.

These mansions were built by Marwari traders, as members of diverse commercial groups from Rajasthan are known throughout India, starting in the mid- nineteenth-century and continuing until shortly before World War II. In addition to the painted mansions, known by the term *haveli* (a word that refers to a courtyard style of house popular in northwestern India),[3] the Marwaris constructed other buildings, such as wells and cow-protection shelters. By the late 1930s, these traders had settled in the

---

1   I am grateful to Carol Henderson and Maxine Weisgrau for their many ideas in understanding *haveli* tourism in Rajasthan, and to David Libby, my husband and in-house editor.

2   Joining the association known as 'English Heritage', for example, allows visitors free access to several hundred historical sites in the United Kingdom.

3   According to Stephen Blake (1991: 45) the term *haveli* derives from Persian, and refers to large walled mansions and open courtyard houses. However, Catherine Asher (personal communication) observes that the term does not appear in the vocabulary of Mughal architecture, and probably originated in early modern Rajasthan to designate a new form of architectural synthesis of Rajput and Mughal domestic styles.

metropolises and had begun to invest in national industrial empires, rather than in embellishing the nostalgic sites of their former homelands. Most of the Shekhawati residences were built after the men migrated from Rajasthan. They housed, for short periods, the women and extended families not among the original migrants. Now largely abandoned and ignored by local residents, the havelis are promoted in tourism marketing as the 'largest open air art gallery' of painted frescoes in the world.[4]

It is not surprising that the painted havelis have been subsumed into tourist destinations in Rajasthan. The houses provide visual clues as to how the extended families of merchants coped with a hot and dusty climate, and how they lived in a society concerned with social status and the seclusion of women. Most tourists do not have access to local homes. Heritage tourism provides an opportunity for outsiders to get a glimpse into the past, and into the images of self and other that Marwari traders projected in the architectural style of their residences.

This paper argues that heritage is predicated upon the social disjuncture between the built environment and local populations. Instead of viewing heritage as something that is presumably acquired or possessed, passed down on account of the noble origins or deeds of a predecessor, I propose, following Johnson (1996) and Edensor (2000), that heritage is brought into being through the cultural practices of tourism and tourist viewing. This approach emphasizes the contingent nature of tourist representations, such as the transformation of understandings of the 'big house' in Ireland from a locus of the gentry, to its construction as a centre of unequal relationships linking the great estate to its tenants and labourers (Johnson 1996) or, as at Colonial Williamsburg, the critique of that destination's representation of slavery (Gable et al. 1992).

In contrast with other forms of tourism in Rajasthan, and South Asia in general, haveli-viewing differs in regards to the kind of interactions visitors might have with nearby residents. Whereas visitors to urban areas in Rajasthan might hope to hear stories of the 'old days' retold by their noble hosts in the palace hotel, and climbers in Nepal look forward to Sherpa hospitality on Himalayan treks, visitors who come to Shekhawati to see the havelis minimize their interactions with local townspeople (Fisher 2004). Guidebooks, which present the master narratives with which tourists pre-arm themselves (see chapter by Karatchkova; also see Chambers 2000, 31) for viewing, while giving a modest amount of historical information about the houses, say next to nothing about the art's interpretation, and nothing about the social relationships embodied in these houses.

Though scholars and curators dispute the artistic merit of the painted murals and frescoes, the Marwari havelis are a popular tourist attraction for foreign visitors. Tourists, unaware of the contentious histories of Marwari capitalism, have little clue that the Marwari past as moneylenders and local creditors have made the havelis less than popular among the less well-off Shekhawati residents (Hardgrove 2004). Narratives promoting haveli tourism keep the nationalist narratives of Indian Marxist history at arm's length, and capitalize on the stereotypes of Rajasthan as an exotic

---

4   The phrase 'open air art gallery' is ubiquitous in tourism marketing and journalistic writing about Shekhawati, as if the entire region were a museum.

land of deserts, forts, and princes, which comprise the master narrative tourists bring to the encounter (see chapter by Henderson).

That cultural, historical, and transnational forces at play redefine heritage to include non-royal merchant mansions is a significant process, involving a variety of actors and cultural conditions relevant to the migration of merchants to urban centres. The case of the painted towns of Shekhawati shows that the production of heritage lies in forgetting, indeed, in erasing history in favor of newly constructed memories of the past (Hobsbawm and Ranger 1983).

The research for this article came about as part of a project on the Marwari community in Calcutta. This research investigated the self-representations that the Marwaris made of their own history and culture, and what interpretations others have made of these narratives (Hardgrove 2004). This chapter revisits some aspects of that research, focused on tourism, and utilizes an interdisciplinary approach that combines ethnographic observation with the historical interpretation of written sources. I made several short trips to the region of Shekhawati in 1996, 1997, and 2000. During those visits I held conversations with local families, foreign tourists, hotel owners, and tour guides.

My research also considers art history, literature and popular travel literature, as well as information on the Internet. In this chapter, I look first at the concept of heritage, describe salient aspects of the Shekhawati setting and examine the origins of haveli tourism. I then turn to a description of three encounters with the havelis: first through the individualized experience common to most travellers, second, through a Shekhawati area guide-mediated experience, and third, through a stay at a Shekhawati ecotourism destination. In the last two cases, I draw extensively upon my own experiences. Finally, I return to a consideration of the migration of the concepts of heritage to encompass a non-royal tourism destination.

Inventing and Re-Inventing Heritage

How is the migration of the concept of heritage from the palaces of the urban elite to the painted houses of middle-class traders and capitalists to be understood? Local and national identity politics, which feature in a number of studies of the construction of 'heritage' (Hobsbawm and Ranger 1983) do not seem particularly salient. When the house owners are absent, locals seem indifferent, and whatever status displays or messages are being produced and consumed, do not seem to focus on the painted haveli as an institution. In looking at the contemporary understanding of these sites, I shall examine how the idea of 'heritage' arises from the tourists' own interaction with a tourist destination, as mediated by guides and guidebooks, as tourists seek increasingly authentic destinations. The saturation of the urban/palace tourist routes in northern India leads to over-visitation at the major tourist sites, and destruction of the uniqueness of the attraction. As a result, tourists seek out 'less touristy' places in their attempts to locate new forms of heritage. In this sense, development of these new tourist locales can be understood, I believe, as an Orientalizing of the peripheral.

Figure 1.1   In Shekhawati most of the tourists' experiences are personal and unmediated, such as this woman tourist peering past laundry to view a painted image on an occupied house. *Photo courtesy of Anne Hardgrove. All rights reserved.*

As signifiers of the 'back regions' of tourist destinations and of the true and intimate sense of the 'authentic' perceived by the tourist, as encounters that are not scripted (MacCannell 1973; Bhattacharyya 1997), these spaces may seem to permit the visitor to imagine personal histories from the built environment. Also, related to this issue, unlike India's major tourist destinations, Shekhawati's small towns and villages lack the usual throngs of eager guides offering their services.[5] Tourists come across these mansions in their owners' absence. Tourists might meet a caretaker or a

---

5   There are now efforts underway to train professional guides, according to the Friends of Shekhawati non-governmental organization website (www.apanidhani.com).

family of renters at the haveli, but in most cases, they are likely to find the building just standing empty: almost, as it were, a stage set onto which the tourist can project his or her imagination.

Further, houses may importantly signify social relationships. As Carsten and Hugh-Jones note,

> [H]ouses come to stand for social groups and represent the world around them…houses are frequently thought of as bodies, sharing with them a common anatomy and a common life history. If people construct houses and make them in their own image, so also do they use these houses and house images to construct themselves as individuals and as groups (Carsten and Hugh-Jones 1995, 1).

It is a far from foregone conclusion that mansions, especially of merchants, would be subsumed into the practices of royalty tourism in Rajasthan, or identified as 'heritage' when they are conspicuously modern. The owners and builders of town-based havelis – of India's capitalist and industrialist class – fall somewhere between the prince and the peasant, the elite and the folk. Why should the painted houses of migrant merchant capitalists be comparable to the grand palaces of the princes? Popular Indian culture depicts Marwari wealth as that of vulgar and uncultured *nouveaux riches* who lack the aesthetic traditions of the Rajput elites. Indian cultural stereotypes depict Marwaris as conniving moneylenders who are physically sedentary and over-indulgent in their consumption of rich foods.

The paintings and drawings on their Shekhawati houses are dismissed as bad taste, according to some art and architectural historians. Gautam Bhatia (1994), for example, pokes fun at the architecturally mixed elements of these structures ('Marwari Gothic') built by the *nouveau riches*. In a study of Rajput palaces, G.H.R. Tillotson dismisses the haveli art as 'vulgar and incompetent' (Tillotson 1987, 22). Local history has little love for the merchant capitalists, either, judging by the accounts of twentieth-century peasant insurgencies in the Shekhawati region against the Marwari moneylenders. This history is still evident in the pervasive indifference to the painted mansions by the contemporary townspeople. As relics of industrial capitalism, the movement of capital, and the trans-regional migration of labour, the houses, as the big houses did for subaltern Irish populations in the 1920s, according to Johnson (1996), represent to contemporary Shekhawati populations the power of moneylenders to whom the peasantry was often deeply indebted. In this context, 'indifference' to the painted houses by locals may be interpreted as a form of resistance.

Shekhawati's development of haveli tourism can be contrasted to the staged heritage of other locations. The Nagarathar (town-dwelling) Chettiar merchant class of Tamil Nadu once built similar big houses and now sponsor a village-style recreation of houses in an open-air museum called Dakshina Chitra, located just outside Chennai (former Madras). Here, groups of school children and tourists can visit relocated and restored 'old' houses. In Rajasthan, Shilpgram ('craftsman's village') on the outskirts of Udaipur established through the West Zone Cultural Centre showcases rural houses. In this museum-like setting, artisans and performers help visitors imagine themselves to be inside a typical village (see chapter by

Snodgrass).[6] The WZCC centrepiece within Udaipur city is a haveli, built by Mewar's mid-eighteenth century Prime Minister Amar Chand Badwa (or Barwa), identified by James Tod as 'a member of the merchant class' (Tod 1971, I, 500–501).[7] The late nineteenth- to early twentieth-century Marwari painted haveli lies somewhere in between these diverse points of reference. In order to follow the trajectory of the understanding of the haveli, it is necessary to review its discovery by the tourism industry, its packaging as a destination, and the contemporary characteristics which colour the tourist encounter.

Getting There

Shekhawati region is about 225 km (150 miles) distant from New Delhi and about 145 km (about 99 miles) distant from Jaipur. The region abuts the recently improved national highway that links these two cities, and that has significantly cut travel times between Delhi and Jaipur. Shekhawati is thus well within the range of the so-called tourism 'golden triangle' of Delhi, Jaipur and Agra. As Shekhawati is a rural region, compared with the urban destinations that dominate India tourism, it appears off the beaten track, 'lost in time.'[8] In fact, Shekhawati is very close to established tourist routes and destinations. Small towns like Nawalgarh, Fatehpur, Jhunjhunu, Mandawa and Sikar have long been connected to telegraph lines (since the 1870s) and to the railway on local routes. It is something of a stretch to think of the Shekhawati towns as isolated from the modern infrastructure of India.

The sense of distance may be heightened, for the foreign tourist in particular, by the few amenities in Shekhawati region geared to this market, though this lack is typical of small-town India. The towns offer a variety of services, including small businesses, banks, schools, colleges, Internet cafés, and bus and railway connections. If tourists do not read Hindi script, they may be unlikely to identify these amenities. Administratively, these towns include tehsil (subdistrict) and subtehsil headquarters for local government. In part, the relative lack of tourism services reflects current tourist practices.

6   I thank Carol Henderson for telling me about the Udaipur example.

7   See www.shilpgram.org/menu/westzone on Bagore ki Haveli, as this is known. The online Mewar Encyclopedia (<www.mewarindia.com>) identifies Amarchand Badwa as a Brahman (a member of the highest ranking, priestly caste group), but does not state his occupation. This source, under the entry for 'West Zone Cultural Centre' cites Bagore ki Haveli, as a 'nobleman's palace', presumably because after Badwa's death, it later came into the hands of the Mewar royal family. Generally, the prime ministers of the Rajput states were drawn from the mercantile groups, as their duties included financing and organizing the finance of state enterprises.

8   IncredibleIndia.org, an on-line tourism website by the Government of India – Ministry of Tourism describes Shekwhati as 'forgotten with the passage of time' ('Offbeat Destinations', www.tourismofindia.com/obd/hiobdshekhawati. For an example of tourist impressions, see the blog by 'Karin-Marijke and Coen', travellers in Shekhawati who on Oct. 22, 2004 under 'Shekhawati-region' posted impressions (www.lk.nl~mailking/iblog)

The railways that reach towns like Jhunjhunu run very slowly. Trains stop frequently and compete with bus routes to transport people travelling to markets, temples, distant family, work, and educational facilities. Hotel accommodations, restaurants, and transportation within the towns cater to the local population, not to the outsider. Tourists find this inconvenient. Most tourists travel by private hired car or jeep for the drive to Shekhawati and back. The fact that the painted houses are located within towns that are perfect for a day trip allows the tourist to explore a less-crowded region than the urban tourist centres. The tourist need not suffer what, to him or her, are the inconveniences of travelling to and staying in villages. Tourists have the option of staying at their nearby palace hotel, or staying in one of a few all-inclusive resorts, where their needs can be met without having to turn to the services of the local town.

Tourism entrepreneurship relating to Shekhawati's havelis dates to the 1980s and seems to have coincided with interest by art and architectural historians, and the appearance of several art books on the havelis, which I describe below. The Indian National Trust for Art and Cultural Heritage (INTACH 1984) produced an ambitious conservation plan for Shekhawati, including a proposal for a 'Shekhawati Wall Paintings Conservation Centre', and a 'Training School for Wall Paintings Conservation' (based on a model in Thailand). A team of experts surveyed the town of Mandawa and prepared a detailed, door-by-door list of its architectural heritage (INTACH 1984: 18). This was followed by a second report in 1985–86, entitled simply 'Rajasthan: Shekhawati' (School of Architecture, New Delhi 1985–86).

A small number of lavishly produced texts by popular writers who praise the art on the haveli walls, popularized Shekhawati in the 1980s. Aman Nath and Francis Wacziarg, for example, produced a beautiful full-colour coffee table book *Rajasthan: the Painted Walls of Shekhawati* (1982). The two went on to create small hotels in the region. Ilay Cooper's *The Painted Towns of Shekhawati* (1994) extensively described the Marwari havelis. An early version of this book was first published in Churu, in the Shekhawati area, as *Rajasthan: the Guide to Painted Towns of Shekhawati and Churu with Street Maps* (1991), and subsequently as *A Mapin Guide to India* (Cooper 1994). It follows guidebook conventions, with a summary of Shekhawati history, including the emergence of the Marwaris (Cooper 1994, 38). Text coverage includes details on the architectural monuments that the Marwaris left behind, including Hindu temples, the domed cenotaphs known as *chhatris*, wells, *dharamshalas* (pilgrim accommodations), shops, and cow protection societies, but the book's focus is a town-by-town guide to the painted mansions.

Entrepreneurs were beginning to be aware of the region's tourism development potential in the 1980s, as it became evident that there was a market for small luxury 'boutique' hotels in rural locations. One hotel in Mandawa dates itself to 1980 (Ramaswamy 2002). The Heritage Hotels Association of India, an organization of palace hotels (converted palaces and forts), which promotes and sets standards for historic preservation values among its member hotels, today lists at least three properties in the Shekhawati region, along with palace hotels in nearby locations such as Jaipur.

Guidebooks published as late as the 1970s and early 1980s do not promote the Shekhawati painted mansions as tourism destinations (see Fodor and Curtis 1974; Crowther 1981). This changed by the 1990s, as Rajasthan began to merit its own guidebooks. The *Lonely Planet Guide to Rajasthan* (Coxall and Singh 1997) devotes over twenty-four pages to Shekhawati. The chapter includes the usual historical summary and descriptions of forts, wells, and cenotaphs, but its focus is the painted havelis, clearly the major point of reference for the reader. This focus also appears in another guidebook, which not only includes ten pages of information on Shekhawati, but also pointedly lists where the most well known images can be found (*Everyman Guide to Rajasthan* 1996).

Rajasthan Government promotion of Shekhawati to foreign tourists also appears to begin in the late 1990s. This followed the earlier trend of seeing cultural heritage promotion both as a means of attracting tourists, and to encourage local appreciation for endangered historical buildings and cultural traditions. In 1999, for example, Rajasthan's Tourism Secretary Lalit Pawar, announced the formation of a '*dharohar sena*' (heritage army) of schoolchildren who would 'adopt' a neighbourhood monument. Under this program, Pawar promised, 'There will not be any more of the 'Panna Lal loves Munni Devi' stuff scribbled on the walls of forts' (The Hindu 1999 Sept. 28).

The 'Unmediated' Tourist Visit

The typical experience of visiting the havelis is one where the tourist simply 'discovers' – for himself or herself – the painted houses while walking along the narrow, twisted streets of the small towns where most havelis are located. Unlike heavily visited tourist sites in India, the majority of the havelis are not staffed with curators, let alone caretakers, so one can wander quite freely without being shepherded around, as is the practice elsewhere. There are no ropes to keep visitors at a distance, no signage, no local guides offering their services, and few schoolchildren asking for cash, pens, and the visitor's name.[9] The fact that these houses are located *in situ* within towns, and not in museums, allows visitors to experience the haveli in ways that are largely not pre-packaged.

In this regard, it is important to note that the havelis thus first came to the attention of Westerners through the lenses of art and art history, architecture and preservation. These lenses have tended to focus on the painted image: it is the 'image' that tourists come to see, and – as the guidebooks' structure indicates – they come to consume

---

9   Car tourists may be buffered from these elements because their driver and/or guide may intervene. Backpacker and cyclist 'blogs' make it clear that children solicit interaction in sites such as Nawalgarh, sometimes unpleasantly, in the view of the tourist, and sometimes in friendly fashion, as the tourist sees it (see blog by John McCabe, www.travelblog.org/Asia/India/Rajasthan/Nawalgarh, Nov. 24, 2005 and Nov. 25, 2005; and the blog ditchtheraf.blogspot.com/2004/10/desert-romance; or www.cyclesydneylondon.com/articles/article15, 'Rajasthan, Shekawati region', 22–00).

specific painted images. Tourist 'blogs' of Shekhawati include mostly photographs that closely frame the paintings and architecture, not the local people or other elements of the small town landscape.

Figure 1.2 **As haveli owners become involved in conservation efforts, signs such as this direct tourists to preserved and restored sites for viewing.** *Photo courtesy of Anne Hardgrove.*

Very few of the houses are set up for formal tourist access, with entry and photography fees. The havelis belonging to some of the most prominent Marwari families include museums and galleries, which mimic the logic of museum exhibitions. Displays of family memorabilia such as honorary degrees and photographs of family members with world leaders, emphasize narratives of personal achievement. The haveli of the industrialist Birla family connects this site with other Birla landmarks in India generally, the Birla colleges, schools and, of course, the famous Birla temples in major cities across India.

In Nawalgarh, the Poddar family established a secondary school at its haveli in 1966, and in 1992, the family restored the frescoes and set up a small museum in the rooms which are separate from the school. A brochure to promote the Poddar museum claimed that it expected about 10,000 foreign visitors in 1997. Also in Nawalgarh, the Morarka family employs a caretaker to greet guests, charge admission, and guide visitors to see the paintings of the structure. The Moraka family foundation, established in 1991, also promotes 'farm ecotourism and heritage conservation', including documentation of the havelis, conservation planning and restoration of the Morarka haveli, with more restorations promised in future (www.morarkango.com/tourism).

Since the havelis are not inhabited by their owners, and are either rented out or simply abandoned, the visitor does not have to deal directly with people with a strong personal stake in the maintenance of the painted mansions. In exploring the havelis, tourists sometimes find themselves asking the resident caretakers for permission to view the paintings. Often the paintings are obscured from view by clotheslines filled with drying sari blouses and petticoats, blowing in the dry hot wind. Children running around and playing games in the houses' inner-courtyards hardly take notice of the visitors, preferring to continue their merriment rather than engage with the strangers holding cameras.

As correspondent Andrew Robinson writes in *The Daily Telegraph* (July 10, 1999):

> .....Many havelis are tucked away in side streets and need to be searched for. Then permission to enter must be sought – normally possible in exchange for some rupees, although inner courtyards, originally the women's quarters, are sometimes still closed. And when you do get inside, the most interesting paintings may require help to locate.
>
> As a rule, hardly any guidance is available on the spot and few people speak any English. Even if you speak Hindi, as my companion did, you are not much further forward (Robinson 1999:6).

Tourists being able to wander alone, with little interference from self-appointed guides and indifference from local residents, is of critical importance in the tourist experience in Shekhawati. It is the feeling that one has found the authentic India – perhaps especially if – laundry drying on crisscrossed clothes lines has to be lifted or pushed aside to view the paintings (Shiner 1994, Waitt 2000). The painted mansions offer the illusion of finding an unmediated experience of an almost-lost heritage that seems divorced from the realities of the present-day residents. This experience is very much that of penetrating the 'back region' of a tourist site (MacCannell 1973). The terseness of the guidebook regarding the paintings themselves, and the relative absence of guides to interpret the paintings, means that the tourist must 'improvise' the touristic performance (Edensor 2000, 335) – in this case, the ritualized seeking, viewing, and photographing of images.

The havelis have the additional attraction of allowing Europeans to see how Indians portrayed their colonial era, yet another 'insider' perspective. Images of Westerners and western technologies are especially popular with foreign tourists, judging by the attention given to these in guidebooks and inclusion in tourist blogs.

This interest apparently fits a Western popular tradition of depicting non-Westerners as humorously incompetent when they try to be western.[10] In a similar vein, Lutz and Collins (1993, 207–212) point out the visual appeal to that magazine's readership of photographs that juxtapose scantily or traditionally-clad natives and

---

10 I am grateful to Carol Henderson for pointing out this connection to me.

modern technology. Clearly, the viewer/tourist is expected to identify with the (western) photographer/colonizer, not the artist/local subject. Guidebooks rarely offer any commentary other than that some images are 'copies' of Western images. In Western eyes, the images are likely to appear quaint (outmoded), naïve (incorrect or poor copies) and kitsch, rather than as entirely within the conventions and aesthetics of the painters themselves, or as a pithy commentary on the West.

Figure 1.3   One of the enduring popular themes for tourist photography is the depiction of Western technology by Shekhawati artists.
Photo courtesy of Anne Hardgrove. All rights reserved.

An Unexpected Bus Trip

My first visit to Shekhawati coincided with a trip to Jhunjhunu's Rani Sati temple, which is very popular with Marwari pilgrims. Seeing the havelis was only an afterthought, something else to do while I was in the area, for in 1996 my commitment was to be seen by others, and to 'perform' as Edensor (2000) puts it, as a scholar: not as a 'tourist.' I chose to stay in a family-run hotel in Jhunjhunu.[11] Before I left, the family insisted that I have at least a one-day tour of some of the area havelis, along

---

11 This reflects both the realities of grant funding for research, which precludes stays in luxury hotels, as well as a long scholarly tradition of preferring to be in more intimate settings

with some of the Marwari temples recently built in the district. Their son would drive me around. Before we set out for the day, my host loaned me a number of expensively produced art books on the area, including the Nath and Wacziarg book, and some books about Rajasthan temples and Hinduism, which I put on the back seat. Thus armed with the 'master narrative' of Shekhawati, we set out.

We drove to towns and stopped and looked at a number of houses. As I viewed the wall paintings, local residents passed by, sometimes murmuring aloud why anyone should be bothered looking at such strange and decrepit houses. They clearly did not expect that I could understand their comments. The son proved to be an engaging guide, regaling me with tales of how officials from the Income Tax Office sometimes raided the temples and insisted on viewing their record books, because their wealth seemed to far outweigh the taxes reported by the business magnate founder. Ironically, to me now, in view of this discussion of the havelis, my guide made a special point, as we drove to some of the local towns, of showing me the newly built and ostentatiously modern mansions of the Persian Gulf returnees, India's *nouveaux riches* of the 1980s and 1990s, who in their home construction demonstrated their new economic and social status (see chapter by Snodgrass).

Only by chance did this trip to the countryside offer me a chance to experience local transport and allow me to recover my privileged position (or so I thought) as scholar, one privy to the unseen 'back stage' of local society. The axle of our air-conditioned car suddenly snapped, and we had to make our way back by bus. With little water on hand, and feeling the responsibility to carry an armful of heavy art and religion books back with me, we walked for a couple of miles under the strong light and heat of the sun to the nearest bus stop. Some mothers with their nursing babies waited with us in a tiny bit of shade. The poverty of the area, including the women co-passengers we talked to as we waited, presented a sharp contrast to the tourism promoted in the area. This was a far cry from the experience of wandering the empty lanes of Shekhawati viewing Indian 'heritage.' The end to the day was also not the way in which a typical tourist would experience Shekhawati, as 'staged tourism' geared to see 'heritage' selectively, in the built environment, among the doings of the rich, and the high and mighty.

Ecotourism and Heritage

My argument is that as tourism expands into new niches – in this case, away from the urban settings of most 'royal' tourism into the rural lanes of Shekhawati – touristic discourse seems to be expanding its definition of 'heritage' beyond its core (royalty), and subsuming within itself the Shekhawati havelis, despite their uncertain position as neither one form of heritage, nor the other. This redefinition involves a migration in the interpretation of the havelis, now viewed as 'traditional', rather than as products of modernity, and hence incorporated into 'heritage', just as in the mid twentieth-

---

such as a family guesthouse, than an anonymous large hotel, in which the performance of self as 'academic' rather than as 'tourist' may be impeded.

century Jaipur became a 'traditional' rather than a 'modern' city (see chapter by Karatchkova). The havelis also, as noted above, seem to be attracting elements of interpretation that incorporate them partially into royal discourses of tourism.

A second strand to the interpretation of the havelis as 'heritage' appears to stem from the global narrative of environmentalism, of ecological preservation, and hence, of ecotourism. This draws from the rural character, at least to visitors, of the Shekhawati region. Ecotourism is an activity generally related to such principles as ecological sustainability, heritage conservation, and social justice. The central experience in ecotourism is viewing endangered plant and animal species, along with contributing to restoration and preservation efforts that aim to protect the plants, animals, and environments where they occur. Ecotourism marketing in Shekhawati plays off the need to save an endangered 'species' (in this case, the paintings) from an indifferent or hostile local population, and off the desire of a niche market of tourists to have a simpler and – to them, more authentic – tourism experience than in a palace hotel.

Possibly the best-known 'ecotourist' enterprise in Shekhawati is a small, full service resort, Apani Dhani, affiliated with the non-governmental organization called the Friends of Shekhawati. The marketing for the resort, available in either English or French, offers the following self-description:

In Shekhawati, [the resort] offers eco-friendly accommodation, excursions and activities with locals such as cooking lessons, initiation to traditional arts and crafts.

Staying with us will enable you to discover daily life and traditions of rural India.

..... [the resort] provides an alternative to the classical hotels.

We are deeply involved in sustainable tourism. We are also a member of The International Ecotourism Society and of Eco Club. http://apanidhani.com/

The marketing discourse of the resort positions this as a counterpoint to the heritage tourism of royalty. Mr. Ramesh Jangid, the owner of the property, described his views in an interview with a British journalist: 'Most travellers get a distorted picture of my country and its people. Agencies from all over the world sell a dream to tourists who want to discover the land of the maharajas. I don't know who is to blame – the traveller who is dreaming, the travel agencies who make them dream, or the local operators who co-ordinate the process' (Wheat 1997).

If the resort is the centre of the hotelier's effort to demonstrate ecological sustainability in tourism practice, the Friends of Shekhawati is the organization that aims to promote conservation values and heritage awareness. European writing about the need for conservation emphasizes the haveli owners' indifference and abandonment of their properties, and even fatal 'improvements' by the towns' residents (Balodis 1998, 27).

French author Eliane Georges notes, in what can be considered a typical statement of this sort:

The Marwaris today have completely abandoned Shekhawati, leaving their havelis in the care of guardians who live sparely without the means to keep people from pillaging them. Destitute squatter families, who, for a couple of rupees, eagerly hasten to open the doors for visitors, occupy some of the houses. An association, founded by Ramesh Jangid and Catherine Ripou, attempts to protect the painted towns and plans for a museum project are under consideration. But the rich Marwaris, upon whom it falls to restore these homes, are much too caught up in the rough and tumble of the great Indian metropolises, to come back into the tiny lanes of Shekhawati (Georges 1996: 44–46; translation by Despina Stratigakos and Antonio Calabria).

I visited this ecotourist resort in the summer of 2000, when I returned to Shekhawati with the purpose of visiting and photographing the painted havelis, along with examples of Marwari philanthropy in the region. I travelled with a graduate student, who was doing research at a nearby sustainable development project. She was interested in the havelis near Nawalgarh. After a few days, we rode the bus there and found our way on foot from the bus stop to the resort.[12] This featured about a half dozen huts built with indigenous techniques, spread around a small compound. The construction of environmentally sensitive lodging was the centrepiece of the resort's ecotourism orientation. As my own first ecotourism experience, my immediate impression in the blistering July heat was the absence of air conditioning. The fans installed in the ceilings of the hut, along with the occasional breeze, provided a little bit of relief from the sweltering heat.

During our time in Nawalgarh, we wandered the town looking for particular images on the walls of the havelis that I wished to photograph, and visited a number of schools founded by Marwari entrepreneurs. The most fascinating part of the visit, at least from my perspective, was to participate in, as well as to observe, how Mr. Jangid interacted with his guests. For these guests, a stay at an ecotourist resort, which is certainly unique in Rajasthan, offered a respite from mainstream tourist practices. Meals were served family style. Mr. Jangid held court around the table with four to six other guests and us. The food – usually dishes of lentils, rice, *chapatti* (flat bread) and vegetables – was served on heavy, hand-made paper bowls and plates, which could be discarded after each meal.

The other guests at the resort turned out to be Europeans, who were more comfortable speaking French than English. It was soon clear that French was the *lingua franca* of the public areas of the resort. I resuscitated my rusty high-school French from the corners of my brain, if just to listen and understand rather than to speak too much. My companion's excellent Hindi did not help her in this situation. Following a discussion she had with Mr. Jangid over how well the floor of our hut had been swept, she spent little time in those evening *salons*.

---

12 Scholarly budgets and preferences, which seek to bring scholars into as close contact with Indian society as possible, feeling this an important element of the research enterprise, privilege transportation options such as the bus and train (often second-class accommodation), rather than hired car or plane.

The ecotourist experience transformed the usual social relationships between tourist visitor and Indian hotel owner. Mr. Jangid's fluency in French – from his years living in France – allowed French-speaking tourists to communicate in their own language, instead of English, which is a second language for both themselves and for most of their local hosts.[13] The power relationships of this experience differed from the usual practice, where a socially subordinate wait staff serves the diners. Mr. Jangid ate his meals right along with the tourists, with everyone sitting at the same table, as social equals, and served by family members – clearly an effort to resist hierarchy. His strained relationship with my travelling companion made it very clear that he resented her attempts to treat him as a mere service provider. Guilt by association prevented me from having as much in-depth conversation with Mr. Jangid as I would have liked.

Occasionally, Mr. Jangid's then twenty-something son would emerge from the family's rooms to converse quickly with his father, and retreat into the shadows almost as quickly as he emerged. Other family members stayed in the background, not speaking much to the guests, if at all, and reservedly expressed their surprise that both my travel companion and I spoke Hindi. This was clearly a typical, conservative Rajput family who remained very much in the background, preparing meals for guests and cleaning their simple rooms. I made a few attempts to talk to them about the guests and the daily routines of the resort, to which they politely answered my questions. But despite the marketing of this experience as contact with Rajasthani family life, it was not the glimpse of rural Shekhawati life that I anticipated again, placing myself in the privileged academic's position – although this vision of rural life clearly met the expectations of the European guests. These give the resort rave reviews. When I reflect on my reasons for talking to the extended family, to ask questions about the day-to-day life of the resort, this was no doubt part of my own discomfort that scholars often feel in being mistaken for tourists.

As the tourist eye shifts from elite, royal sites to other places, the ideas of rural development, environmental protection, the preservation of haveli art and non-profit organizations all meld together. Heritage in this venue is very much a marketable tourism commodity, yet placed within a global rhetoric of responsible tourism. In the case of the abandoned deteriorating havelis, ecotourists have the potential to realize a self-gratifying and almost civilizing mission: to save a heritage that, the ecotourist is led to believe, most Indians (aside from their host and a few others they might meet) do not appreciate enough to save. The emphasis in Shekhawati tourism is on architectural preservation. The Morarka Foundation, which also promotes ecological values, approaches this from the standpoint of developing sustainable 'green' technology. Every effort is made to preserve the built environment that resulted from Marwari economic ascendancy in the late nineteenth-century. In this setting, the ideas of preservation and conservation, part of the ecotourism experience,

---

13 It is worth noting that the resort website lists newspaper clippings about its heritage preservation in three languages: English, French, and German (www.apanidhani.com).

are materialized through the idea of saving the heritage of the built environment as a source of future revenue.

Multivocal Messages and Heritage

Today, the Marwari community is located in the metropolises of Mumbai, Calcutta, and other major cities. Both domestic and international tourism play a role in how Marwaris represent their pasts, and how the Shekhawati havelis draw upon the multivalent messages of historical tourism of Rajasthan. Such activities help mediate the historical relationships between Marwari and Rajput royal cultural traditions. Although as a group the Marwaris have maintained their financial success, individual families have tended to neglect the houses, perhaps seeing them as no longer being of value to the family. Shekhawati residents blame the absent Marwaris for the lack of upkeep, suggesting in this their cynicism for Marwari philanthropy in the region. A growing number of thrift and pawnshops in Jaipur and New Delhi retail valuable household objects scavenged from the houses, for antique-hunters seeking carved doors or home furnishings.

For the Marwaris, the creation of the houses and their paintings marked their meteoric rise as the capitalist class of modern India, and in Rajasthan, replacing the Rajputs as the dominant economic group. Paintings on early Marwari havelis contain scenes of folk tales, daily activities, and Indian epics. Images of Hindu gods such as Krishna and his consort Radha are especially common, and reflect popular religious movements in the region. Whereas Rajput paintings place greater stress on rulers, courts, and battles, the Marwaris claim their authority through their religious devotion. Later, pictures of trains, cars, and planes also represent a shift away from the royal purview of feudalism, in the latter case to a market-based capitalist and cosmopolitan perspective. In this way, the Marwari painted houses could be simultaneously traditional – like the royal palaces – yet also portray the hybrid world in which Marwaris found themselves. For Marwaris, the houses were an effort to establish social respectability through the built environment. This is the message of the houses and their paintings intended by their creators.

The Marwari families whom I got to know in Calcutta had little interest in going back to Rajasthan to visit their homes. In the past, perhaps until the 1960s or so, families might return for important ceremonial occasions at places important to the ancestral lineage (see chapter by Cort). These cultural practices are in line with traditional Indian forms of tourism such as pilgrimages to ancestrally important holy sites. These stories told by Calcutta Marwaris, however, seemed more symbolic than historical. One did not need to know Rajasthan well to claim allegiance to the ancestral homeland of one's family.

The messages that tourists perceive, however, are quite different. The migration of heritage from the palaces to the havelis is predicated on the disjuncture of old houses and modern populations. In the case of the havelis, the message that something is 'old' is underscored by its state of disrepair and abandonment. Almost all the tourist literature on the havelis incorporates a pervasive theme of local indifference and the neglect of wealthy Marwari families, depicted as uninterested in saving the heritage of the painted houses. Travel writer Robinson notes,

> In 20 years of travel in India, I have rarely encountered such blank indifference to local history. It is as if the enterprising Marwaris who left Shekhawati and the people they left behind belong to separate worlds. Year by year the murals are vanishing beneath coats of whitewash, election graffiti and general grime. If their owners in the cities do not take action soon only photographs will be left. (Robinson 1999: 6)

Though the tone of this author's remarks carries the easy glibness of the foreigner, the words raise questions about the relationships between romanticism, the mobilization of the past, the construction of identity, and the politics of belonging, all key issues in the discussion of heritage tourism (Edwards 1998). At first glance, one could read into this journalistic statement the colonial trope of India's faded glory as something unrelated to the contemporary inhabitants, a theme of decay and indifference that echoes through much of the tourist marketing literature on havelis.

The mansions fall between the established touristic tropes of the prince or the peasant, the urban or the rural. In this regard, and given the global middle-class propensity of distain for the tastes and style of the nouveau riche, the havelis are more likely to migrate upward into the category of the fort or palace, to be reinvented as mini-palaces for tourist consumption, than to migrate downward as exemplars of a 'peasant' or 'nomad' culture. This migration would be consistent with the master narrative of Rajasthan tourism: royalty. Non-royals come into this narrative only as 'local colour' and as 'bit players', as 'gypsy' musicians, nomads, performers, and crafts artists. The havelis clearly do not fit this latter story line.

Yet, the havelis' interpretation is also uncertain, for they also fit a second important narrative of Western tourism, at least, and that is ecotourism. This narrative positions the wall paintings as akin to endangered species, 'nature' to be saved from the very people who would otherwise destroy it. The ecotourist narrative is predicated upon a civilizing narrative where outsiders (and a few discerning insiders) appreciate disappearing architecture, which modern Shekhawati residents are indifferent about saving. The narratives of the local histories, of the reasons for local townspeople's indifference, are far beyond the scope of what the tourist wants to hear. The moral economy of this second narrative positions the tourist as a 'saviour', and patron to the paintings, rather than as a potentially disruptive influence in local society, as suggested by local commentary and polite indifference toward intruders in family courtyards.

By the 1990s, the term 'haveli' had acquired a cachet of cosmopolitanism coupled with a selective and colourful notion of tradition: restaurants, upscale shops and catalogues for house wares and clothing ranging from Canada to East Asia, used the term to appeal to consumers with the cultural capital to purchase goods laden with the symbolic value of tradition refashioned. The haveli connoted a stopping place in a journey across exotic destinations, of products reworked to appeal to cosmopolitan sensibilities, without losing the signs and symbols that, to these consumers, connoted 'tradition.' Sometimes these marketers emphasized the ephemeral nature of these goods, produced by vanishing crafts experts (turning to higher-paid factory labour), or representing vanishing tastes, as local peoples turn to machine-made goods and plastics. Exporting the term with these connotations ties into Orientalist representations of luxury and exoticism, and to the theme – as seen with the havelis themselves – of protecting something that is soon to disappear.

References

Balodis, J. (1998), 'Rajasthan's Beautifully Decorated Towns are in Disrepair as Inhabitants Choose Progress over Preservation', *The Canberra Times*, 22 February, A2.

Bhatia, G. (1994), *Punjabi Baroque and other Memories of Architecture* (New Delhi: Penguin).

Bhattacharyya, D. (1997), 'Mediating India: An Analysis of a Guidebook', *Annals of Tourism Research* 24:3, 371–389.

Blake, S.P. (1991), *Shahjahanabad: The Sovereign City in Mughal India, 1639–1739* (Cambridge: Cambridge University Press).

Carsten, J. and S. Hugh-Jones (1995), *About the House: Lévi-Strauss and Beyond* (Cambridge: Cambridge University Press).

Chambers, E. (2000), *Native Tours: The Anthropology of Travel and Tourism* (Prospect Heights, IL: Waveland Press).

Cooper, I. (1991), *Rajasthan, the Guide to Painted Towns of Shekhawati and Churu, with Street Maps* (Churu, Rajasthan, India: Girish Chandra Sharma & Sons).

—— (1994), *The Painted Towns of Shekhawati: A Mapin Guide to India* (Ahmedabad, India : Mapin).

Coxall, M. and S. Singh (1997), *Rajasthan: A Lonely Planet Survival Kit* (Hawthorn, Victoria, Australia: Lonely Planet Publications).

Crowther, G. (1981), *India: A Travel Survival Kit* (Hawthorn, Victoria, Australia: Lonely Planet Publications).

Edensor, T. (2000), 'Staging Tourism: Tourists as Performers', *Annals of Tourism Research* 27:2, 322–344.

Edwards, J. (1998), 'The Need for a "Bit of History": Place and Past ·in English Identity', in Nadia Lovell (ed.) *Locality and Belonging* (New York: Routledge).

Everyman Guide to Rajasthan (1996) (London: Everyman Guides).

Fisher, James F. (2004), 'Sherpa Culture and the Tourist Torrent', in Sharon Bohn Gmelch (ed.) *Tourists and Tourism: A Reader* (Long Grove, IL: Waveland Press, 373–388).

Fodor, E. and W. Curtis (eds.) (1974), *Fodor's India* (New York: David McKay Company, Inc).

Gable E. et al. (1992), 'On the Uses of Relativism: Fact, Conjecture and Black and White Histories at Colonial Williamsburg', *American Ethnologist* 19:4, 791-805.

Georges, E. (1996), *Les Petits Palais du Rajasthan* (Paris: Editions du Chene).

Hardgrove, A. (2004), *Community and Public Culture: The Marwaris in Calcutta c.1897–1997* (New York: Columbia University Press; and New Delhi: Oxford University Press).

Hobsbawm, E. and T. Ranger (eds.) (1983), *The Invention of Tradition* (Cambridge: Cambridge University Press).

Indian National Trust for Architecture and Art Conservation (INTACH) (1984) Shekhavati: A Project for Conservation under the Auspices of INTACH; A summary report.

Johnson, N.C. (1996), 'Where Geography and History Meet: Heritage Tourism and the Big House in Ireland', *Annals of the Association of American Geographers* 86:3, 551–566.

Lutz, C.A. and J.L. Collins (1993), *Reading National Geographic* (Chicago: The University of Chicago Press).

MacCannell, D. (1973), 'Staged Authenticity: Arrangements of Social Space in Tourist Settings', *American Journal of Sociology* 79:3, 589–603.

Nath, A. and F. Wacziarg (1982), *Rajasthan: the Painted Walls of Shekhawati* (New Delhi: Vikas and London: Croom Helm).

Ramaswamy, Anindita. (2002), 'Hotel Mandawa: the Painted Palace', *Outlook Traveller* [website], www.outlooktraveller.com/aspseripts/mag

Robinson, A. (1999), 'Travel India: Heat, Dust and Fading Glory', *The Daily Telegraph* 10 July, 6.

Shiner, Larry (1994), '"Primitive Fakes," "Tourist Art," and the Ideology of Authenticity', *Journal of Aesthetics and Art Criticism* 52:2, 225–234.

School of Architecture, New Delhi (1985), Rajasthan: Shekhawati (New Delhi: Indian National Trust for Culture and Art Conservation (INTACH).

The Hindu (1999) 'Schools to adopt Monuments in Rajasthan' *The Hindu* 28 September.

Tillotson, G.H.R. (1987), *The Rajput Palaces: the Development of an Architectural Style, 1450–1570* (New Haven: Yale University Press).

Tod, J. (1971), *Annals and Antiquities of Rajast'han, Edited and with an Introduction by William Crooke*. In 3 vols. (London: George Routledge and Sons).

Waitt, G. (2000), 'Consuming Heritage: Perceived Historical Authenticity', *Annals of Tourism Research* 27:4, 835–862.

Wheat, S. (1997), 'When a Holiday is a Way of Life', *The Independent* 2 March , <http://www.apanidhani.com/alter/holiday.htm>

Chapter 2

Ghost Towns and Bustling Cities: Constructing a Master Narrative in Nineteenth-Century Jaipur

Elena Karatchkova

Travel writing has, for at least two centuries, been an important form of mediation of tourist activity. Travel narratives, including travel publications, personal travel accounts, guidebooks, travel magazines, and oral narratives offered on site by tour guides, are capable of constructing *tourist spaces* out of ordinary geographical places. Travel narratives in tourist spaces over time proliferate and challenge each other; they also converse with one another (Edensor 1998).

This chapter reconstructs the development of the dominant travel narrative, or, as I alternately refer to it, the marketing discourse, of Jaipur and Amber, from the early nineteenth-century to the present day. I first discuss how contemporary guidebooks present Jaipur and Amber as tourist destinations and the contemporary marketing discourse that these descriptions reflect. I then examine the historical roots of this discourse, by illustrating how nineteenth-century European travellers of various backgrounds and different nationalities represented Jaipur and Amber.

This approach documents the historical emergence and the contemporary continuity of two themes in the genre of travel writing about Jaipur and Amber: the image of Amber as deserted and abandoned, in contrast to Jaipur as the 'modern' city. Jaipur is familiar to travellers. Amber is strange, unfamiliar, and its 'otherness' encapsulated in a set-piece which, as will be seen, is repeated for over a century. This dichotomous view continues in the oral narratives of tour guides at both locations.

This chapter analyses the content of both nineteenth- and twentieth-century sources. Nineteenth-century sources used for this discussion include the published accounts of Reginald Heber (1783–1836), Anglican bishop and missionary; Victor Jacquemont (1801–1832), French naturalist; Prince Aleksei Soltykoff (1806–1859), Russian diplomat turned painter; Thomas Hendley (1847–1917), colonial administrator. Rudyard Kipling (1865–1936), the author; and Edwin Arnold (1832–1904); English poet, journalist and travel writer. Twentieth-century materials discussed are tourist publications and contemporary guidebooks. These latter include thematic English language publications featuring tourist sites of Jaipur, such as *Majestic Jaipur* (Wheeler 1998) and *The Taj Magazine,* issued by the Taj Group of Hotels. I also reference magazine and newspaper articles published in Jaipur that feature tourism issues. Finally, I use the results of my fieldwork in Jaipur and Amber from 2000 to the present, including interviews with people involved in a variety of positions in the tourism industry.

Jaipur and Amber as Tourist Destinations

Jaipur (population 2.3 million in 2001) is the capital of the state of Rajasthan. Formerly, Jaipur was the capital of the princely state of the same name. Jaipur is best known to international tourists and tourism entrepreneurs as the third destination in the 'golden triangle' (to tourism entrepreneurs) of New Delhi, Agra and Jaipur, the most popular tourist circuit in north India.[1] Government and civic entities have long recognized the city's tourist potential and have been keen to develop its infrastructure, quality of the tourism experience, and heritage significance. Newspapers frequently debate various plans to improve Jaipur as a 'tourist-friendly' destination.

Amber (alternatively Amer), a short five miles northeast of Jaipur, is routinely included in the itineraries of domestic and foreign tourists. Tours package a visit to Amber as a half-day outing along a picturesque road, with the exotic treat of an elephant ride up the winding pathway and through the gates of the old fort-palace complex. This image is widely reproduced in tourism documents promoting Jaipur, Rajasthan, and India generally (see chapter by Henderson).

Amber (current population around 15,000) was the capital of the Dhundhar kingdom from the tenth century A.D. until 1728. Dhundhar kingdom was also known as Amber kingdom until the new capital of Jaipur was built during the reign of Sawai Jai Singh II (1699–1743). Amber was then and remains today a two-level structure. Its magnificent fort-palace perches high above the town. The town itself lies at the bottom of the hill. Amber bears much resemblance to many small Indian towns, with its bustling shops selling sweets, drinks, toys, and other inexpensive goods geared to holiday travellers. Some of Amber's residential buildings and temples predate the fort-palace complex by as much as three hundred years. Although the fort-palace complex, now managed by the State Ministry of Tourism, is kept in a relatively good condition, the town suffers from neglect by these same authorities.

In the 1990s a group of architects, stimulated by a local heritage society, began to conduct surveys on Amber and its environs. Following a survey, in 1996 the architectural firm Abhikram produced the Amber Conservation Plan whose goal was to preserve and develop the town as a 'Heritage Zone'. Among other developments the plan suggested creating guided tours along specific routes within the town walls, the oldest part of the city, but implementation of the plan was halted owing to bureaucratic resistance.[2] These efforts helped to include Amber in an ambitious

---

1   In 2001, 173,000 foreign and 656,000 domestic tourists visited Jaipur according to the Department of Tourism, Government of Rajasthan (Indiastat.com).

2   This data was obtained as a result of my personal communication with Nimish Patel and Parul Zaveri of Abhikram, who generously opened their company archives and allowed me to work in them for three days during a visit to Ahmedabad.

Figure 2.1 View of the old town of Amber looking upwards towards the fort-palace citadel. Some structures in the old town predate the hilltop complex by a century. *Photo courtesy of Elena Karatchkova.*

Rajasthan Urban Infrastructure Development Project involving the Government of Rajasthan and the Asian Development Bank (RUIDP 2005). Tentative allocations for Amber were estimated at approximately US$2 million, with US$8 million estimated for Jaipur's development.[3] Amber town has been slated for construction of sewer lines, and preservation efforts aimed at the fort's and the town's main features.

Tourism Discourse on Jaipur and Amber

Colonial travel writing largely ignored Amber as a population centre and described it as desolate and abandoned.[4] Today's tourism marketing discourse acknowledges the town, but selectively: it mentions just two or three of its heritage monuments. Groups of organized tourists arriving from Jaipur usually enter and depart the fort-palace complex of Amber unaware of the town's population. Occasionally backpackers and tourists can be seen browsing Amber's streets, but their favorite guidebooks, such as *Lonely Planet Guide* (Choy and Singh 2002*)* ignore Amber town as a tourism destination.

Tourism marketing discourse resembles what Lyotard refers to as master narratives (Lyotard 1984), which are rigid, standardized, and formulaic narratives that claim objectivity and authority. A master narrative is also reductive, in that it usually develops one theme at the expense of other possible themes and meanings. Examples from tourism include the familiar 'Rome: The Eternal City', or 'Red Square – Heart of the Soviet Motherland.' Master narratives reference historical or archeological research to create a sense of objectivity. Tourism writing invokes authority with the use of earlier travel accounts embellished with abundant quotes from past travellers.

Contemporary tourist publications share these distinguishing features with master narratives by emphasizing one theme for each location, and specifying the landmarks that should be seen. These publications share the same interpretation of each location and support these interpretations with identical historical references. As a result, most tourists arrive at a tourism destination already armed with its master narrative (Bhattacharyya 1997).

The contemporary master narrative for Jaipur and Amber is 'royalty'(Ramusack 1994). This theme is ubiquitous in tourist publications, such as *Majestic Jaipur* (Wheeler 1998). Royal personalities are emphasized, as in Jaipur: *The Royal City* (Singh, 1998, 43). One article on tourist attractions of Jaipur features a full-page photograph of Maharaja Bhawani Singh, in full regalia, with his wife and daughter, all identified as 'the present royal family' (Kanwar 2000, 36–37).

---

3   This data is based on personal communication with Poonam Verma, an architect working for INTACH on behalf of Abhikram, in February–March of 2003.

4   For example in November 2005, the online Wikipedia description calls Amber a 'ruined town', citing as its source the 1911 *Encyclopedia Britannica* (Wikipedia 2005 http:// en.wikipedia.org/wiki/Amber%2C).

All guide books recommend tourist attractions in Jaipur that are either connected with royalty or interpreted as such (see chapters by Bautès, Henderson and Jhala). Jaipur's City Palace, partially converted into a museum, displays the luxurious lifestyles of the former rulers. According to most guide books, *Hawa Mahal* ('the Palace of the Winds') was supposedly built for the royal women. Gaitor town, situated about five miles away from Jaipur, is the royal cremation site for the ruling dynasty. And Amber is, of course, their former abode.

Tourist Spaces in the Making: Travel Narratives 1800–1860

I now turn to the *process* of production of this marketing discourse, or tourist spaces in the making. During the nineteenth-century, the unique first impressions of travellers gradually became fixed in the rigid frames of a master narrative. This process was abetted by the technological changes that transformed travellers to India into tourists. Early nineteenth-century travellers endured the hardships of travelling in palanquins or on horse- or elephant back, accompanied by guards to protect them against robbers. By the early 1870s, rail service connected Jaipur with Delhi and Agra, and with Mumbai. Thomas Hendley's guidebook marks the transition from arduous overland animal-powered travel to leisure tourism via rail in Rajasthan. One of the features of guidebooks becomes rail schedules and accounts of rail journeys. Thus for example, Hendley's *The Jeypore Guide* (1875) includes two chapters on railway travel: 'Railway Journey from Jeypore to Ajmere', and 'Railway Journey from Jeypore to Agra and Delhi', describing attractions worth seeing along the way.

A variety of English and other travellers came to Jaipur from the eighteenth century to around the 1820s, largely on official missions.[5] For example, Mountstuart Elphinstone (1770–1859) passed through the Shekhawati region of Jaipur territories in 1808 en route to his mission in Afghanistan, but he did not visit the capital. Elphinstone scarcely describes the towns he passes through in Shekhawati and Bikaner, save to note that they are fortified (Elphinstone, 1815, 8–10). James Tod, the author of the much-quoted *Annals and Antiquities of Rajast'han* (1829, 1832) says that he visited Jaipur in 1807 (1829, 4), but this published description of Jaipur and Amber uses very similar language as that used by Reginald Heber in his published descriptions of the same locations published the year before in London and Philadelphia (Heber 1828, 2:4).

The foundational and most detailed descriptions of Jaipur and Amber were authored by Reginald Heber, who became the Anglican Bishop of Calcutta in 1822. After an almost-six month sea voyage to India with his wife, Amelia (then pregnant with the couple's second child), Heber arrived in India in the fall of 1824. Soon after this, he undertook a long journey through the Upper Provinces of India to get acquainted with his diocese. According to his account, he travelled by boat up the

---

5   The earliest written European traveller's account seems to be authored in 1745 by a Portuguese scientific advisor to Maharaja Jai Singh II, according to Sarkar (1984).

Ganges, by horse, palanquin, and elephant on occasion. Heber's letters and travel journal were edited and published posthumously by his wife (Heber 1828).

The city of Jaipur, soon to celebrate its first century anniversary, impressed Heber favourably:

> The city is a very remarkable and striking one. Being all the work of one sovereign, Jye Singh [Jai Singh][6], it is on *regular plan* with one *very wide street*, crossed at *right angles* by three others, with a square in the centre of the town, which serves as a market place. The houses are generally two stories high, but some three and four with ornamented windows and balconies, and many of them finely carved. They are interspersed with some *handsome temples* in the same style with those of Benares [Varanasi]... [Italics added] (Heber, 1828: II, 4).

Two days after recording these observations, Heber headed for Amber, accompanied by Colonel Raper, the Jaipur British Resident (the East India Company agent in charge of political affairs), Residency Surgeon Dr. Simpson, and two ministers of the Jaipur court. Heber describes Amber as:

> ...a *small ruinous town*, overgrown with trees, and intermingled with towers and temples, and over it[...]a *noble old fortified palace*, connected by a long line of wall and tower, with a very large castle on the highest part of the hill...the town...which almost entirely consisted of temples, and had few inhabitants but *grim and ghastly Yogis*, with their hair in *elf-knots*, and their faces covered with chalk, sitting *naked and hideous*, like so many *ghouls*, amid the *tombs* and *ruined houses*. A *narrow winding street* led us through these *abodes of superstition* [italics added] (Heber, 1828: II, 12).

The fort and palace complex at Amber produced a more favorable impression on Heber than did Amber Town. Today, there is hardly a tourist publication that does not reproduce the following quote from Heber:

> I have seen many royal palaces, containing larger and more stately rooms, many, the architecture of which was in a purer taste, and some which have covered a greater extent of ground ... but for varied and *picturesque effect*, for *wild beauty* of situation, for the number and *romantic singularity* of the apartments, and the strangeness of finding such a building, in such a place and country, I am able to compare nothing to Umeer [Amber] ...[italics added] (Heber, 1828: II, 12).

Heber's descriptions laid down the template for future descriptions: the clean, wide, regularly laid streets of Jaipur *versus* the winding and narrow streets of Amber; Jaipur's 'handsome temples' *versus* Amber's 'abodes of superstition.' Heber stresses the romantic beauty of the Amber fort, but does not comment likewise on Jaipur's fortifications.

---

6   The currently accepted spelling of proper and geographical names is indicated in brackets here and throughout.

Heber initiated another convention of writing about Amber when he described his visit to one of its oldest temples – *Shila Devi ka Mandir* – which he, along with most European travellers, simply called 'Kali's temple.'

> ...[our guide] led us some little distance up the citadel, then through a *dark low arch* into a small court, where to my surprise, the first object that met my eyes was a *pool of blood* on the pavement, by which a *naked man* stood with a *bloody sword* in his hand ... The guide ... cautioned me against treading in the blood, and told me that a goat was sacrificed here every morning. In fact a second glance showed me the *headless body* of the poor animal lying before the steps of a small shrine apparently of Kali. The Brahman was officiating and tinkling the bell, but it was plain to see, from the embarrassment of our guide, that we had intruded at an unlucky moment... The guide told us on our way back that the tradition was that, in ancient times, a man was sacrificed here every day; that the custom had been laid aside till Jye Singh [Jai Singh] had a frightful dream, in which the destroying power appeared to him and asked him why her image was suffered to be dry? The Raja, afraid to disobey, and reluctant to fulfill the requisition to its *ancient extent of horror*, took counsel and substituted a goat for the human victim... [italics added] (Heber 1828: II, 13–14).

Heber's account is a classical first-person narrative where events and encounters are seemingly described as they occur. Every minor episode constitutes an event; and Heber effortlessly switches from village descriptions to personal encounters, from ethnographic data to local gossip.

From this publication onward, every nineteenth-century European who published an account of Amber writes about the ritual sacrifice in Kali's temple. Two examples, the French botanist Jacquemont and the Russian Prince Soltykoff, illustrate the variations on the themes established by Heber. Ironically, each of these visitors enters the Kali temple at the very moment of sacrifice, but describes the experience in different narrative styles. The tone of shocked sensibility culminates in Edwin Arnold's *India Revisited* (1886). Arnold devotes almost three pages to this 'horrid propitiation',[7] which 'the ladies would by no means view' (Arnold 1886, 154–156).

Victor Jacquemont, an equally prolific writer on Rajasthan, was a young, unmarried Frenchman who travelled to India to collect botanical specimens. Jacquemont suffered injuries from a fall from a horse shortly after his departure from Jaipur, and the effects of this accident, combined with severe dysentery, contributed to his death of liver abscesses in December, 1832 in Mumbai. His letters were published in Paris in 1833 and were a great success (Jacquemont 1833, 1834). Jacquemont's account of Rajasthan was first published in the *Journal des Debats*, and subsequently as *Voyages et Voyageurs* (Cuvillier-Fleury 1856). English language writers of the nineteenth-century and early twentieth-century often allude to Jacquemont's account of Jaipur and Amber (for example see Imperial Gazetteer of India 1908: vol. 5, 290).

Jacquemont's voyage to India on board a French Government corvette lasted for six months. He arrived in 1829, but bureaucratic delays held him in Calcutta until

---

7   The sacrifice of animals in public temple rituals was banned by the Rajasthan state authorities in 1975.

1831. Jacquemont's comments in his letters indicate that he was aware that as a French national (a country which had been England's great rival in the not-so-distant past), he may have been viewed with suspicion by his British hosts. With far more modest equipment and a smaller entourage than most travellers, Jacquemont crossed India from Calcutta to Delhi and Punjab and proceeded into the Himalayas as far as Ladakh.

On his return from the north, Jacquemont rested in Delhi and resumed his journey to Bombay through what was then Rajputana. Jacquemont's letters written between December 1831 and May 1832 provide a lively sense of the journey along the way (Jacquemont 1936). The detailed account of his four-day stay in Jaipur (March 1–4, 1832), is in his posthumously-published Journal in a segment entitled 'Dans Le Rajpoutana', which covered his travel from Delhi to Alwar, Jaipur, Ajmer, and Chittor en route to Malwa and Bombay.

In another publication, (Jacquemont 1934), in a chapter entitled '*Jeypour-Amber, Des Avantages de la Domination Anglais'* ['Jaipur and Amber: Of the Advantages of British Rule' written in 1832], Jacquemont first comments that '*Jeipour est une ville moderne'* ('Jaipur is a modern town'), followed by a description of its founder, Maharaja Jai Singh. Jacquemont notes that Jaipur has streets that meet at right angles and are exactly oriented to the cardinal points of the compass (Jacquemont 1934, 33). He describes the rows of shops with workmen industriously occupied inside, and the solid characteristics and neatness of the urban environment:

> ... The ordinary houses have been built with the stone of the hillocks around. The houses of a higher rank, built of the same materials, are plastered with a lime cement of brilliant whiteness[8]. The cement is sometimes polished like stucco ...Most of the temples and palaces have facings of white marble. *There is no hut, no ruined building, no rubbish heap.* The city has the look of what it really is, *an entirely new town*, which has not yet been subjected to the horrors of war. In general, the architecture of Jaipur is of very elegant style [italics added] (as quoted in Sarkar, 1984, 208; see also Jacquemont 1934, 33–34).

Jacquemont was a proponent of modern values, including industrious labour. In his view, Jaipur is a modern, industrious and clean city. Jacquemont's scientific training shows in his attention to details about construction materials, such as white marble and red sandstone.

Jacquemont's narrative style changes when he reaches Amber, described poetically as a sad ruined city, still visited occasionally by the royal family now residing in Jaipur (Jacquemont 1934, 34). Jacquemont next describes the palace temple complex, and the infamous Kali temple. He informs the reader of the presence in the temple of devout 'Brahmans and fakirs' who daily offer a goat to the goddess Kali, a practice that – the reader is told – replaced human sacrifice in Amber. He

---

8   Jaipur would acquire its famous pink colour only in the second half of the nineteenth century, during the reign of Sawai Ram Singh (r. 1859–1880).

states however that human sacrifice was recently practiced in the Himalayas and is still practiced by the indigenous tribes of central India (Jacquemont 1934, 35).

He then goes on to describe the palace of Amber, built during the reign of 'Radjah Man-sing'[9] (r. 1589–1614). Jacquemont feels that this palace represents a truly Indian architecture, likened to that which he saw in Kashmir (Jacquemont 1934, 35). He makes brief mention of the women's quarters, noting that the Jaipur Rajputs are stricter than other Indians in enforcing female seclusion.

A description of landscape adds mood to the melancholy picture he paints of Amber:

> The winter has turned the country-side brown [this was March 1–4], and framed round by these *wild* hillocks the lake, with its white marble kiosks and the *magnificent* verdure of its gardens, forms a *ravishing* tableau' [italics added] (cited in Sarkar, 1984, 209).

> The city of Amber has fallen into ruin. We can call it a city, marked by the *fatal providence*, visited by *desolating plague*, without an inhabitant, without one voice except the *monotonous murmur* of the prayer of a Brahman who has remained faithful to one of his old temples [italics added] (in Sarkar, 1984, 209).

Jacquemont recorded his impressions, in letters and diaries, of his travels throughout northern and central India, and acknowledges James Tod's voluminous works on Mewar. He waxes enthusiastic about Jaipur, calling it, 'without comparison, the finest city in India' (Jacquemont 1834: v.2, 273). It is probably its modernity, comparable to European cities, that most favorably impresses him.

The Russian Prince Aleksei Soltykoff (1806–1895),[10] visited Rajasthan some thirteen years after Jacquemont, in 1845. At age eighteen, in 1824, Soltykoff joined the diplomatic service with the Russian State Collegium for Foreign Affairs (Alaev 1985, 3). After diverse short posts in Europe and the Middle East, Soltykoff realized that a diplomatic career no longer attracted him and he would rather be a traveller and an artist. At thirty-four he retired to Paris, engaged in drawing and painting, and started to plan his trip to India, which he undertook in 1845.

In 1848, Soltykoff published a selection of his letters to a family member from India in French, the language used by nineteenth century elite Russians (Soltykoff 1848). The same book was translated into Russian and published three years later in Moscow in Russian in 1851 (Saltykov 1985 [1851]). The book was an instant success in Russia: it enraptured the reading public, and earned Soltykoff the nickname 'the Indian' among the Russian and French aristocracy. The book was then republished in several subsequent editions in France (e.g. Saltykov 1851, Soltykoff 1858). Soltykoff

---

9   Man Singh of Amber was the most famous and successful general of the Mughal Emperor Akbar.

10   When he published his works in French and these works were subsequently translated into English he used the spelling 'Soltykoff.' His works translated into Russian today use the currently accepted transliteration from Cyrillic script, 'Saltykov.'

also published several editions of an album of his drawings created during his travels in India (Soltykoff n.d. a and b; Saltykov 1859).[11]

In a short letter dated December 4, 1845, he describes Jaipur as 'a beautiful city built in a perfectly Moorish style' (Saltykov 1985, 164–165).[12] The same letter contains an account of his visit to Amber, 'an old city reinforced with a fort amidst the slopes of stony hills, reminiscent of Granada and the Alhambra' (Saltykov 1985, 165). As the previous visitors did, Soltykoff includes a detailed description of his visit to the Kali temple:

> I entered a heathen temple, where preparations of a victim for the sacrifice were underway: it was a goat. Sixty years ago the victim would have been human. They brought the victim and positioned it in front of the idol; the Brahmin poured some water on its head and, muttering prayers, scattered around yellow flowers. Then a child and another adult dragged the goat to a place covered with sand, where they instantly severed its head off with a razor-like knife…The head and the first blood went into a copper bowl, which they placed in front of the idol and closed the curtain. The idol sits in a sanctuary deep within a rectangular yard. When the curtain was drawn, the animal's neck was lowered into a pit to drain the rest of the blood. *We left and ate our breakfast in a pleasant garden adorned with a red marble kiosk* [italics added] (Saltykov, 1985, 165).

This description adopts the stance of an objective observer with a strong stomach. Future authors visibly increase the drama around the sacrifice, add detail and even change the reported facts. The passage above is characteristic not only of the typical bravado of a young Russian aristocrat, but also of Soltykoff's personal style.

As Russian and French travellers to India, Soltykoff and Jacquemont stood outside British society there. Heber's sensibility too stood somewhat outside the preoccupations of official society, for his mission was to the Anglican Church and to his flock.[13] Each of the three writers makes it clear that he possesses a somewhat independent, if not critical, stance toward British policy. All three also were well travelled; Heber visited Moscow prior to his trip to India, Jacquemont spent some time in North America, and Soltykoff's diplomatic resume reads like a map of Europe and the Middle East. In a sense, too, these three individuals represent a pre-Victorian sensibility that lacks that era's intense moralizing about ritual and social practice. Although many things would change with the advent of Victorian attitudes and the post-1857 transformation of India's political and economic relationships to the British rulers, it appears that images of Amber and Jaipur remained constant.

---

11 The bibliographic sources for Soltykoff listed in this chapter are for the editions consulted, and are referenced as they appear in English-language electronic databases and catalogues. *Voyages dans l'Inde* published in 1851 in French transliterates his full name as 'Aleksiei Dmitrievich Saltykov, knaz'; other editions of his work transliterate his full name as 'Alexis Soltykoff, prince'.

12 Translations from Russian are by this chapter's author.

13 For example see Heber 1829: 286–287 for his comments on the insulting and denigrating manner in which most British residents treated Indians.

Figure 2.2   Students of the Rajasthan School of Art produced the illustrations for the first 'Jeypore Guide' in preparation for the visit of the Prince of Wales in 1876. Today its prominent signage contains the English name rendered in *deva nagari* script with the Hindi 'Postgraduate Fine Arts College' directly beneath.
Photo courtesy of Elena Karatchkova. All rights reserved.

This is illustrated in the works of two authors, both British, who travelled to this area in the late nineteenth-century.

Travel Writing after 1870

Thomas H. Hendley served in various official capacities in Rajputana for over a quarter century. He held several offices in Jaipur, including Agency Surgeon and Consulting Physician to the newly opened Mayo Hospital, and would eventually be named Administrative Medical Officer for the whole of Rajputana and a Lieutenant Colonel in the Indian Medical Service (Hendley 1876; Hendley 1897). A member of the Royal Asiatic Society, he wrote several books and pamphlets on arts and crafts of the area, including 'Memorials of the Jeypore Exhibition of 1883' (which he organized) and a *Handbook to the Jeypore [Jaipur] Museum*[14] (Hendley 1895),

---

14 Today known as the Albert Hall Museum.

an institution he was instrumental in founding. Hendley's *Jeypore Guide* (1876) was initially prepared for the Viceroy's visit to Jaipur in December of 1875. Unsurprisingly, it celebrates many of the infrastructural improvements introduced by the British in the previous decade. In December 1875 only the first 40 of its 146 pages were printed; the printing difficulties were soon surmounted, and the entire book was printed early 1876 (Hendley, preface dated January 28, 1876). The Jeypore Guide is small – 4 by 6 inches – and slim enough to slip into a pocket. It includes a fold-out map that shows Jaipur and Amber, along with their points of interest. Illustrations for the book were executed by students at the Jaipur School of Art (now the Rajasthan School of Art) another of Hendley's local projects. The book includes a table of distances around Jaipur. An appendix lists hotels, carriage and guide hire rates.

Interestingly, the copy of Hendley's guide book to which I had access appears to have been used by a traveller to Jaipur in 1881. This individual used a heavy red pencil to underscore and mark descriptions of particular personal interest, such as palace interior décor, religious ritual, and the staging of animal fights. The owner used the guidebook's pages as a reminder of what was seen on what particular day. This particular copy of the guidebook provides a glimpse into the role of guidebooks as constituting a dialogue between guidebook and tourist practices.

At the outset of Chapter One, Hendley refers to Jaipur as the 'modern capital' (Hendley 1876, 1) described as a '*spacious* and *magnificent* city', where 'the *wide streets* lined with houses of tolerably *regular form*, the cupolas, the *mathematical plan*, the over-hanging hills and forts, the gaily dressed people, and above all, the clear sky combine to form a *most pleasing impression*' (Hendley 1876, 5). These descriptions echo Heber's accounts of the city, which Hendley acknowledges. Hendley notes Jaipur's 'unusual regularity of plan', and favourably comments that the arcades of Jaipur's main thoroughfares are more aesthetic than the current efforts by the British builders in the Public Works Department' (Hendley 1876, 6).

A chapter called 'Modern Institutions' links the modernity of the city to the Maharaja's vision. Many subsequent authors make similar statements as this by Hendley, which demonstrates clearly the British perception of the modern ruling prince.

> Perhaps the great interest taken by the Maharaja of Jeypore *in introducing modern institutions into the country has done more to attract the attention of the outside world* than even the beauty of his capital and the hospitality he has ever afforded to the visitors. While determining, that in his hands Jeypore should be made, by the addition of handsome public buildings, gardens, etc. still more attractive, he has not neglected the comfort and true prosperity of its citizens, who have now to thank a beneficent Chief for the blessings of an abundant supply of pure water, well lighted streets, medical attendance for the poor, with excellent accommodations when sick, and good education for their children [italics added] (Hendley, 1876, 122).

Travel accounts of the last decades of the nineteenth-century and the beginning of the twentieth-century confirm that modern institutions were just as strong an attraction for British tourists in Jaipur as scenery or architecture. Amber's appeal is entirely different. Hendley introduces the chapter on Amber 'the ancient capital' with the remark:

> The first view of Amber, from the Southern entrance, seems to bring the traveller into a new world. The *gloomy grandeur, and solidity*, of the *venerable* fort, palaces and town, suggest the thought, that the architects, worked for fame and *immortality*; whereas *modern Jeypore* inspires ideas of *change, and constant activity* (itself a virtue), necessary to prevent the ravages of time upon its less substantial edifices... [italics added] (Hendley 1876, 36).

Hendley draws a contrast between Amber's builders, whose idea is to 'leave a name' for themselves in stone monuments, whereas today's ruler of Jaipur finds satisfaction in the intangible monuments of modernization: schools, 'moral improvement' and – last but not least – the 'magnificent Mayo hospital, his city water and district irrigation works' (Hendley 1876, 37).

Of Amber, Hendley states, 'There is an indescribable charm about this beautiful forsaken town, alone in the picturesque valley, which the visitor can never forget' (Hendley 1876, 38). He completes his description of Amber with the Kali temple, which he identifies with its actual name:

> The temple of Silla Devi, (the stone goddess, the shrine of the female essence of Shiva), a little to the west of the top of the high flight of steps leading to the Palace, is very ancient; here a goat is daily sacrificed, the substitute, according to tradition, for the human victim formerly offered to the goddess.

> Bishop Heber tells us in his Journal, that his guide stated 'that the custom had been laid aside till Jey Singh had a frightful dream, in which the destroying power [Kali] appeared to him, and asked why her image was suffered to be dry? – he took counsel, and substituted a goat for the human victim, with which the 'dark goddess of the azure flood' was graciously pleased to be contented' (Hendley, 1876, 46).

Hendley's reference to Bishop Heber contributes to the signal features of the master narrative, the use of earlier sources as authorities and their disconnection from their complex original contexts. This simplification of Heber, coupled with Hendley's hymn to modernity, establishes the pattern of the master narrative which contrasts Jaipur with Amber.

Hendley, while primarily occupied with his official position as physician and director of the Mayo hospital, was very much concerned with the city's modernization. Sometime in the early to mid-1880s he was visited by the son of a colleague, who was just starting his career as a journalist. The young man – in his early twenties – was Rudyard Kipling (b. 1865), who was writing a series of travel sketches for the Lahore *Civil and Military Gazette* and the Allahabad *Pioneer*. These appeared in 1887 and 1888 and were subsequently collected and reprinted as Kipling's *Letters of Marque* (1899). Unlike Hendley, Kipling was not a colonial administrator. Born in India, and returned to it after an English education, Kipling was at this time primarily a journalist documenting the British colonial world and the characters that threaded their way through it.

Letters of Marque is a fictionalized narrative disguised as journalism. Kipling's protagonist is a hypothetical Englishman, described as 'one of a few thousand Englishmen in India', who decides to see more of the country and, among other places, visits Jaipur. This humorous and satirical account (Condé, 1993) includes considerable description of Jaipur and Amber. Kipling's description of Jaipur develops the themes of it as a *planned city* and the theme of Jaipur as a *modern city*. With typical hyperbole, Kipling asserts:

> Jai Singh built a 'pink city'[15] set on the border of a blue lake, and surrounded by the low red spurs of the Aravali [mountains] – a city to see and puzzle over … with *huge streets straight as an arrow,* sixty yards broad, and cross streets *broad and straight.* … Later on came a *successor, educated and enlightened by all the lamps of British Progress* who with the help of his British employees[16] … built gas-works, set a-foot a School of Art, a Museum, all the things in fact which are necessary to Western municipal welfare and comfort … (Kipling, 1899, 18–19).

Kipling's account of Amber includes the pros and cons of a *ticca-ghari* (horse carriage) versus an elephant ride, and he suggests the best time of departure from Jaipur:

> Rise very early in the morning, before the stars have gone out, and drive through the sleeping city till the *pavement* gives way to *cactus and sand,* and *educational and enlightened institutions* to mile upon mile of *semi-decayed Hindu temples* – brown and weather beaten – running down the shores of the great Man Sagar Lake, wherein are more ruined temples, palaces and fragments of causeways … it is a fitting prelude to the *desolation* of Amber [italics added] (Kipling, 1899, 27).

This description adds a metaphoric dimension to the distinction between the two cities: a journey from Jaipur to Amber becomes one from the present to the past, from the light of modernity into medieval darkness.

Kipling devotes eight full pages to Amber's description, quotes the poet Byron and concludes with a note of nostalgia:

> There may be desolation in the great Indian Desert to the westward, and there is desolation upon the open seas; but the *desolation of Amber is beyond the loneliness of either land or sea.* Men by the hundred thousand must have toiled at the walls that bound it, the temples and bastions that stud the walls, the fort that overlooks all, the canals that once lifted water to the palace, and the gardens on the lake of the valley... [italics added] (Kipling 1899, 32–33).

After visiting Amber, Kipling's Englishman returns to Jaipur to observe yet a new sign of modernity, 'His Highness the Maharaja's Cotton Press' that 'somehow…did

---

15 cf footnote 8.

16 In particular, Kipling names Col. Swinton Jacob, the Superintending Engineer of the State of Jaipur.

not taste well after Amber. There was aggressiveness about the engines and the smell of the raw cotton' (Kipling 1899, 33).

Kipling's *Letters of Marque* also registers an important new tourism phenomenon, the 'Globe-Trotter', the middle-class tourist on vacation. His portrait is sarcastic and surprisingly familiar:

> ... there is no reverence in the Globe-Trotter: he is brazen. A Young Man from Manchester was travelling to Bombay... and finding that he had ten days to spare at Bombay, conceived the modest idea of 'doing India',... Then he explained that he had been 'much pleased' at Agra, 'much pleased' at Delhi and, last profanation, 'very much pleased' at the Taj... With rare and sparkling originality he remarked that India was 'a big place and that there were many things to buy' (Kipling 1899, 12).[17]

Finally, the Globe-Trotter is signally ignorant of India. Unlike the British residing in India, the 'Globe-Trotter' must rely on his guidebook:

> He [the Globe-Trotter] 'reads-up' – to quote his own words – a city before he comes to us, and, straightaway going to another city, forgets, or, worse still, mixes up what he has learnt – so in the end he writes down the Rajput as Mahratta [Maratha], says that Lahore is in the North-West Provinces and was once the capital of Sivaji [Shivaji][18], and piteously demands a guide-book on all India, a thing that you can carry in your trunk y'know – that gives you *plain descriptions of things without mixing you up* [italics added] (Kipling, 1899, 17–18).

Kipling's narrative of tourism in the late nineteenth-century marks a significant transformation: an ignorant tourist has taken the place of the educated *traveller* of the past. This tourist demands a simple master narrative, even though, as Kipling reminds the reader throughout the *Letters of Marque*, India is complex.

A decade after Hendley wrote his *Jeypore Guide*, he was visited by the noted poet and translator Edwin Arnold (Arnold 1886, 144). Unlike Kipling, who wrote for the British residents in India, Arnold's account of his 1885–86 trips to India, which includes a visit to Jaipur and Amber ,was intended for a British audience in England. Arnold's ornate Victorian prose style took fire as he entered Rajputana, which he characterizes as the 'land of romance and chivalry' (Arnold 1886, 133).

His eight page description of Amber (Arnold 1886, 151–158) begins with the trip to Amber on elephants supplied by the Maharaja. Accompanied by Hendley, Arnold describes Jaipur and Amber, both viewed simultaneously from the Mahadev temple. From this vantage point he describes Jaipur as a populous city 'in full vitality' (Arnold 1886, 152) and Amber more dramatically as:

---

17 By the 1880s it was possible to stop at Jaipur in the evening for a quick tour of the palace, take in Amber early the next morning, and be back at the train station to make the 11 a.m. train to Delhi, as Robert Bacon did in 1881 (Scott 1923).

18 Shivaji, (1630–1680), Maratha ruler of the seventeenth century.

...a city dead and silent, nine-tenths of its stone built-buildings tumbled and ruined as though by an earthquake, wild weeds growing over its mansions and temples, and the ancient streets choked with wild fig-trees and broken blocks of carved marble and sandstone. Some hundreds of Brahmans still loiter about the least dilapidated abodes, and there is a little bazaar; but otherwise the only inhabited edifices left in Amber are the fort, the palace, and one or two temples (Arnold 1886, 152).

He goes on to describe the now-obligatory visit to the Kali temple. The priests attempt to prevent their entrance to the temple, but Hendley arranges for Arnold's party to view the sacrifice (Arnold 1886, 155). He notes that the women in his party refuse to enter the temple, and he opines about human sacrifice in India and describes in detail the goat sacrificed by grim-faced priests. His book includes one photograph of Amber and none of Jaipur. His photograph of Amber is the view across the valley of the long ramp up to the Amber Palace Gate, which continues to be a photographic icon to the present day for travellers to Amber (see Henderson this volume).

Conclusion

The accounts by Heber, Jacquemont and Soltykoff originated as letters to friends and family or personal journals. They are peppered with literary references and comments about the personalities and politics of the day, and are not above a little gossip. These early travellers viewed their experiences as potentially hazardous adventures, which in fact they were, before the construction of railroads, the advent of the steamship, and the building of the Suez Canal. In fact, Heber and Jacquemont died in India of illness or injury within months of their journeys to Rajasthan.

The accounts of Hendley, Kipling and Arnold are explicitly written for a travelling audience either in India or Great Britain. They mention the works of Heber, with which they are obviously familiar. They consolidate and embroider the key themes of the Amber narrative in contrast with that of Jaipur, as a dichotomy of modernity *versus* antiquity, of science and knowledge *versus* medieval obscurantism and superstition, and of enlightened monarchy *versus* oriental despotism. These narratives single out and describe Kali's temple and the ritual of goat sacrifice with single-minded persistence for well over a century. In British eyes, Kali worship represented the most repulsive side of Hinduism and everything considered to be the obverse of modernity (Van Woekens 2002). Kali's temple neatly embodies this past, and contrasts with the 'handsome temples' of Jaipur as a symbol of the present.

The association of both destinations with royalty is set into motion by Heber, Jacquemont and Soltykoff, who were received by the Maharaja. The unofficial and less distinguished visitors of the second part of the nineteenth-century sought similar experiences, but could only view royal lifestyles through a visit to Amber or, upon permission, to the Jaipur palace.

The contemporary version of this master narrative deletes the modernism of Jaipur and conflates both locations as ancient and royal. It stresses 'travelling into the past' and witnessing the luxurious and exotic lifestyles of royalty, without much distinction drawn between Jaipur and Amber. No longer is Jaipur viewed as a city that was 'modern' as founded: its only 'modern' elements are those of the present day (see for example the treatment of Jaipur in the *Rough Guide to India* 2003, 145–147). The contrast between the two cities fades; both now are seen by travel discourse as ancient and traditional.

Ironically, the 'modernity' of Jaipur, so prominent in nineteenth-and early twentieth-century writing, now is being effaced by a narrative that privileges historic preservation. This narrative emphasizes 'tradition'-in part comprised of pride in Jaipur's history, but also cognizant that Jaipur's most prized asset, as a tourism destination, is its designation as a historic heritage city.

Since 2000, there have been well-publicized efforts to restore Jaipur's 'traditional' appearance. The touchstone of tradition, as this is being constructed, appears to be the mid-1870s: no one proposes to restore Jaipur's original 'brilliant white' colour, such as Jacquemont reported in the early 1830s. United States President Bill Clinton's 2000 visit provided the impetus for city authorities to tear out merchant stalls that intruded under the arcades and walkways along the thoroughfares in the vicinity of the City Palace, and to institute uniform signage over the arcade storefronts. These are now all in a uniform Hindi script, and English-language signs are no longer permitted. City authorities also gave the town a fresh coat of pink paint.

'Operation Pink', as the renovation and restoration efforts targeted at the city centre in 2000 were called, reflects a selective reading of Jaipur's history. The past is pink, not white; Jaipur is traditional, not modern, Amber is a tourist destination of 'temples and ruined mansions', not an inhabited community (*The Rough Guide to India* 2003, 160). Priests, goats, and sacrifices have vanished from view. Kali's temple is a photo-op on the exit from the fort-palace complex.

In India in general, and in Rajasthan in particular, contemporary Western tourists seek exotic, out of the ordinary experiences, something that they are unlikely to find at home. They do not come to India in search of a cotton press, a nuclear plant, or whatever may be the metaphor of progress today. They seek the past, and that is precisely what tourism-dependent municipalities provide.

References

Alaev, L.B. (1985), 'Predislovie [Introduction]', in Saltykov, A.D. *Pis'ma ob Indii.* [Letters From India] (Moskva: Nauka, 3–8)
Arnold, E. (1886), *India Revisited* (London: Trubner & Co).
Battacharyya, D. (1997), 'Mediating India: An Analysis of a Guidebook', *Annals of Tourism Research* 24 (2), 371–389.
Caine W.S. (1898), *Picturesque India. A Handbook for European Travellers* (London and New York: George Routledge & Sons).
Choy, M. and S. Singh (2002), *Rajasthan* (Melbourne, Australia: Lonely Planet Publications).

Condé, M. (2004), 'Constructing the Englishman in Rudyard Kipling's *Letters of Marque*', *The Yearbook of English Studies* 34:1, 230–239.

Corbey, R. (1993), 'Ethnographic Showcases, 1870–1930', *Cultural Anthropology* 8:3, 338–369.

Cuvillier-Fleury, A.-A. (1856), *Voyages et Voyageurs* (Paris: M. Lévy Frères).

Edensor, T. (1998), *Tourists at the Taj: Performance and Meaning at the Symbolic Site* (London & New York).

Elphinstone, M. (1815), *An Account of the Kingdom of Caubul, and its Dependencies in Persia, Tartary, and India; comprising the view of the Afghaun Nation. A History of the Dooraunee Monarchy* (London: Printed for Longman, Hurst, Rees, Orme and Brown)

Heber, R. (1828), *Narrative of a Journey through the Upper Provinces of India*, vol. I, II. (Philadelphia: Carey, Lea & Carey).

Hendley, T.H. (1876), *The Jeypore Guide* (Jeypore: Raj Press)

—— (1895), *A Handbook to the Jeypore Museum* (Calcutta: Central Press Company Ltd).

—— (1897) [2001], *The Rulers of India and the Chiefs of Rajputana* (New Delhi: Low Price Publications).

Hunter, W.W. and J.J. Sutherland, et al. (eds.) (1908), 'Amer', vol. 5, *Imperial Gazeteer of India* (Oxford: Clarendon Press).

Imperial Gazetteer of India (1908) (Oxford: Clarendon Press).

Jacquemont, V. (1833), *Correspondance de Victor Jacquemont avec sa famille et plusiers de ses amis. Pendant son voyage dans l'Inde (1828–1832)* (Paris: Librairie de H. Fournier).

—— (1834), *Letters from India: describing a journey in the British dominions of India, Tibet, Lahore and Cashmere during the years 1828, 1829, 1831,....* (London: E. Churton).

—— (1841–1844), *Voyage dans l'Inde, par Victor Jacquemont, pendent les annees 1828 a 1832...* (Paris: Firmin Didot freres).

—— (1934), *Etat Politique et Social De L'Inde du Sud en 1832*: *Extraits de son 'Journal de voyage.' Avec une introduction de M. Alfred Martineau* (Paris: Societe de L'Histoire des Colonies Francaises et Librairie Ernest Leroux).

—— (1936) *Letters from India 1839–1832* (London: Macmillan & Co).

Kanwar, D. (2000), 'Jaipur: The Evergreen Pink City', *The Taj Magazine*, 29: 2, August.

Kipling, R. (1899), *Letters of Marque* (New York & Boston: H.M.Caldwell).

Lyotard, J.-F. (1989), *The Post-Modern Condition: A Report on Knowledge* (Minneapolis: University of Minneapolis Press)

Ramusack, B. (1994), 'Tourism and Icons: The Packaging of the Princely States Rajasthan, in C.B. Asher and T.R. Metcalf (eds.), *Perceptions of South Asia's Visual Past* (New Delhi: Oxford & IBH).

RUIDP [Rajasthan Urban Infrastructure Development Project] (2005), 'Project Cities.' www.ruidp.org/project-cities.

Saltykov, A.D. (1851), *Voyages dans l'Inde*, 2nd Edition (Paris. L. Curmer, V. Lecou). [See also Soltykoff]

—— (1985) *Pis'ma ob Indii* [Letters From India] (Moskva: Nauka)

Sarkar, J. (1984), *A History of Jaipur* (Delhi: Orient Longman)

Scott, J.B. (1923), *Robert Bacon Life and Letters* (Garden City, NY: Doubleday).

Singh, R. (1998), *Jaipur: The Royal City* (Jaipur: Piyush International)

Singh, S. and M. Coxall (2002), *Rajasthan* (Melbourne: Lonely Planet Publications).

Soltykoff, A., Prince (1848), *Lettres sur l'Inde* (Paris: Amyot). [See also Saltykov].

—— (1985) [1851], *Pis'ma ob Indii* (Moskva: Glad. Red. Vostochnoi lit-ry Izd-va 'Nauka.'

—— (1858) *Voyages dans l'Inde* (Paris: Garnier Freres).

—— (n.d.a.), *Souvenirs de l'Inde, 25 sujets* (Paris: Victor Lecou libraire-editeur).

—— (n.d.b.), *Habitants de l'Inde: dessines d'apres nature* (Paris: H. Gache).

—— (1859), *Indian Scenes and Characters: From Drawings Made on the Spot* (London: Smith, Elder).

Tod, J. (1829), *Annals and Antiquities of Rajast'han*, Vol I. Reprint of 1829 Edition (London: G. Routledge and Sons).

Van Woerkens, M. (2002), *The Strangled Traveler: Colonial Imaginings and the Thugs of India* (Chicago: The University of Chicago Press).

Wheeler, S. (1998), *Majestic Jaipur* (New Delhi: Prakash Books).

Chapter 3

Travel, History, Politics and Heritage: James Tod's 'Personal Narrative'

Jason Freitag

If any part of a land strewn with dead man's bones have a special claim to distinction, Rajputana, as the cockpit of India, stands first. ... The tangled tale of force, fraud, cunning, desperate love and more desperate revenge, crime worthy of demons, and virtues fit for gods, may be found, by all who care to look, in the book of the man who loved the Rajputs and gave a life's labours in their behalf. (Kipling 1899, 8–9)

It is not possible to discuss travel writing, its history and function, in Rajasthan without attention to one of the key figures in the field of Rajasthani historiography, James Tod. Lieutenant-Colonel James Tod (1782–1835) was Political Agent to the western Rajput states then comprising Kota, Bundi, Udaipur and, briefly, Jodhpur and Jaisalmer, from 1818 to 1822. Many historians consider Tod to be the originator of modern Rajasthani historiography. Tod's massive *Annals and Antiquities of Rajast'han*, published in two volumes 1829 and 1832, is a now-classic British history cited as authoritative by many scholars. In his work, Tod constructed the image of chivalrous, heroic, martial, and romantic Rajputs that became stereotyped in English and Indian historical discourses and literary imaginations. Historians have referred to Tod as 'The founder of modern historiography on Rajasthan' (Bhattacharyya 1973: 426), '*rajasthan ke itihas ke pita*', 'the father of the history of Rajasthan' (Singhvi 1992), and even as 'the Herodotus of the History of Rajasthan' (Vashishtha 1992).

Tod made travel and interaction with the peoples he met an integral part of his official and historical programs throughout his time in India. A significant component of the *Annals* is the personal narrative by Tod that forms a distinct subsection within the text (Tod 1987: II, 760–928 and 1987: III, 1621–1827). Tod's accounts of his travels in Rajasthan incorporate many of the conventions of the travel genre.[1] Beyond this, however, I demonstrate how this narrative, in the form of a travel diary,

---

1   It was very common at this time for authors of accounts of Indian states to include their travel diaries as a separate section in the text. For an account of nineteenth-century travel writing, see David Seed, 'Nineteenth-Century Travel Writing: An Introduction', 2004 *Yearbook of English Studies*, 34(1):1–5; and Jean Viviès, *English Travel Narratives in the Eighteenth Century: Exploring Genres,* Tr. Claire Davison, Ashgate (2002). I have used the William Crooke three volume edited version of Tod of 1920, reprinted in 1987 as this has a

advances Tod's historical and political program, namely, to establish the nationhood and independence of the Rajputs of Rajasthan. I argue that Tod uses the genre of the travel narrative to mark the boundary between the centre and the periphery of his historical project, seen in the historical genre of the *Annals* proper. This provides the history of the princes and the courts, while Tod's personal travel narrative provides the history of peoples at the margins. This latter topic is marginalized both physically, because segregated in the text, and discursively, because of a change in genre.

The necessity of this travel narrative to Tod's historical project becomes clear as the marginality of Indians in the colonial context enters view. Tod counters the prevailing Orientalist attitudes of his day – that Indians are incapable of historical consciousness and therefore also of achieving the freedom of the modern nation-state – as he argues for the historical consciousness as well as the nationhood of the Rajputs. It is here that the travel narrative becomes a crucial component in the construction of Tod's argument for Rajput independence.

The sense that history suffuses every aspect of Rajasthan – including its inanimate objects – is an ever-present aspect of Tod's travel diary. Tod's reader is always in the presence of history in the diary, down to the rocks and streams that are underfoot. The reader does not just follow Tod as he progresses along the roads of Rajasthan, but also as he travels through its history. Further, Tod as the storyteller, not only has the power to bring us along on his journey, but also to include himself in the tales.[2]

This chapter is drawn from a biographical and historical project on Tod that seeks to locate his work in the large-scale context of the pressures facing the East India Company at the start of the nineteenth-century (Freitag 2001). In this chapter, I will focus on a close reading of the personal travel narrative in the Annals. This reading will demonstrate how Tod crafted this travel diary to support his advocacy of Rajput statehood. This chapter first summarizes the place of Tod in current historiography and briefly examines Tod's background. I describe the structure of the Annals and Tod's travel narrative. I then take a close look at Tod's narrative of a journey from Udaipur, capital of Mewar, to the border of that state, in order to see how this travel writing relates to issues of marginality and centricity in the text.

James Tod's Historical Project

Praise for Tod is noteworthy now for being centred in India, and also is prominent in tourism literatures on Rajasthan, which extensively cite the *Annals*. Scholars in England and America still read Tod, whose work is often the first place a researcher will explore when investigating some aspect of Rajput history. Criticism of Tod has taken two broad forms. One line of criticism seeks to correct Tod's factual identifications, such as with William Crooke's 1920 edition of the *Annals* (Tod 1987). This editor changed Tod's

---

wider availability than reprints of the 1829 and 1830 texts (Tod 1829, 1820). All citations to Tod in this chapter are from the 1987 edition reprint.

2   For more on Tod's relationship to the Rajputs, and the Rajput history he is constructing, see Freitag (2001), especially chapters 1 and 4.

spellings to conform with twentieth-century norms, identified names, dates, and places and especially – relevant to current scholars – corrected Tod's etymological flights of fancy, such as Tod's remarks about the derivation of certain words. Crooke often derides Tod's speculations on the relationships between the Rajputs and various peoples from the ancient 'western' world (i.e. the Scythians or the Celts).[3] This criticism, while unavoidable as new historical information comes to light over time, challenges only the details, leaving the underlying narratives and assumptions intact.

The second criticism of the *Annals* examines its Orientalist biases, shared with most other texts of the period, in order to comprehend how Orientalism functions in Tod. A recent debate involves Ronald Inden's discussion of Tod's 'Feudal Rajputs' in *Imagining India* (Inden 1990, 172–176) and Norbert Peabody's extended response (Peabody 1996). Inden explores Tod's concept of feudalism in the Rajput polity within the Orientalist framework, and finds power-laden binaries at work in the construction of British histories of India. Peabody challenges Inden's dichotomies and argues for a nuanced continuum of categories in Tod's text. Peabody looks to the way that these categories are woven into discourses on nationalities in the *Annals*. In the end, though, neither author takes Tod as the subject or contextualizes this writing in respect to his historical or political project, but rather views his work as an exemplar text in a larger debate on the nature of Orientalist knowledge.

It is important to see Tod in some historical context before turning to his text, as this provides some background to Tod's political agenda. There is not a rich store of biographical detail for James Tod. He traces his ancestry to the time of Robert the Bruce (1274–1329), and is proud of the family's brave service rendered to the Scottish hero. This background sets the stage for the heroic notions of Scottish chivalry that form an integral part of Tod's self-identification.[4] Tod's valorization of his Scottish background also was implicated in larger-scale processes of the time. The large number of Scots in the East India Company service attests to the realization that travel and career success were intimately related for Scots in this period. In her study of three prominent officials, Tod's peers Thomas Munro (1761–1827), John Malcolm (1769–1833) and Mountstuart Elphinstone (1779–1859), Martha McLaren (2001) identifies a series of career patterns and intellectual attitudes that, she argues, form a Scottish school of Indian administration.

The impetus to join the service of the East India Company was the hope for social and economic advancement of a kind not possible in the metropolis, given English aristocratic domination of political and social life (McLaren 2001, 8–9). The best way to advance quickly was to produce well-written reports demonstrating familiarity with Indian history (which required facility in Asian languages), that could serve the Company's increasing need for expert knowledge on the Indian territories as it became more involved in governance than trade. Tod's career path clearly followed a similar pattern. Following his arrival in India in 1798 at the age

3   See Freitag (2001), especially Ch. 4, 'Interpretation.'
4   See Chapter 1 of Freitag (2001), pp.28 and 48–52.

of 16, Tod rose from lowly cadet status to the rank of Lieutenant-Colonel in the East India Company Army by the time of his departure from India in 1825.

The Scots had a clear sense of their position within the growing sense of being British, a new identity that began to develop at the start of the nineteenth-century, and the inclusiveness that was necessarily a part of this term. John M. MacKenzie notes in this regard, 'Scots were also perhaps crucial to this new identity...from the early eighteenth century the Empire was never anything other than British, a setting for common action by the component populations of the British Islands' (MacKenzie 1999, 273–274). At the same time, many of these men – Tod in particular – felt the historical weight and importance of the difference bestowed on them by their Scottish traditions. As a Scot largely raised in England and as a sojourner who was to spend almost his entire adult life in India, it is not unsurprising that Tod was quite conscious of his own dislocation, on the margins of his Scottish identity; the society of his Rajput friends; and on his return to England, of the society in which he found himself.

McLaren notes that the Scottish moral philosophers provided the framework underlying the position that 'the human nature of Indians was essentially the same as that of Europeans and equally capable of improvement if the system of government provided the right framework for progress' (MacKenzie 1999, 242). Hence, these administrators tried to support Indian institutions, and install systems of government appropriate to the developmental stage of Indian political consciousness (MacKenzie 1999, 253). In Tod's case, as Political Agent to the Western Rajput States, one of his stated goals was to protect the rights of the native princes and allow them to continue to rule in their traditional provinces in as undisturbed a way as possible, a position that emerges strongly in the *Annals* and in his official dispatches (Freitag 2001).

Mapping The Annals

Tod succinctly asserted his political project in writing the *Annals* in the first volume's dedication to King George IV:

> The Rajpoot princes, happily rescued, by the triumph of the British arms, from the yoke of lawless oppression, are now the most remote tributaries to Your Majesty's extensive empire; and their admirer and annalist may, perhaps, be permitted to hope, that the sighs of this ancient and interesting race for the restoration of their former independence, which it would suit our wisest policy to grant, may be deemed not undeserving Your Majesty's regard (Tod 1987: I).

Tod's view was that the independence of the Rajputs, as chronicled by the historian who lived among them (himself), should be restored as a sign of the triumph and power of the British imperial project. Tod's work as political agent was intimately involved in the reconstruction of the Mewar court. In fact, he was often accused by his colleagues and superiors of being too deferential to the native princes (Freitag 2001, 35–38).

The *Annals* was originally published in two volumes. Each volume is composed of eleven books, and each book covers a major area of study (Tod 1829, 1832). Book I describes the geography of Rajasthan. This volume sets the physical stage for the work, details the landscape, climate and agricultural production of the region, and summarizes the results of the surveys Tod undertook early in his career. In his cartographic work, and his rhetorical presentation, Tod literally 'worlded' Rajasthan for his readers. Previous European knowledge of the area was minimal, so Tod needed to introduce the terrain both as the entry point into his study, and as a precondition for travel in the area.[5] In Tod's work, the geographic entity of Rajasthan becomes an object that can be studied and known, a spatial domain in which to operate, and thereby laid open to invite the reader along on the journey that is to come. This was a standard element of the genres of official reports and travel writing at the time.

Tod follows the geographical section of the *Annals* with a consideration of the 'Royal Races' of Rajasthan (the ruling lineages of each of the Rajput states), a discussion of the 'Feudal System of Rajasthan' (political institutions), and presentation of the histories of each of the states of Rajasthan. Mewar, the most important of these states in Tod's narrative, receives the most attention (twenty-four chapters and an appendix), while Jaisalmer and Bikaner receive the least, three chapters each. Two appendices present an assortment of materials – translations of land grants, temple inscriptions, legal announcements, letters exchanged between Tod and various local princes and a selection of treaties between the British East India Company and the Ranas of Udaipur (January, 1818), Jodhpur (January, 1815), Jaisalmer (December, 1818), Jaipur (April, 1818), Kota (December, 1817) and Bundi (February, 1818). Though this material is historically and archivally of interest to assess the British relationship with the princely states, these texts are presented in the order just given. Tod does not explain their ordering or presentation or, at this point, the very complex relationships of internal politics of each state or between each state and the British, discussions of which are found elsewhere in the text.[6] These compendia reflect the author's envisaged historical project: the archival aspect of the *Annals*, which presents a wealth of information without analysis or comment, as if a repository waiting for visitors, rather than as a politically-inspired document.

Tod's personal narratives are his accounts of his time in India, and comprise the last major component of the text. The publication of the travel diary seems to put Tod squarely in the genre of travel writing as practiced by his contemporaries. Tod introduces himself as a sympathetic character in these passages. As Viviès (2002, 106) notes in his work on eighteenth century travel writing, travel narratives succeed through 'the link the author develops between his text and the reader.' Margaret

---

5   For instance, earlier maps reversed Chitor and Udaipur. See Tod 1987 ; I, 3). For more on cartography and knowledge in India, see Edney 1990.

6   These treaties suggest a picture of the various material exchanges between the British and the Rajputs. Although outside the scope of this chapter, I note that Tod's list is in order of his notion of 'racial purity, and therefore priority, which he attributes to these Rajput 'races', by which he means the ruling lineages, or families, of each state.

Hunt describes this process as a collapse of the difference between the reader and the writer (Hunt 1993, 336) as Tod's perspective becomes that of the reader, who is there, in the moment, with Tod.

Tod treats his reader to tales of his party being attacked by a bear, a tiger and an elephant. Tod reports his brushes with death, negligent elephant drivers, sickness and attempted poisoning, which increase his journeys' hazards. Tod includes in the travel diary important details of his meetings with local princes, the minutiae of court protocols, and an episode, of which the author is justifiably proud, in which he performed the *rajtilak* ceremony to install the eleven year old Rana of Bundi (Tod 1987: III, 1740–1744). Tod also includes translations of inscriptions, as well as histories of small village regions and petty kingdoms in his personal narrative.

This type of material is also the stuff of Tod's posthumously published *Travels in Western India* (1971), his second major work. Originally published in 1839, it was based on travel from Udaipur to Mumbai in late spring of 1822. Tod was at this time bound for England on medical leave, and he never returned to India. Though *Travels in Western India* includes a great deal of historical and cultural material, scholars and others have relegated this work to the sidelines. It is scarcely cited in tourist literature, for example, compared with the prominence of the *Annals* as an authoritative source in tourism guidebooks.

In the 'Personal Narrative' in the *Annals*, Tod's approach to the individual areas that he visits mirrors the treatment he provides of each of the major states of Rajasthan in the historical sections of the *Annals*. This microstructure involves a number of elements. The first is a moving gaze: here, the daily travel in short stages. In the larger work, the gaze moves over large territories, between each of the different states. Second, Tod maps the geographical terrain, sometimes including the longitude and latitude measurements, but always including a detailed description of the landscape, vegetation, and current travel conditions – features that would not be unusual in a contemporary traveller's diary or Internet blog (see chapter by Hardgrove). Tod usually next describes and discusses the human terrain, including who lives in the area and a catalogue of their special characteristics. He names individuals and includes their comments in the text. Finally, the segments end with a short statement of the present-day condition of the land. As with the historical segments of the *Annals*, this structure adopts the position of neutral observer. In important ways, this discursive technique gives Tod important leeway in developing his political argument, through the choice of images and language.

This is a flexible form, however. As journal entries, Tod's style appears much more relaxed than in the more self-consciously historical sections of the work. It is more personal, inviting the reader to travel with him. And, as will be seen, he braids history into his narrative of travel in ways that heighten the reader's identification with the author and, hopefully, engages sympathy for the Rajputs and others whom Tod meets on his travels.

Travel, History and the Margins

I will now focus on the ways in which Tod's discourse on his peregrinations presents the relationship between centre and margin in his historical imagination, and thus builds his argument. The first thing to notice about the personal narrative is the way in which it simultaneously emphasizes its timeliness, and undermines its sense of daily chronology. The histories of the individual Rajput states feature a narrative that is in strict chronological order of the reigns of the rulers or the major events (usually battles) of their time. The personal narrative adopts a chronological form as well, not of the large time scale of historical events, but rather the daily course of the travels, exactly as one would expect from an actual travel diary.

On October 11, 1819, Tod left Udaipur on a two-month tour of the countryside, from which he returned on December 19. This is a dramatic change in the form of the narrative, and one would expect its substance to follow suit. In general, it does, as the reader learns about the composition of the travelling party, the merits of Tod's contingent of Skinner's Horse Cavalry, and the honor guard sent by the ruler of Mewar to accompany him to the border. In the middle of this description, though, Tod presents the following passage:

> We reached the camp before eight o'clock, the distance being only thirteen miles. The spot chosen (and where I afterwards built a residence) was a rising ground between the villages of Merta and Tus, sprinkled with trees, and for a space of four miles clear of the belt of forest which fringes the granite barriers of the valley (Tod 1987: II, 762).

The typical elements of a travel narrative are here. Tod notes the distance travelled and the rough location of the camp, as well as something about the beauty and composition of the valley below. The jarring element is the mention Tod makes of the place where he *will* build a residence. This observation could only have come after all the travel was done, and it therefore denies the spontaneity of the travel diary form. The after-the-fact narrative belies the aspects of live action that give a travel tale its sense of immediacy, as if the reader were present with the author as the author experiences the events he is chronicling. This temporal break draws attention to the form of the narrative, as opposed to its substance.

This sudden break in the diary format switches attention to the omniscient narrator required by the genre of historical narrative. Time, though used here as a marker of travel and immediacy, can simultaneously undermine that purpose in its reference to the end of the story. Tod sacrifices the sense of being in the moment of the trip to signal the historical character of the personal travel narrative. Not only have events ended, but the author is now reflecting back on his travels from some later position. The shift is subtle, but the trappings of travel writing are, I argue, now being used in the service, or at least idiom, of history.

Tod's mirroring in the personal travel narrative of the overall structure in the Annals, that is daily travel, geography, human terrain, and the current state of the land, also underscores this connection between travel and history. A good example of this analysis comes in the treatment of Samecha region, visited on October 18 (Tod

1987: II, 773–776). Tod presents his reader with a lush description of the landscape, summed up by his observation that 'Nature has been lavish of her beauties to this romantic region' (Tod 1987: II, 774). A short description of the area's agricultural production and techniques of terrace cultivation follows. Tod next provides his analysis of the 'Rajput Bhumias' (landowners), whom he describes as Kumbhawats, 'descended of Rana Kumbha' and therefore 'though undistinguishable in dress from the commonest cultivator, I [Tod] did homage to their descent' (Tod 1987: II, 776). Tod spent his day with these people recalling their history and noting that they had suffered depredations at the hands of the Marathas, but that today they truly were the 'real allodial tenants of the land.'

Finally, Tod notes:

> I conciliated their good opinion by talking of the deeds of the old days, the recollection of which a Rajput never outlives. The assembly under the fig tree was truly picturesque, and would have furnished a good subject for Gerard Dow (Tod 1987 II: 776). [7]

The elements of a good travel narrative are present. One can almost see the painting, a camp of turbaned Rajputs and uniformed British seated in a circle amidst the lush vegetation. Maybe they are depicted sharing a smoke. The romance of this scene is unavoidable, but Tod gives his readers more information for he recounts their conversation. The men are discussing history, which seems to be the life-breath of the Rajput. History, here, has the function of bestowing legitimacy and authority to the teller of historical tales. As Tod will go on to say of the landscape of his next location, the mountainous region of Kelwara where Mewar's then-ruler took refuge when driven from the ancient capital of Chitor, 'There is not a rock or stream that has not some legend attached to it, connected with these times' (Tod 1987 II, 776).

Kelwara, the next stop on Tod's tour, illustrates the key relationships among power, narrative and history in the travel diary. Again, the microstructure I outlined above is present, as Tod includes a detailed description of the landscape, complete this time with temperature, barometer and longitude and latitude readings of the Kumbhalmer [Khumbalgarh] Fort. It is this presence of the fort that touches off a lengthy digression on the long and valorous history of the area. Tod again foregrounds himself in the text as an historical actor, noting that he peaceably took possession of the fort for the British on his arrival in 1818 by ending a dispute over back pay owed its armed garrison of Rajputs. The fact of this action, mentioned by Tod, serves again to foreground the history of the area, and in this case especially, Tod's role as an agent of, and in, that history.

As the reader follows Tod's progress, each digression from the present moves further back into history. A description of the temples and monuments along the roads leads Tod into a complex discussion of the thirteenth century Rajput heroes Prithiraj and his wife Tara Bai. After recounting five pages of the exploits of Prithiraj and

---

7   Gerard Dou (alternative spelling Dow) (1613–1675) was a Dutch genre and portrait painter who enjoyed a great deal of popularity principally for his scenes of domestic middle-class life.

Figure 3.1   Engraving of the Khumbalgarh Fort on the border of the then Mewar-Marwar territories, in Romantic style from a sketch produced by Tod's travel companion, Patrick Young Waugh for the first edition of *Annals and Antiquities of Rajast'han*. Image reproduced courtesy of the British Library.

Tara Bai against the 'Afghan' rulers (what is sometimes termed the Delhi Sultanate), October 20 arrives and with it, the frontier of Marwar.

At the Margin

The next major stop on the tour provides a dramatic vignette that exemplifies Tod's use of the travel diary form within the historical project of the Annals. After a day of travel, Tod's Indian guides found a place they thought appropriate for the party to stop for the night. Here, there would be 'shade from the dews and plenty of water.' The most compelling element of this place to Tod, however, was that the terrain ahead was treacherous; it should not be treated lightly. Tod notes there are:

> ...but darkness and five miles more of intricate forest, through a path from which the slightest deviation, right or left, might lead us into the jaws of a tiger, or the toils of the equally savage Mer, decided us to halt. We now took another look at the group above-mentioned. ...it was impossible to contemplate the scene before us without a feeling of the highest interest. From twenty-five to thirty tall figures, armed at all points, were sitting or reposing in groups round their watch-fires, conversing and passing the pipe from hand to hand, while their long black locks, and motley-fashioned turbans, told that they belonged to Marudesa [i.e., the 'land of death', Marwar, also called Jodhpur] (Tod 1987: II, 788).

The prospect of further miles of dense forest at the end of a long, fatiguing day is topped only by the presence of the 'savage' tribesmen as a reason to come to a halt. There are elements of a swashbuckling adventure story in this passage. As darkness falls in a dense forest, the travellers encounter the spectre of wild 'plundering' natives who belong to the 'region of death' (Tod 1987: II, 788). Danger is everywhere palpable. But danger is seductive – at least to Tod, and as the British party pitches camp, hungry and tired, he is drawn to the scene.

'I soon left them [his companions] in happy forgetfulness of tigers, Meras [Mers], hunger, and all the fatigues of the day, and joined the group to listen to the tale with which they enlivened the midnight hour' (Tod 1987, 788). The lure of the tale, their history, is too much to resist. Not only does Tod stop to enter the world of the savage, the travel narrative halts here too. Tod pauses to invite his reader into this world. 'As there may be no place more appropriate for a sketch of the mountaineers, the reader may transport himself to the glen of Kumbhalmer, and listen to the history of one of the aboriginal tribes of Rajast'han' (Tod 1987: II, 789).

This rhetorical manoeuvre places Tod in an authoritative and insider position from which he can continue his narrative, even in the middle of danger, while the reader follows along from the comfort of his or her armchair. It is also an important narrative move, for Tod now inserts more than eight pages of Mer history into the account of his personal journey. The crucial interplay of the travel narrative and the historical narrative is vividly on display, as they intertwine in the text.

Substantively, the history of the Mers comes in an important place. Tod's party is at the border between Mewar and Jodhpur, between Mewar, where his diplomatic credentials hold, and Jodhpur, where he was until recently credentialized. [8] Mewar is a state with good relations with the British, while Jodhpur's are rocky (Tod 1987: II, 1092–93, 1101–1103). Not only is he at the physical margins of Mewar state territory, Tod presents himself in a sense at the human margins as well, in more than one sense. At this point in the narrative, Tod emphasizes that we are not in the pomp and civilization of the court of the Rana, but in the woods around a 'rude altar' (Tod 1987: II, 788). Tod sees Mers as one of Rajasthan's aboriginal peoples; their 'primitive' state is on display as, by association, is that of the territory into which Tod has just moved.

I contend that it is not accidental that the Mers are also in the margins of the *Annals*. The Mers appear not in the main historical discourse of the Mewari court, but at the end, in the outskirts of a personal – and therefore *not* official – narrative. Tod's history of the Mers occurs only when he leaves Udaipur. The Mers exist out of the geographical centre of the text, and their appearance in the travel journal signifies their displacement from the conceptual centre of the work as well. In this sense, the travel narrative needs to be read not simply as the record of Tod's journey, included in the spirit of inclusiveness, of leaving no detail, however small, out of the *Annals* history project, but rather as a clear demarcation, or roadmap, of what is centrally important in the text and what is marginal to it. By implication, as well, Tod marks what is centrally important as history and what is marginal.

Conclusion

In the tale of ten days of journey, Tod provides what appear to be the beginnings of an adventure story and a continuation of the historical project he undertook in the *Annals*. More significantly, Tod has given his reader a way to read this conceptual world that clearly relates the travel narrative to the historical project of the *Annals*. The centred, stationary portions of the text hold the authoritative position, while the marginal, mobile portions of the text define its periphery. This discursive structure underscores in yet one more way the construction of royal courts as the focal organizing structure of history in Rajasthan.

Yet Tod cannot resist his fascination with the margins, and with the 'marginal' people within them, people who may be recruited into history and hence into the centre. The diary is where Tod provokes the reader's emotional identification with himself, as Tod introduces himself as a character who reacts to and reflects on his day-to-day adventures, and the people he meets during his travel. In the end, it is the

---

8   At this point Tod was only accredited to Mewar, not to Jodhpur, so he was crossing a diplomatic line as well. As Tod recounts in the personal narrative, the visit was amicable (1987: II, 848–849).

history that is so omnipresent in his journeys that Tod sees as the ultimate measure of the worth and value of the Rajputs themselves. After another in the series of encounters with these embodiments of Rajput tradition, in this instance, the ruler of Ghanerao, Tod makes the following extended observation:

> It is after such conversation that the mind disposed to reflection will do justice to the intelligence of these people: ... If by history we mean the relation of events in succession, with an account of the leading incidents connecting them, then are all the Rajputs versed in this science; for nothing is more common than to hear them detail their immediate ancestry or that of their prince for many generations, with the events which have marked their societies. It is immaterial whether he derives this knowledge from the chronicle, the chronicler or both: it not only rescues him from the charge of ignorance, but suggests a comparison between him and those who constitute themselves judges of nationalities by no means unfavourable to the Rajput Tod 1987 II, 802).

In response to the developing notions of Indians as a people without and in some sense incapable of historical thought, Tod constructs the Rajputs as a self-consciously historical people.[9] In every case, Tod's interlocutors are deeply aware of their own ancestries and of the great events in the lives of their lineages and their state. They are, as Tod reminds his reader, fully capable of structuring this knowledge into a recognizably historical chronicle. As such, Rajputs raise themselves out of the realm of 'ignorance' and take their place among peoples who have a nationality. They become people with history and as such may claim statehood.

The immersion into the historical worlds of the Rajputs that Tod experienced in his personal journeys, travels that took him from the centre to the margins, from kings to tribal peoples, was not simply an antiquarian's or adventurer's indulgence, but form a crucial element in Tod's project of recognizing and defining a 'new' – that is to say, *ancient* – nation. The travel narrative was an integral part of this evaluation, for in this Tod demonstrates the depth of the historiographic consciousness of the inhabitants of Rajasthan. Even casually-met individuals display the historical sensibility that forms the meeting ground between British Agent and Rajasthani, men of two different worlds.

Ultimately, Tod's personal travel narrative is thoroughly immersed in the Rajput reclamation project that Tod practiced in his official career as well as in the central and historical portions of the *Annals*. Travel writing served as a physically and rhetorically enabling device that not only mapped the cultural geography of Rajasthan and the historical geography of Tod's text, but in the process provided the ground for bestowing a national, and therefore in Tod's view, a modern, character on the Rajputs and the associated groups in the outlying areas. Through the possibilities of the travel diary genre, Tod was able to build his case for his political argument of the Rajputs as a modern people. It is ironic, then, that in today's tourism literature,

---

9   Ronald Inden's, 'Hinduism: The Mind of India', chapter 3 in *Imagining India*, Cambridge, MA: Blackwell (1990) is an extremely useful overview of this discourse of the essential otherworldliness of the Indians.

Tod's writing is used selectively and authoritatively to represent Rajputs, and other Rajasthanis, as traditional subjects and as people who are outside history.

References

Bhattacharyya, S. (1973), 'James Tod', in S. P. Sen (ed.) *Historians and Historiography in Modern India* (Calcutta: Institute of Historical Studies, 416–424).

Edney, M.H. (1990), *Mapping an Empire: The Geographical Construction of British India, 1765–1843* (Chicago: University of Chicago Press).

Freitag, J. (2001), 'The Power that Saved Them from Ruin and Oppression: James Tod, Historiography and the Rajput Ideal', Doctoral Dissertation, Middle East Languages and Cultures Department, Columbia University.

Hunt, M. (1993), 'Racism, Imperialism and the Traveller's Gaze in Eighteenth-Century England', *The Journal of British Studies* 32:4, 333–357.

Inden, R. (1990), *Imagining India* (Oxford: Basil Blackwell).

Kipling, R. (1899), *Letters of Marque* (New York: Charles Scribner's Sons).

MacKenzie, J.M. (1999) 'Empire and Metropolitan Cultures', in A. Porter (ed.) 'The Nineteenth Century', *Oxford History of the British Empire*, Vol. III (Oxford: Oxford University Press).

McLaren, M. (2001) *British India & British Scotland, 1780–1830: Career Building, Empire Building, and the Scottish School of Thought on Indian Governance* (Akron, Ohio: University of Ohio Press).

Peabody, N. (1996), 'Tod's Rajast'han and the Boundaries of Imperial Rule in Nineteenth-Century India', *Modern Asian Studies* 30:1, 185–220.

Seed, D. (2004), 'Nineteenth-Century Travel Writing: An Introduction', *Yearbook of English Studies* 34:1, 1–5.

Singhvi, J. (1992), 'Rajasthan ke itihas ke pita Karnal Tod', in H. Bhati (ed.) *Itihasakara Jemsa Toda: vyaktitva evam kritiva* (Udaipur, India: Pratap Sodh Pratisthan, 168–172).

Tod, J. (1829), *Annals and Antiquities of Rajast'han*, vol. I, Reprint of 1829 Edition (London: G. Routledge and Sons).

—— (1830), *Annals and Antiquities of Rajast'han*, vol. II, Reprint of 1832 Edition (London: G. Routledge and Sons).

—— (1987), *Annals and Antiquities of Rajast'han, or the Central and Western Rajput States of India*, Reprint of 1920 Edition, ed. William Crooker (Delhi: Motilal Banarsidass).

—— (1971) *Travels in Western India*. Reprint of 1839 Edition (Delhi: Oriental Publishers).

Vashishtha, V. K. (1992), 'James Tod as Historian.' in G. N. Sharma and V. S. Bhatnagar (eds.) *The Historians and Sources of History of Rajasthan* (Jaipur: Centre for Rajasthan Studies, University of Rajasthan, 152–164).

Viviès, J. (2002), *English Travel Narratives in the Eighteenth Century: Exploring Genres,* trans. Claire Davison (Aldershot, England: Ashgate).

Chapter 4

Virtual Rajasthan: Making Heritage, Marketing Cyberorientalism?

Carol E. Henderson

Anyone who searches the Internet for 'India' swiftly discovers that tourism is an important topic. Search engines rapidly assemble lists of websites containing the word 'India' 204 million 'hits' (or successful searches), or the word 'Rajasthan' 1,570,000 'hits.'[1] On some websites, there might be a few bars of music as a camel scurries across the screen. A flashing logo invites the visitor to a seasonal festival. These websites lure the visitor to enter, with links to information on history, dance, music, art, architecture, ethnic diversity and cultural traditions of India. The Internet – scarcely known to most potential travellers to India as recently as a decade ago – has emerged as a critical marketing tool in contemporary tourism.[2]

Rajasthan's emergence as a tourism destination in India coincided with the rise of the Internet as a medium for marketing within the past decade. In the mid-1980s, the development of the desktop computer boosted usage and promoted efforts to create better links between users and systems (Leiner et al. 2000). These efforts resulted in development of the World Wide Web (www), or Internet, released in 1991, followed by development of the 'search engines' which allow one to navigate (or 'surf') the Internet.[3]

India gained its first connection to the Internet at this time. Improvements in telephone and satellite networks, along with hardware and software developments, brought computers not merely to universities and to government offices, but into the commercial, NGO (non-governmental organization) and personal sectors. One result has been the proliferation of websites that promote India-based tourism businesses to an international market.

---

1   These two searches were conducted using Google (www.google.com), a proprietary search engine, 7 October 2005.

2   I would like to express my appreciation to the readers of this chapter, who encouraged me to explore how to approach the provision of information on the Internet, and especially to think about how we might study this phenomenon. I would particularly like to thank Barbara J. Price and Maxine Weisgrau, who so ably commented on the several versions of this paper. Previous research in India was supported by funding from the American Institute of Indian Studies, and by the U.S. Educational Foundation in India (Fulbright).

3   For more, see tutorial at the website of University of California Library (2004).

The Internet functions much as do print and audio-visual media, with the important difference of potentially unlimited images and links between websites. These include formats that permit a reader to send a query and get a near-instant response. Yet, as with non-Internet communications, marketing on the web mediates the tourism experience by directing the tourist's gaze to certain elements and by defining the destination (Chambers 2000; Urry 1990, 1, 145). The promised destination competes in this information market with others, all of which try to inspire enthusiasm for travel to a desired location.

Tourism promoters, such as governments and tourist agencies, are not the only ones to use the Internet to elaborate upon tourism. Travellers create websites containing stories, photos, and video images. Web logs ('blogs') recount their adventures. Participatory formats allow travellers and interested parties to comment on one another's remarks. The Internet also includes websites with related concerns, such as non-governmental organizations (NGOs) and academics. Although the topic is outside the scope of this chapter, it should be noted that aspects of consumers' and non-marketer websites on tourism may assume elements of a counter-discourse to marketers' efforts.

Boosters of the Internet in its earliest days saw the 'information superhighway', as it was dubbed, as having a utopian potential to revolutionize social relationships (Escobar 1994; Rosenzweig 1998, 1550; Wilson and Peterson 2002, 450–451; see also Ginsburg 1994, 12). A number of studies of user groups, almost entirely in Western countries, followed (Brunn 2005; Escobar 1994; Hakken 1999; Herman and Swiss 2001; Kelty 2005). It soon became evident that in many ways, the Internet mirrored existing social relationships (Brunn and Cottle 1997; Christiansen 2003; Jackson and Purcell 1997; Nakamura 2002). Some worried that the Internet might heighten globalizing and homogenizing pressures felt generally in media (McChesney 2000; see also Said 1978, 26).

This chapter examines Rajasthan tourism marketing discourse on the Internet and its relationship to discourses of heritage. Marketing discourse of course aims to attract visitors through its use of images and text, while heritage discourse may link to broader political and identity issues. 'Sun and sand' destinations, for example, routinely depict pristine beaches fringed with palms, blue seas, and attractive European American couples. European urban destinations highlight historical landmarks (the Eiffel Tower) and art (Michelangelo's David). Asian destinations emphasize historic architecture such as the Taj Mahal with images of Asian animals (tigers, elephants, pandas), and persons clad in non-Western dress. Many tourist marketing images have become iconic: a gondola signifies 'Venice'; St Basil's Cathedral in Moscow's Red Square, 'Russia'; guards in Beefeater uniform, 'London.' All are highly selective images and deflect tourist attention from politicized heritage conflicts (e.g. conservation, environmental damage, inter-ethnic or religious conflict).

Efforts to market India as a tourism destination frequently use Rajasthan images. The idea of Rajasthan as exemplifying authentic 'Indian' culture,[4] of pre-British

---

4   For example, Singapore Airlines used an image of the Amber fort-palace in advertising its air service in India, even though Jaipur is not among its destinations. In the Orientalist

Hindu India appears in tourism discourse at least as early as a 1974 travel guidebook: 'Nowhere will he [the tourist] see people more intrinsically Indian and more true to their traditions than the Rajputs' (Fodor and Curtis 1974, 252–252). This idea tracks back certainly to James Tod's two-volume *Annals and Antiquities of Rajast'han* (1914a, b [originally published in 1829 and 1832]) and forms an important theme in his treatment of the Rajput polity (see chapter by Freitag).

Most Rajasthan marketing websites discussed below were produced in India. Their designers are aware of the multiple dimensions of marketing images, and of the partial and selective nature of those presented to tourists. These images, for many Rajasthanis, are equivocal. On the one hand, a man plowing with a camel could represent 'tradition;' yet such an image can also signify poverty and 'backwardness' – terms used specifically in the state's development discourse about Rajasthan, one of India's poorer states (Henderson 1998; Hooja and Joshi 1999).

This chapter reviews the Orientalist discourse on travel writing, guidebooks, and print marketing as the general context within which Internet marketing has emerged. I next describe how features of the Internet affect the consumption of marketing images by potential tourists and constrain potential research strategies and outcomes. Core data in this chapter's analysis of images was produced using a search of websites aimed at European American markets in 2002 and 2005. This portion of the analysis, following Cohen (1993), uses a general content analysis approach. The chapter then identifies the general features of Internet marketing images as these are most likely to be viewed by consumers. Semiotic analysis of verbal and visual manifestations of key motifs provides insights into how they recapitulate general themes linked to Rajasthan as a destination.

This paper is informed by a reading of historical travel accounts, tourism guidebooks, and marketing promotional materials relating to India generally and to Rajasthan specifically. My own research background on Rajasthan has been in the area of economic development, but it is very difficult to travel about Rajasthan without encountering various discourses on tourism, as seen from the perspective of local people, and to experience this phenomenon directly. Prior research conducted on wool production and consumption generated data on the marketing of textiles as souvenirs. Informal conversations with tourists, with Indian friends who have engaged in tourism entrepreneurship, and my own encounters with tourist destinations also provide background to the following discussion.

Orientalism, Travel and Marketing Discourses

In recent years, scholars have focused on how the perspective of Orientalism informs the discourses of colonial and post-colonial regimes. The key logic of Orientalism, according to Edward Said (1978, 40, 42) originates in Western notions of opposition between itself and the discursive field it identifies as 'the East', or

---

model, all images become dehistoricized and are equivalent.

Orient. The colonial encounter promoted stereotypes of Asian societies as stagnant (contrasting with 'modern' Western societies), as sexually ambivalent (contrasting with Western 'manly vigour' and self-control), and as despotic (contrasting with Western democratic political institutions). Following Said, a host of studies examine how Orientalist discourses infused Western thought about Asia (Bandyopadhyay and Morais 2005; Bhattacharyya 1997; Inden 1986; Spivak 1988; Breckinridge 1989).

Orientalist thinking infused travel writing from the inception of tourist travel to India. To the late Romantic traveller of the 1840s, Indian scenes were reminiscent of the past, filled with decaying monuments, fallen palaces, and overgrown forts. These early travel writers constructed a view of heritage as something handed down unchanged from the past. To the Romantic writers, India's 'picturesque' features included numerous references to royalty and their properties, and the dangers of wildlife, such as snakes and tigers. The commodification of Rajasthani destinations appears in guides such as the early twentieth-century *Imperial Guidebook to India*, which refers to Udaipur as both the 'City of Sunrise' and as the 'Lake District of India' (Murray 1904, 173). This reference recalls a popular English tourism destination associated with the Romantic poets which would have been familiar to Murray's readers.

Lutz and Collins' analysis of the production and consumption of images in the popular magazine *National Geographic* suggests mid-to-late twentieth-

Figure 4.1   Tourists on elephant approaching Amber Palace (c1980), an iconic tourism activity documented by travellers to Rajasthan from the end of the nineteenth century to the present. *Photo courtesy of Maxine Weisgrau. All rights reserved.*

century continuities with the Orientalist position. The magazine's middle-class and middlebrow readers – who are the target for India tourism marketing efforts in North America – see a tradition-bound, timeless society (Lutz and Collins 1994, 80, 91, 111). The pervasive influence of Orientalist themes appears in travel guides (Bhattacharyya 1997; Echtner and Prasad 2003).

The persistence of Orientalist discourse about India is not likely to be lessened by its recent marketing as a cultural heritage destination, one which features a convincingly authentic past that, tourists accept, 'portray[s] the past in the present' (Nuryanti 1996, 250). Its validity on the basis of archaeological, ethnohistorical or other evidence is less significant than how the tourists feel about the site's authenticity (Gable and Handler 1996). The cultural heritage destination 'adds value' to the past – especially things that are disappearing – by transmitting it into an exhibition of itself. (Kirshenblatt-Gimblett 1995, 370). Cultural heritage may be embodied in the built environment, in the enactment of customs transmitted through seemingly unbroken inheritance, and even as inscribed on the bodies of those who are the bearers of these traditions. Tourists experience this commodified past through audiovisual, print and Internet media; directly through visits to the destination, viewing and photographic sites and spectacles; and the purchase of souvenirs (Chhabra, Healy and Sills 2003; Edensor and Kothari 1994; Johnson 1999; Poria, Butler and Airey 2003; Waitt 2000).

Despite marketers' efforts to present a convincing 'experience', it may fail because of interactions at the destination (Chronis 2005; Edensor 1998; MacCannell 1973). The tourist is not simply a passive captive of the marketer's presented 'destination.' Residents of destinations also are not inert. They too negotiate the images and scripts that they present to visitors (Bruner 2001; Taylor 2001). Gita Mehta (1979) noted how surprised Indians were by the behaviour of 1960s hippies in India, who violated Indian norms. Another example of this process appears with respect to textile arts in India. Certain cloth prints, the wearing of which is being discarded by members of some groups, because these prints signal their stigmatized social status, have reemerged in the tourism context as fashionably associated with 'tradition.' The textile sells well to tourists precisely because in their minds, it epitomizes India: It is woven and printed by hand (western cloth by machine); the cloth is made of a natural, not synthetic, fiber; the textile design conforms to tourists' notions of 'traditional' as opposed to 'modern' designs. There are many 'traditional' patterns which local folk find attractive, and that in no way attract tourists' aesthetic appreciation. In fact, tourist demand can promote production of new 'old' patterns for this market.

On-site interactions may subvert the tourist's experience. A case in point is the discourse about the sexual harassment of European American women tourists (see chapter by Weisgrau in this volume). Tourists express dissatisfaction at perceived intrusions of modernity, noise, rubbish, and some commercial transactions at sites. Tourist satisfaction is greatest the most closely the site conforms to their expectations. As Chambers (2000, 31) points out, tourism marketers work hard to convey a familiar script about the destination and to deliver it.

Efforts may be taken to limit guides, touts' and souvenir-sellers' access to tourists. Tourist organizations and site managers may attempt to standardize narratives and to enforce codes of dress and behaviour by their employees. There may be efforts to educate tourists as to appropriate behaviour. Governments and tourism development associations enforce standards and encourage adherence to historic preservation values. Efforts are made so that the site better conforms to the claims made in tourism marketing.

In 2001, the Government of Rajasthan ordered the removal of non-conforming elements in the main tourist areas of Jaipur, then sent in work crews who accomplished the job when the building owners stalled. Strongly Rajasthan-oriented trade associations such as the Heritage Hotels Association, set standards for members that emphasize historic preservation (Taft 2003). Most recently, hotel corporations have created luxurious enclaves offering attractions such as puppet shows, elephant rides, dance exhibitions, and dinners, such that the tourist need never leave the hotel grounds, yet feel as if she or he has enjoyed an 'authentic' Rajasthani experience.

Here, as elsewhere, the market for tourism services subdivides into specific sectors: high-end (Westerners and wealthy Indians), middle-class, and low-end. There is a diverse array of domestic tourists, largely drawn from the Indian middle class, but urban working class and rural people also may combine travel with leisure (Gold 1988). The European American tourism market with which this chapter concerns itself is one in which potential India travellers stand out as high income, highly educated consumers seeking diversion from destinations such as the Mediterranean, Caribbean or Mexico. Traditional print marketing aimed at this consumer appears in magazines appealing to this group. Print marketing tends to feature 'India', rather than specific Indian states.

An extensive advertising and marketing campaign of 2001 sponsored by the Government of India's Ministry of Tourism called 'Eternally Yours' emphasized the spiritual transformation that results from visiting India. Advertising targeted at persons of Indian descent living abroad, called 'Non-Resident Indians' or NRIs promised: 'Discover India. Discover Yourself' with the words below an attractive Rajasthani couple superimposed over an image of the Taj Mahal – set against the background of a blue, two-toned image of a tiger![5] More recently, this campaign shifted to 'Incredible India.' Colourfully-draped camels waded through sparkling blue waters in front of the Taj Mahal. This advertising campaign, by a combination of Indian and international advertising agencies, also emphasized India as a spiritual resource for the world (Goorha 2005, Stamler 2001).

Each state within India also promotes tourism. The states attempt to establish specific identities or 'brands' for themselves, such as Kerala, 'God's Own Country' (Kerala Tourism Development Corporation 2006) and Uttar Pradesh's 'Amazing Heritage. Grand Experiences.' (Uttar Pradesh Government Department of tourism 2006). This a shift from the 2002 'Cow Belt' theme – an image likely to confuse a European American tourist, whose 'cow belt' is probably a midwestern U.S. state.

---

5   This ad was collected from an issue of *India Today*, 2001.

Figure 4.2   **Despite the selling of Rajasthan as authentic and spontaneous, considerable discussion and 'back stage' management often occurs. These traditional performers at an NGO-sponsored all-Rajasthan conference are discussing performing artists' work conditions and the future of the arts.** *Photo courtesy of Carol E. Henderson. All rights reserved.*

Goa preens itself as a 'perfect holiday destination' (Goa Government of Department of tourism. 2006), while Rajasthan's current motto, developed since 2002, is 'Simply Colourful'.[6]

Towards Rajasthan Internet Tourism Marketing

Information about tourism in India is accessible on many different kinds of websites. Government sites, businesses, non-governmental organizations, scholarly institutions, and others include information on or about tourism.[7] Many Government of India, state government, and even district-level websites include tourism information and links to tourism service providers.[8] Since 1999, India's Ministry of

---

6   www.rajasthantourism.gov.in.

7   These websites include the domain of the 'dot-gov', (.gov), 'dot-com' (.com and .co [in Great Britain]) and 'dot-net' (.net), dot-org. (.org), dot-edu (.edu) and others that re just now being defined.

8   India's Ministry of Tourism webpages as of 2002 included www.tourisminindia.com and www.tourindia.com. Rajasthan's government tourism website as of 2006 was <www.

Tourism has maintained at least one website. The states' versions of this, such as the Punjab Tourism Development Corporation and the Rajasthan Tourism Development Corporation promote to both potential tourists and potential investors.[9] Tourism trade associations also promote destinations and services.

The largest category of websites devoted to India tourism lies in the private ('.com' or '.co') sector. These include business organizations, travel agencies, and publishers. NGOs ('.org') and educational institutions ('.edu') have a much smaller presence on the Internet. Most of these sites are in the English language, reflecting marketing's orientation to the European American consumer. This is true for websites both on India, generally and Rajasthan, particularly. For example, in 2002, German language websites for India listed only 350,000 sites (compared to 16 million for English) and French language websites listed only 87,000 websites. Indian-language websites, such as Hindi, similarly appeared to lag, reflecting the domination of the English language among Internet users and the groups most likely to visit India.

Several characteristics of web-based information and search engines used to generate data for this chapter are problematic from the standpoint of research methods. Looking first at this field of information as a whole, it is much less 'fixed' than print, in some respects more like orally transmitted information. The potential set of websites changes, as old websites are discontinued or edited, and new ones appear. Web designers modify existing sites. A user's access to websites reflects his or her computer's operating system and software, the software that sustains particular websites, that is used to browse the web, and used to 'read' it. Not all search engines gain access to all sites. An individual user's preferred search engine, or browser – and different versions of this – determines search outcomes.

The search engine used to identify websites for this study, Google.com, was selected over competitors such because, as of data collection in 2002, Google maintained the biggest search engine data base.[10] 'Paid' advertising clearly is separated from the list generated by the search procedures. Generally, the mathematical algorithm used in generating and ordering the results list of any keyword search, measures the relative density (how many times) with which a keyword occurs (also referred to as 'relevance') , and keywords' distance from one another in a website text. The search keywords are alphanumeric sequences (ABCXY). There is no protocol for searching visual images available to casual users at the present time.

Initially, I thought to conduct a content analysis of sites, through a stratified random sampling procedure. The basic premise behind this procedure is that any particular object, out of a field of any number of objects, will have an equal chance of being selected as any other object. The technique of random sampling was not consistent with efforts to approximate the results an ordinary user is likely to gain, compared with the results one might gather with special programming. Although

---

rajasthantourism.gov.in>.

9   <www.rajasthantourismindia.com/rtdc>

10 For a discussion of search engines, see University of California Library (2004 and 2006).

the search engine might generate several million 'hits' on any particular keyword search, there was no way for a casual web searcher, one using just the publicly available software with Google, randomly to identify and sample these 'hits.' The results list itself as produced is in a non-random order.

Research on user behaviour indicates, however, that individuals using a search engine view few websites on a results list before initiating new searches (Huberman *et al.*, n.d.; Adar and Huberman n.d). The top ten sites on a search results list in numerical order are the most likely to be looked at by any individual.[11] This may even be a generous overestimate. Such behaviour is a practical response on the part of the user: the further from the top of the list, the less likely the selected search terms (e.g., 'Rajasthan' and 'tourism') are to occur in close proximity to one another and the less likely the site will be about information of interest.

In the English-language marketing of South Asian tourism destinations, the number of search hits for countries by that country's name, plus the word 'tourism' (e.g., India tourism or Bangladesh tourism) are India (571,000 'hits'), Pakistan (210,000 'hits'), Nepal (200,000 'hits'), Bangladesh (150,000 'hits'), and Sri Lanka (143,000 'hits').[12] Looking within India, Rajasthan, with 30,800 'hits' of the state name plus 'tourism' is in the number six position, behind Delhi (136,000), Kerala (51,900), Kashmir (47,300), Goa (36,000), and Punjab (35,100).[13] One caution is that these search procedures are not useful in calculating the relative significance of tourism in the real world. The search procedures capture only what is on the Internet. Pakistan tourism arrivals of international tourists are about ten percent of India's (Buing 2002). The conflict in Kashmir has greatly reduced that region's significance in India tourism.

Included in 30,800 websites were both the terms 'Rajasthan' and 'tourism.'[14] However, the results list from this that could be viewed with this procedure contained only 764 sites. I compiled this list of websites as the basis for a preliminary overview of the website content. These 764 websites comprise approximately 2 percent of the 30,800 successful 'hits.' Most of these websites were commercial, produced and owned by companies selling trips and tours to Rajasthan. 646 of the 764 sites were proprietary sites ('.com' or '.co'). It turned out that most of the non-proprietary websites sold tourism services, too. At the time the search was conducted, there were no strict rules relating to website suffixes (say, .com vs. .org), although site designers usually matched the suffix to the organizational type.

---

11 In a survey of undergraduate students in my 'Introduction to Cultural Anthropology' course in 2001, only two (out of forty) indicated that they would look at more than twenty websites on a results list. Another two would look at more than ten. About half of the remainder said that they would look at numbers one to ten, and the other half said that they would look only at the top five.

12 Based on a Google search of these terms conducted on 17 September 2002.These numbers have subsequently skyrocketed.

13 Data based on a Google search 5 October 2002.

14 This does not guarantee that the websites have any relation to the topic of tourism in Rajasthan – just that these two strings of characters are present in the website.

Looking at the list of 764 websites, only five non-proprietary websites appeared in sites 1–100. Of these five websites, three marketed tourism services and were commercial. Four non-proprietary websites were identified in websites 101–201. Two of these proved to be commercial. Thus, in websites numbered 1–200, only four sites were not related to tourism marketing. The frequency of non-proprietary websites increased in the next block of websites, fourteen out of websites numbered 201–300. Seven of these, however, comprised commercial sites. In the next block (numbers 301-400), there were only four non-proprietary websites.

There were 65 non-commercial websites in the remainder of the list (numbers 401-764). Overall, non-commercial websites comprised slightly more than ten percent of the total, but almost all of these websites occurred at the end of the results list. These last included government websites, that of a UK-based NGO concerned with tourism issues, and most academic websites.

As noted above, the websites 1–10 were the most likely to be viewed by persons searching the Internet for information on tourism and Rajasthan (see Appendix A). In the following description, these websites will be referred to simply according to their position in the list, e.g., 'website 1', 'website 2', and so on, through website 10. The general visual characteristics of the home page on each website were tabulated in terms of: main colours used, layout, and specific images. Of particular interest was the banner, or top of the page, and the images and text located there. Overall, the text and images on the page were noted. Observation then was made of the pages contained within the site and links to other sites for further information.

The Orientalist's Sentimental Journey

The theme of the past is omnipresent in the tourist marketing discourse on Rajasthan where 'heritage' (the word) looms large as an unchanged entity. Rajasthan is in a 'time warp' (website 4). The tourist can 'Journey through the Royal Past' (website 1). By spending a night in a Rajasthan hotel, the tourist is 'Reliving the past' (website 9). The tourist can even take the 'Lost World' tour where '...the people and culture [are] completely isolated, hence completely unadulterated' (website 7). The reader is told that, 'Rajasthanis are sturdy, cheerful and simple folks relatively untouched by the fast pace of modern times' (website 1). After all, this website explains, '[t]he culture in Rajasthan is predominantly medieval.' After visiting Rajasthan and entering the past, one website warns, tourists may find it difficult to rejoin the 'modern [w]orld' (website 7). Depictions of modern technology are conspicuously absent and contrast with adjacent Haryana state whose government-sponsored tourism website bills itself as 'A Pioneer in Highway Tourism' and highlights such activities as 'Golf Tourism', 'fast foods', and even a 'Newsbyte' (Haryana Tourism Corporation Limited 2006).

Three key motifs realize the theme of the past and will be discussed in some detail below: 'royalty', 'colour', and 'camels'.[15] Sometimes, all these elements combine in a single passage on a website, as with the remarks:

> Think about Rajasthan and the picture of people clad in brightly *coloured* clothes riding *camels* through the ever-lasting stretches of sand seem to invite you to the land of *kings*. A stay at any of the magnificent forts and splendid *palaces* of the *Maharajas* of the bygone centuries, now a part of the India heritage will for sure turn you into a *prince* or *princess* for a day. (website 8).[16] [italics added]

The theme of the past appears in each visual and verbal image. 'Royalty' offers a pathway to Rajasthan history. Contemporary royals, or ex-royals, have no status as such in governance although as individuals they may play important roles within society (see chapters by Jhala and Bautès). 'Colour' as a motif contrasts with the putative drabness of modern life. 'Camels' symbolize a step backward in time, through the image of the desert caravan and non-modern technology that they represent.

Visual images on the web page underscore the idea of the past. Pages are densely crowded with images, much as an Oriental carpet stereotypically is packed with tightly knotted designs, as opposed to the minimalism of modern carpet design. The visual imagery of almost every website home page features historic architecture such as forts and palaces. Women and men wear traditional garb. Women's jewellery, in ostentatiously traditional designs, and men's turbans, are emphasized in images. Photographs of hand woven and printed fabrics highlight their pattern and design. The camel, the horse, and sometimes oxen appear to be the only form of transport. Pages might include a design element from traditional art, such as a warrior mounted on his prancing steed – a figure which is almost iconic in contemporary marketing of Rajasthan.

The present is notably absent. Modern structures, like the new government building in Jaipur, do not appear. People on the Rajasthan tourism websites are not depicted chatting on their cell phones, watching television, or in settings such as bus stops, banks, or shopping arcades with electric lighting. Rural people's adoption of plastic buckets, rubber shoes, and tractors goes unnoted. It is as if the contemporary world does not exist.

The colours used on these pages are the same as in the clothing worn by individuals in photos on the websites: deeply saturated yellows, golds, pinks, and reds. Lighting of subjects tends to a warm yellow or golden, evoking the sepia tones some Western publications use to denote 'old-fashioned' photography. The visual imagery and use of colour distinguishes Rajasthan tourism websites from other Indian states', such as

---

15 This portion of the analysis draws on the contents of the first ten websites (Google Search 12 September 2002).

16 Themes of tourism and heritage featured from 2002 and in 2006 on the Rajasthan State Government website, for examples see Rajasthan Government (2006).

the blues, greens and tans of the websites promoting Indian beach destinations and the blue skies and snowy mountains of the Himalaya states.

The Past is Royal

Text and visual images reinforce the message that Rajasthan is a place where one will encounter royalty, will live like royalty, and can enter a royal past. Although the motif of royalty has long appeared in conjunction with elite tourism, as Ramusack (1995) notes, today's marketing emphasizes that royalty is accessible to all budgets. Websites invite visitors to 'feel like *royalty*', to 'live like a *prince*', to 'take a *royal* retreat and be the *king* or the *queen*', and to 'get carried away into the opulent world of the *Maharaja*s' (Sites 2, 3, 6, 9 and 4) [italics added]. Failing this, the tourist might be associated with 'the land of kings' [Rajasthan] and to 'be entertained by the royal family' (Sites 7).

The names of tours and excursions highlight this motif: 'Journey through the Royal Past' (website 1), 'Royal Honeymoon' (websites 3, 10), 'Forts and Palaces' (websites 4,5,8), 'Royal Glories', 'Castles and Camels' (website 4), and 'Maharaja Retreat' (website 8). Visitors can travel on the Palace on Wheels. At day's end, tourists sleep in a 'Palace Hotel.' Honeymooners can become a 'prince and princess' in a 'fairy tale', and reenact a romantic legend' – 'now with you as the role model!' (website 7).

Royalty, history, and heritage are never far apart in this virtual Rajasthan, as presented on the Internet. The link is explicit: these websites present Rajasthan's history as *royal* history. Website 5 calls visitors to 'visit the monuments [forts and palaces] that stand testimony of the Royal Past.' Another website tells the tourist, 'history lies enshrined in its forts'.[17] Website 4 introduces Rajasthan as the 'Land of Royalty' and immediately follows this title with the statement that 'History abounds in Rajasthan.'

The 30,800 sites identified in the base search 'Rajasthan' and 'tourism' found 22,247 references to the term 'royal' and its closely associated terms.[18] There were 7,855 references to 'heritage', not including the terms 'Heritage Hotel' and Heritage Hotels' (3,745 'hits'), a term coined by the hotel operator's association of that name and promoted by them (Taft 2003). Another set of synonyms that relate to the theme of history is 'tradition', 'traditions,' and 'traditional' (10,050 'hits').

The web pages offer little in the way of substantive history. Few dates or names clutter the page. Absent are Rajasthan's other pasts, such as its history of peasant struggles, as part of India's nationalist narrative, and of the histories of diverse social groups. Tourism marketing presents non-royal groups as 'people without history' (Wolf 1982). They supposedly have always done what they do, in an unchanged universe (for an alternative account, see chapter by Snodgrass). Tourism marketers

---

17 This is for a tour entitled 'Exotic Rajputana', website 2.

18 In addition to 'royal', these terms are 'royalty', 'palace', 'maharaja', 'maharajah', 'prince', 'princes', 'princess' and 'princesses.'

invite visitors to fantasize a selective, highly romanticized past and to project it onto the present as a spectacle to be consumed.

A Colourful Past

The second motif associated with Rajasthan tourism marketing is 'colour.' Bright visual images reinforce the idea of colour. Indeed, Rajasthan's Department of Tourism is currently billing the state as 'colourful.' The term 'colour' and related words invite one into an exciting world. Colour signals that a visual as well as emotional feast is to be experienced. 'Colour' represents the exotic: this is an out-of-the-ordinary place, where emotional responses are stronger than in everyday life. Visual images on the websites underscore this through their use of highly saturated colours.

Rajasthan tourism marketing discourse asserts, life is 'still alive with *colour, joy*, regality, people, art and culture' (website 2) [italics added]. The guest encounters the '*colours* of *joyous celebration* and *gay abandon*' (website 9) in this place, where '*life vibrates* to the sound of music and sways in a profusion of *colours*' (website 10) [italics added]. Many adjectives modify colour terms. Colours are 'bright', 'lively', 'dazzling', 'brilliant', 'sparkling', 'swirling', and 'vivid': sound images filled with excitement and motion. 'Colour' connects the visitor with the past, which possesses more of this quality than does modernity (website 10). Rajasthan is a 'magnificent spectacle of *colour*, music, and festivity', an 'oasis of *colour*', typified by '[*colourful* costumes, festivals and customs*' (website 9) [italics added].

The discourse of colour extends to 'branding' major destinations: Jaipur, the 'Pink City', Jaisalmer, the 'Golden City' and Jodhpur, the 'Blue City', which is also the 'Sun City.' In this discourse, bazaars and markets are colourful. So are villages and towns. So are the people. The bodies of Rajasthani women and men embody the past, for they wear bright clothes conspicuously marked as 'of the past', which an urban Indian man or woman might put on only for a special event. The tourist is invited to view 'a kaleidoscope of brightly turbaned men' (websites 2 and 9). The turban symbolizes an exotic locale. Women wear 'colourful swirling *ghagras*' (skirts) (website 2). Animals wear clothing, too. At the fair one encounters '[c]olourfully attired elephants, camels, and horses (website 9). Mention of colour occurs many times in descriptions of festivals and fairs.[19] The tourist is invited to experience '[j]oys, celebrations, *colours* and customs' (website 7), and to 'enjoy the *colours* of festivity' (website 5) where one may view '*colourful* cultural performances' (website 7).

Victor Turner's discussion of liminality and celebration seems apt in thinking about the tourism discourse on colour in Rajasthan (Turner 1969). Terms such as 'spectacle', 'costumes', and 'festivals' clearly demarcate regular time from festival time, the 'time' to be consumed by the tourist. These statements draw the tourist into a fantasy that she or he has entered a touristic dream-time, similar in some

---

19　Some of these fairs were invented by the Rajasthan Tourism Development Corporation, while other 'new' fairs piggyback on preexisting events in novel kinds of way. See Hobsbawm and Ranger, (1983).

respects to the liminality of time experienced by pilgrims in their journeys (Turner and Turner 1978).

Colour in its diverse spellings (colours, colour, colourful, etc.) recurs 8,317 times in the base set of 30,080 websites containing 'Rajasthan' and 'Tourism.' The most frequently used colour term is – surprisingly – green (4,550 hits), followed by red (4,480), white (4,330), and gold (3150), followed by (in this order) black, blue, and yellow, with pink trailing. Red, bright pink, and gold are the most frequently viewed colours in the websites: no need, perhaps, to name these colours?

The Past is a Camel

The third motif in websites is the camel. This image appears to be a relatively recent addition to marketing discourse, as camels or activities related to them are not strongly marked (if, indeed, present) in guidebooks published prior to the 1980s. In websites, camels sit next to brightly clad women and men. Strings of camels climb the sand dunes and march into the sunset. Travel by camel recalls an older world prior to the invention of the internal combustion engine, the Asian silk routes, and even a royal connection, as some websites remind the reader that the sixteenth century Mughal emperor Humayun crossed the Rajasthan desert this way. If the trip to Rajasthan is an escape from the everyday (Turner and Turner 1978), then the camel safari is an escape-within an escape – a refuge that mediates tensions of the tourism experience.

The recently popular camel safari appears to have stimulated this marketing motif. This activity grew out of camel rides offered to tourists at livestock fairs such as at Pushkar. The term 'safari' is borrowed from Africa, and is associated with masculine adventures. Instead of offering big game to shoot or photographic images of these now-protected species to 'bag', the camel safari offers the sensations of closeness to the rural life, of romance, and of freedom from the social strictures of urban life in spaces that are relatively free of the disjunctures in the urban environment that so distresses travellers.[20]

Safaris divide into the day-trip by camel to a designated location where a picnic lunch is offered, and overnight outings. Both activities promise controlled and scripted encounters with local people. For example, the tourists will be 'garlanded' by villagers upon arrival (reminiscent of the Hawaiian tourist practice of putting leis around the necks of arriving tourists), and the 'chief' of a village will 'ceremonially' share the *chillum* (tobacco pipe) and *hookah* (water pipe) with the visitors. The tourists may be permitted a quick glimpse around the village. In one case, the tourism entrepreneur simply built a 'heritage farmhouse' for this purpose (website 2).

---

20 E.g. the perception of (in no particular order) dirt, poverty, crowding, modernity and social transgressions such as in-your-face touts and – for women – sexual harassment. Of course, cities (as every villager knows) are where the wealth is, and where one can get lost and escape the monotony of small-scale society.

Overnight safaris include travelling between one or more destinations and camping out while *en route*. An important activity is each night's halt, camping in tents, complete with cocktails and dinner. Each night there is a campfire with music and dance by local performers. The big attraction clearly is not the travel by camel, even described as unpleasant in the discourse by marketers, but the overnight halts. The tourist is called to 'adventure' (websites 3, 8) – but one that is keenly romantic (websites 3, 4, 9, 10). Website 9 titles its camel safari, 'Romantic Rides through the Desert', an 'escape from the tamed world.' We find that 'the safaris traverse... totally rural terrains still ruled by its romantic past of chivalry, love, and passion' (website 10). In fact, some tourist entrepreneurs note that they sometimes take routes that avoid settled areas – possibly because those are too modernized. Resistance by villagers to tourist invasions is motivated by several factors. Villagers feel inadequately compensated (although they may be paid for their services unknown to the tourists). Villagers perceive tourists as uncivilized and amoral, people they do not want in their own backyards.

The adventure of the safari is to give the tourist the sensation that she or he is getting close to the real life of rural people:

....the Romance of the Desert overwhelms. Life vibrates to the sound of music and sways in a profusion of colours. Sturdy moustached men in colourful turbans, cheerful women in multi-hued skirts, caparisoned camels... Enticing Gair, Fire and Snake dancers, Folk musicians and festive gaiety. (website 10).

The evening rituals draw the group together and foster new friendships:

Night camping under the open starry sky can be an extremely romantic idea. The camel driver would happily cook for you, make you comfortable in the tent and relate romantic tales. Be a gullible listener to ward off boredom. Maybe some vagrant group of balladeers and musicians find you. For a small tip they can be excellent company. Try to catch up on lost sleep.... (website 3)

So, how close to Rajasthan can one get on the camel safari? The websites turn coy:

Prefer riding a male camel. What if your female camel is pursued by males! Desert loneliness has strange, unpredictable side effects. (website 3)

The camel safari explicitly promises freedom, camaraderie, and communion between the tourist and the fantasy destination. The term 'safari' would seem to position this as a masculine activity that evokes Hemingwayesque images of the big-game hunter. The landscape lies open to a male gaze (Urry 1990, Pritchard and Morgan 2000). Yet the websites' images and text contradict this expectation, in favor of ambiguous sexuality. Instead of the externally-directed activities of hunting, tracking and shooting game (either with a gun or a camera), visitors on the camel trip are directed instead to the internally-directed emotions of romance and the feeling, not of mastering the desert, but of becoming one with it by 'truly experiencing' rural life.

The desert is a wild, stark place to the tourists, but one that includes village settlements and promises of nightly luxury. The camel drivers, cooks, and guides are males, who deliver a mixture of masculine services (guiding, controlling the camels) and feminine services (cooking, making the guest comfortable in the tent). The female camel ridden by the tourist may become the object of the male camel's gaze and pursuit, when it is the (male) tourist rider who should pursue others. Transgression of gender norms may not only be permitted, but encouraged. Hence, perhaps the snickers by villagers when the camel safari is mentioned, and the swift change of topic to how much money tourists are willing to pay to ride around on a camel!

Toward Cyberorientalism?

The Internet's creators and many early enthusiasts perceived the information superhighway as evolutionary and subversive, so decentralized that no single group could dominate. This promise has taken some unexpected turns since those days. More information is available on Rajasthan to more people than ever before on the Internet, but it is segmented. Tourism marketing of Rajasthan unabashedly promises an Orientalist fantasy. In this, marketing representations of Rajasthan on the Internet have much in common with earlier guidebook and travel writing narratives.

The appeal of nostalgia, however false for tourists who lack cultural experiences of India, is overt. Tourists are invited to step into the past. Virtual Rajasthan is a land where the clock stopped long ago. It is also a place of sexual ambivalence as seen through the lens of the camel safari. Here, the webpage designers consciously engage a fantasy of freedom from social norms. The third great theme of Orientalist discourse, rule by despots, is not marked in tourism discourse, for the obvious reason that it contradicts the promise of being the king or queen for a day.

Marketing discourse turns away from the political and economic realities embodied in the fortified compounds and palaces to the fantasies of royal hotels and guesthouses. The only narratives in which labour enters the discourse of the past are those which feature rulers' paternalistically helping famine relief. There is a veil drawn over other aspects of the royal past. Tourists do not want to hear about this. Many older Rajasthanis who experienced the era of royal rule would just as soon not talk about this time, too.

The more successfully the tourist operator keeps the visitor's gaze away from these kinds of contemporary and past realities and the more successfully the destination can be scripted, the greater the chances of tourist satisfaction. Here, there is a collusion between interests. To some extent, the tourist operator's 'virtual Rajasthan' intersects with his or her personal vision of Rajasthan: pride in the built environment of the past, arts and crafts, and performance arts traditions, of honourable hospitality extended to visitors. Similarly, the tourist's 'virtual Rajasthan' intersects with the presentation of built sites, the consumption of material goods such as textiles and wooden *objet d'arts*, and the enjoyment of musical and dance evenings. The tourist as defined by the tourism marketing websites is one who would partake of Rajasthan's historical heritage and who wishes to experience, in close proximity, this culture.

How successfully these goals are accomplished depends on the extent to which the tourist perceives marketing's pastiche of Orientalist stereotypes about 'the East', 'India', and 'Rajasthan' as realized in the tourist journey. In Rajasthan, as tourists discover (and comment on blogs and conversations among themselves), there are many challenges to the fulfilment of the promised fantasy-destination. On the Internet, however, these distractions may be ignored: NGO websites, academic sites, and trenchant commentary on current social conditions are distant from the words and images of tourism marketing for Rajasthan. Yet this image of Rajasthan heritage, repugnant as it may be to critics of the Orientalist position, is neither a compelling necessity nor foreordained, as seen in addition of themes and their reworking as marketing responds to shifts in tourism services and demand.

Appendix A

List of websites cited in the text. Top ten websites generated in Google search for sites containing the terms 'Rajasthan' and 'Tourism'. Search conducted 5 October 2002.

1. www.rajasthandiary.com
2. www.rajtourism.com
3. www.rajasthanhub.com
4. www.rajasthan-tours.com
5. www.tourism-rajasthan.com
6. www.travel-rajasthan.com
7. www.destinationrajasthan.com
8. rajasthan.indianvisit.com
9. www.rajasthanholiday.com
10. www.rajasthan-india.com

References

Adar, E. and B.A. Huberman, (n.d.), 'The Economics of Surfing', http://www9.org/final-posters/31/poster31/.html. Accessed 27 February 2007.

Bandyopadhyay, R. and D. Morais (2005), 'Representative Dissonance: India's Self and Western Image', *Annals of Tourism Research* 32:4, 1006–1021.

Bhattacharyya, D.P. (1997), 'Mediating India: An Analysis of a Guidebook', *Annals of Tourism Research* 24:2, 371–389.

Breckenridge, C. (1989), 'The Aesthetics and Politics of Colonial Collecting: India at World Fairs', *Comparative Studies in Society and History* 31:2, 195–216.

Bruner, E.M. (2001), 'The Maasai and the Lion King: Authenticity, Nationalism, and Globalization in African Tourism', *American Ethnologist* 28:4, 881–908.

Brunn, S.D. and C.D. Cottle (1997), 'Small States and Cyberboosterism.' *Geographical Review* 87:2, 240–258.

Buing, N. (2000) 'Picking Up the Crumbs', *Dawn* http://www.dawn.com/events/century/soc7.html

Chambers, E. (2000), *Native Tours: The Anthropology of Travel and Tourism* (Prospect Heights, IL: Waveland Press).

Chhabra, D., R. Healy and E. Sills (2003), 'Staged Authenticity and Heritage Tourism', *Annals of Tourism Research* 30:3, 702–719.

Christiansen, N. (2003), *Inuit in Cyberspace: Embedding of Offline Identities Online* (Copenhagen: Museum Tusculanum Press, University of Copenhagen).

Chronis, A. (2005), 'Coconstructing Heritage at the Gettysburg Storyscape', *Annals of Tourism Research* 32:2, 386–406.

Cohen, E. (1993), 'The Study of Touristic Images of Native People: Mitigating the Stereotype of a Stereotype', in D. Pearce and R. Butler (eds.) *Tourism Research: Critiques and Challenges* (New York: Routledge, 36–69).

Echtner, C.M. and P. Prasad (2003), 'The Context of Third World Tourism Marketing', *Annals of Tourism Research* 30:3, 660–682.

Edensor, T. (1998), *Tourists at the Taj: Performance and Meaning at a Symbolic Site* (New York: Routledge).

Edensor, T. and U. Kothari (1994), 'The Masculinisation of Stirling's Heritage', in V. Kinnaird and D. Hall (eds.) *Tourism: A Gender Analysis* (Chichester: John Wiley & Sons, Ltd.,164–187).

Escobar, A. (1994), 'Welcome to Cyberia: Notes on the Anthropology of a Cyberculture', *Current Anthropology* 35:3, 211–231.

Fodor, E. and W. Curtis (eds.) (1974), *Fodor's India 1974* (New York: David McKay Company, Inc).

Gable, E. and R. Handler (1996), 'After Authenticity at an American Heritage Site', *American Anthropologist* 98:3, 568–578.

Ginsburg, F. (1994), 'Culture/Media: a (Mild) Polemic', *Anthropology Today* 10:2, 5–15.

Goa, Government of. Department of Tourism (2006), 'Home Page' of website http://www.goatourism.org. Accessed 26 August 2006.

Gold, A.G. (1988), *Fruitful Journeys: The Way of Rajasthani Pilgrims* (Berkeley: University of California Press).

Goorha, P. (2005), 'Tourism Ministry Hires 15 Agencies for Rs. 70 cr Incredible India Campaign', *AgencyFAQs!* 15 June, 2005 http://www.agencyfaqs.com/news/stories/2005/06/15/11742.html

Hakken, D. (1999), *Cyborgs@Cyberspace?: An Ethnographer Looks to the Future* (New York: Routledge).

Haryana Tourism Corporation Limited (2003), 'Home Page' of website http://www.haryanatourism.com. Accessed 26 August 2006.

Henderson, C. (1998), 'The Great Cow Explosion in Rajasthan', in W.S. Balée (ed.) *Advances in Historical Ecology* (New York: Columbia University Press, 349–375).

Herman, A. and T. Swiss (eds.) (2001), *The World Wide Web and Contemporary Cultural Theory* (New York: Routledge).

The Hindu (2004), "Foreign Tourists' Arrival Up by 47% in Rajasthan', The Hindu 26 November. Online edition, http://www.hindu.com/2004/11/26/stories/2004112608540500.htm

Hobsbawm, E. and T. Ranger (eds.) (1983), *The Invention of Tradition* (Cambridge: Cambridge University Press).

Hooja, R. and R. Joshi (eds.) (1999), *Desert, Drought and Development: Studies in Resource Management and Sustainability* (Jaipur: Rawat Publications).

Huberman, B.A., P.L.T. Pirolli, J.E. Pitkow and R.M. Lukose, 'Strong Regularities in World Wide Web Surfing', www.3.org/Protocols/HTTP-NG/1998/02/1998-02-surfing-final.pdf.

Inden, R. (1986), 'Orientalist Constructions of India', *Modern Asian Studies* 20:3, 401–446.

Jackson, M.H. and D. Purcell (1997), 'Politics and Media Richness in World Wide Web Representations of the Former Yugoslavia', *Geographical Review* 87:2, 219–239.

Johnson, N. (1999), 'Framing the Past: Time, Space and the Politics of Heritage Tourism in Ireland', *Political Geography* 18, 187–207.

Kelly, C. (2005), 'Geeks, Social Imaginaries, and Recursive Publics', *Cultural Anthropology* 20:2, 185–214.

Kerala Tourism Development Corporation (2005), 'Home Page' of website http://www.ktdc.com. Accessed 26 August 2006.

Kirschenblatt-Gimblett, B. (1995), 'Theorizing Heritage', *Ethnomusicology* 39:3, 367–380,

Leiner, B.M. et al. (2000), 'A Brief History of the Internet', http://www.isoc.org/Internet/history/brief.html, 12. © Internet Society

Lutz, C.A. and J.L. Collins (1993), *Reading National Geographic* (Chicago: The University of Chicago Press).

MacCannell, D. (1973), 'Staged Authenticity: Arrangements of Social Space in Tourist Settings', *American Journal of Sociology* 79:3, 589–603.

McChesney, R. (2000), 'So Much for the Magic of Technology and the Free Market: The World Wide Web and the Corporate Media System', in A. Herman and T. Swiss (eds.) *The World Wide Web and Contemporary Cultural Theory* (New York: Routledge, 5–35).

Mehta, G. (1979), *Karma Cola: Marketing the Mystic East* (New York: Simon and Schuster).

Murray, J. (1904), *The Imperial Guide to India, Including Kashmir, Burma and Ceylon* (London: John Murray).

Nakamura, L. (2002), Cybertypes: Race, Ethnicity, and Identity on the Internet (New York: Routledge).

Nuryanti, W. (1996), 'Heritage and Postmodern Tourism', *Annals of Tourism Research* 23:2, 249–260.

Poria, Y., R. Butler, and D. Airey (2003), 'The Core of Heritage Tourism', *Annals of Tourism Research* 30:1, 238–254.

Pritchard, A. and N. J. Morgan (2000), 'Privileging the Male Gaze: Gendered Tourism Landscapes', *Annals of Tourism Research* 27:4, 884–905.

Rajasthan. Government. Department of Tourism (2006) 'Home Page' of website RajDarpan – The Official Web Portal, Government of Rajasthan. http://www.rajasthan.gov.in. Accessed 26 August 2006

Ramusack, B. (1995), 'The Indian Princes as Fantasy: Palace Hotels, Palace Museums, and Palace on Wheels', in C.A. Breckenridge (ed.) *Consuming Modernity: Public Culture in a South Asian World* (Minneapolis: University of Minnesota Press, 66–89).

Rosenszweig, R. (1998), 'Wizards, Bureaucrats, and Warriors: Writing the History of the Internet', *American Historical Review* 103:5, 1530–1552.

Said, E.W. (1978), *Orientalism* (New York: Pantheon Books).

Spivak, G.C. (1988), 'Can the Subaltern Speak?' in C. Nelson and L. Grossberg (eds.) *Marxism and the Interpretation of Culture* (London: Macmillan, 271–313).

Stamler, B. (2001), 'A New Campaign from Oasis stresses the wonders of India for potential American Tourists', *The New York Times* 28 June, C-6

Taft, F. (2003), 'Heritage Hotels in Rajasthan', in S. Singh and V. Joshi (eds.) *Institutions and Social Change* (Jaipur: Rawat Publications, 127–149).

Taylor, J.P. (2001), 'Authenticity and Sincerity in Tourism', *Annals of Tourism Research* 28:1, 7–26.

Tod, J. (1914a), *Annals and Antiquities of Rajast'han*, vol. I (London: Routledge and Sons, Ltd).

—— (1914b), *Annals and Antiquities of Rajast'han*, vol. II (London: Routledge and Sons, Ltd).

Turner, V. (1969), *The Ritual Process: Structure and Anti-Structure* (Ithaca, NY: Cornell University Press).

Turner, V. and E. Turner (1978), *Image and Pilgrims in Christian Cultures, Anthropological Perspectives* (New York: Columbia University Press).

University of California Library (2004) 'Three Basic Families of Search Tools', (tutorial on types of search tools) http'//www.Lib.berkeley/edu/TeachingLib/Guides/Internet/Tools/Tables.html. Copyright Regents of the University of California. Accessed 28 September, 2006.

University of California Library (2006), 'Recommended Search Strategies', (tutorial on 'finding Information on the Internet') http://www.lib.berkeley.edu/TeachingLib/Guides/InternetStrategies. Previously accessed June 2001.

Urry, J. (1990), *The Tourist Gaze: Leisure and Travel in Contemporary Societies* (London: Sage).

Uttar Pradesh Government. Department of Tourism (2006), 'Home Page' of website http://www.up-tourism.com. Accessed 28 September, 2006.

Waitt, G. (2000), 'Consuming Heritage: Perceived Historical Authenticity.' *Annals of Tourism Research* 27:4, 835–862.

Wilson, S.M. and L.C. Peterson (2002), 'The Anthropology of Online Communities,' *Annual Review of Anthropology* 31, 449–467.

Wolf, E.R. (1982), *Europe and the People Without History* (Berkeley: University of California Press).

Part 2
Tourism, Transgression and Shifting Uses of Social Capital

Introduction to Part 2

Carol E. Henderson and Maxine Weisgrau

Tourism particularly relates to how individuals and groups mobilize social capital in the cultural politics of identity. Early tourism scholarship emphasized the negative ways in which mass tourism, in places which previously received few such travellers, affected local populations. The arrival of the tourism juggernaut, in these views, distorts previous social relationships, destabilizes cultural sensibilities, negatively affects environmental quality, and creates conflict.

Settings that market 'heritage' may be particularly vulnerable to such problems, particularly where heritage is closely tied to properties of the physical landscape. Industrialization in and around Agra is criticized as ruining air quality, blamed for damaging the Taj Mahal and ruining tourists' views of the site. In Jaipur, city planners were so concerned about the deterioration of the heritage components of the spaces in and around the walls of the Pink City that they forced the removal of signage, stalls, and add-on constructions. There has been great concern over pollution in the Ganges River at Varanasi, which detracts significantly from pilgrims' and tourists' experience of the waterfront at this holy site of Hinduism.

Of no less local concern are ideas about the transformations prompted by tourism that affect the spaces of identity and meaning in which people live. Usually, this focuses on social transgressions relating to sexuality or social hierarchy: children are warned not to beg from adults; women's social status may be demeaned by consorting with foreign men; non-elites may suffer social sanctions if tourism entrepreneurship brings them new forms of wealth that others feel are inappropriate to persons of their social status. Ideas of what is right and proper – that constitute valued components of cultural heritage – also become arenas of debate.

These four chapters look at how tourism intersects with local perspectives on tourism entrepreneurship, providing a more nuanced and contemporary vision of scholarly analysis than studies that focus purely on tourists' or elites' perspectives. A key theme here is the interrelationship between ability to mobilize social capital and social identity. Tourism, unsurprisingly, proves to be a mixed bag of costs and benefits. What one group might perceive as a cost, another sees as a benefit. Even in one tourism designation there is plenty of diversity. The diverse instances in these case studies, largely focused on the city of Udaipur in central–south Rajasthan, could be repeated across India, with some variation.

As Bautès outlines the situation, the vision of Udaipur's 'Old City,' the primary tourism destination, is dominated by one elite player: the former ruling house. Other significant groups negotiating for voice in planning the tourism vision of the Old City include wealthy merchant families, local and state government agencies, well-connected (on the national and international scene) non-governmental organizations (NGOs), non-royal Rajput families and both Indian and multinational hotel corporations. The former royal house's property interests in the core tourism zone dwarf those belonging to these other groups. The dominant group's definition of the resource and its management of space combine to identify Udaipur's 'heritage' in this instance as one of royalty. This vision dominates the planning for the city's primary tourist destination. The casual visitor may not know that the voices of city residents, along with the other interests in local tourism may not hold equal sway in the on-going debates over how Udaipur might be presented to tourists as a heritage site.

Moving from the top to the bottom of the social hierarchy, Snodgrass finds that members of formerly Untouchable groups have found a niche for themselves performing for tourists in the big hotels and in display spaces, such as the 'cultural village' on the outskirts of Udaipur. In this performance, there is intense discussion of costume (what to wear), music (which accompaniments work best), and selection of material to perform. A very important assertion of their identity is through claimed historic association with Udaipur's ruling house.

The group's portrayal of a seemingly unchanged tradition, as Snodgrass shows, largely begins and ends in the performance space. The group migrated to Udaipur, adopted a performing art outside their traditional range, and renamed themselves. They have emphasized as cultural heroine a woman, whom a traditional story links to the royal family of Udaipur, even though members of this group never enjoyed a patron-client relationship with Udaipur royalty.

Recently, members of this group have shifted their tourism earnings from a social display that is specific to membership in their group, to investment in real property and consumer goods. Snodgrass makes clear that this shift was facilitated, in part, by developments that enhanced this group's security in property ownership. Today, tourism produces enough cash income that performers can now surround themselves with solid homes, good educations for their children, the latest appliances, and motor vehicles – all the markers of Indian middle-class lifestyle.

Yet, there are limits to their ability to realize these aspirations. They are unlikely to meet as social equals any member of the elite families who are also involved in tourism – and some of whom, reflecting an older generation's feelings, are critical of these aspirations to upwardly mobility. Yet, by moving to a city far from their village homes and by changing their name, the performers have obscured the most stigmatizing elements of their former identity.

Sex, class, and race intersect in the play of gender and identity identified by Weisgrau. Youthful Rajasthani men find that they can gain access to substantial resources through their personal connections with Western foreigners, particularly women. Clearly, a little English, an attractive demeanour, self-confidence, and a sociable personality are great assets. So too is the understanding of the gulf between wages and income in the tourists' home countries, and what the young man is most likely to be able to earn in the non-tourist economy of Udaipur. The best case scenarios seemed to be those where tips, gifts, and earnings could help a family to retrieve a lost social position, and to achieve or to sustain middle-class status.

Interestingly, Indian women's accounts of these relationships focused on those that most transgressed social hierarchy (as if a member of the group Snodgrass studied took up with a foreign woman). It was not the infidelity, or the time away from his own family, that was of such concern, but rather that the 'wrong sort' might wind up as a guest in the best hotel in town and thus, symbolically, become one's social equal. This is a cautionary tale about who gets access to foreigners and also a story about how to realize resources in an economic environment, where other possibilities are monopolized by Udaipur's dominant group.

Jhala writes of the mobilization of identity (as a Rajput, as a king) in the construction of heritage in the tourism industry. Jodhpur city is also a place where there is an important property owner – the Maharaja's family. As in Udaipur, people complain that elite families capture the bulk of the tourism resource for themselves, to the detriment – they say – of everyone else. Yet some of the most outstanding tourism assets of Jodhpur – unlike Udaipur – are physically separated from the city centre. Tourism in Jodhpur is much less compact than in Udaipur and dominance of one group is mitigated by its larger business community (Jodhpur is twice the size of Udaipur), the presence of a large military installation, and regional government offices, such as the Rajasthan High Court, located here.

We cannot conclude a discussion of Udaipur and Jodhpur without noting elite Rajput cultural identity politics. Members of the former ruling groups are acutely aware of one another's' presentation of heritage. As Jhala shows, an important component of the Maharaja of Jodhpur's birthday celebration showcases elements in a specifically royal idiom – understandable and relevant only to the claims and counterclaims of status among members of that group. There is a certain amount of jostling for prestige among Jaipur, Jodhpur, and Udaipur's royals. While Udaipur may have the 'advantage' of a seemingly clear ground for the assertion of identity, other business and governmental groups compete with these elites. This arena of competition in India's increasingly privatized economy provides distinct possibilities for how new forms of identity will be mobilized into this competition for control over the representation of local heritage.

Chapter 5

Exclusion and Election in Udaipur Urban Space: Implications of Tourism

Nicolas Bautès

This chapter analyses various spatial aspects of tourism growth in the city of Udaipur (population 389,317) in southern Rajasthan, the capital of the district of that name and of the former princely state of that name.[1] I examine the political, social and economic relationship between tourism and territory, in particular the impact of tourism on the city's urban layout, the resulting uneven economic development and its political consequences. In this chapter, I discuss tourism as a social phenomenon encouraging the economic specialization of particular areas and modifying social relationships between those areas involved in tourism and others. Territory is seen as the spatial dimension of power in this instance, under the impact of the growth in tourism.

An examination of localities within Udaipur city, using tourism as key, gives a good idea of recent changes in the urban power structure and its impact on urban planning. This study highlights the negative impact of tourism development on the city's spatial system, in particular the effective dismemberment of the tourism district, as I shall term the sections of the city which have tourism assets, from the rest of the urban centre. This disjuncture between the tourism and non-tourism sections of the city directly results from the importance of tourism in the urban economy and its key role in particular sections of the city. The issues to be addressed are similar to those faced by other urban tourism destinations in the world, although obviously, prospects and outcomes, will vary from one location to another.

The development of tourism in Udaipur should be seen in the light of various strategies aimed at territorial control.

This chapter assesses tourism's impact on the townscape as a whole, by analysing the impact of tourism and comparing its effect on the attractive urban heritage areas with those lacking such assets. It appears that the tourism-oriented projects implemented by dominant social actors tend to be linked to changes in the dynamics of the urban landscape. Key actors have chosen their strategies to increase their power and to reinforce their position in the social system. Projects directly or indirectly related to tourism also provoke changes that inhibit the balanced development of the

1   I would like to thank Carol Henderson and Maxine Weisgrau for their valuable comments and suggestions on this paper.

urban territory as a whole, the nature of tourism, and its development in the medium term.

In Udaipur as elsewhere, the growth of tourism is a major factor in urban development. My thesis is that tourism plays a significant role in the organization of urban space in Udaipur, in the way key actors present this space in development and tourism discourse, and in their related activities. Tourism is the economic sector in which the interests of the dominant social forces in the city converge. Unsurprisingly, its control is a major objective for numerous organizations.

Many private individuals, civic groups, and government actors are aware of tourism's major contribution to economic development. They regard tourism as a way to promote the city, attract visitors, and encourage urban innovation. By highlighting and selling the city's history, primarily in the form of its historic urban landscape, tourism helps to redefine the local population's relationship with the districts in which they live. However, by basing the local economy largely on activities requiring the preservation of particular elements of the town, tourism tends to reinforce existing social and spatial disparities. In this process, Udaipur's territorial dynamics can be seen as a process of selection and exclusion of particular areas.

This chapter is based on information collected between 1999 and 2002. The data come from a variety of sources: town planning documents, Rajasthan Ministry of Tourism publications, statements by municipal officials, discussions with members of NGOs working on projects encouraging sustainable town planning in the city, and interviews with Indian and non-Indian tourists, tourist industry professionals (hotel managers, tourist guides, businessmen, etc.), and numerous city and regional inhabitants. My field work included a questionnaire-based survey and a series of interviews with 140 tourists (64 Indian nationals and 76 non-Indian nationals). It also established which sites, in the tourists' view, best reflect their image of Udaipur. The field work examined tourist behaviour at these sites to determine various aspects of the process by which the sites had been chosen. The conclusions in this paper are based on data collected during these interviews, on local and regional sources, and newspaper accounts collected during the term of fieldwork.

This chapter starts with a description of Udaipur as a tourist destination, marketing images of tourism in Udaipur, and the key attractions as these are perceived by tourists. I include a description of the tourist district, as defined by tourist perceptions and behaviour patterns. The chapter then moves to a consideration of the exclusionary processes that contribute to the rather narrow definition of the tourist district as seen in these accounts. The 'City within a City' Project proposed by the Maharana Mewar Charitable Foundation (MMCF) provides a case study of the operation of processes that define certain parts of the city as the 'tourism district', while others are excluded.

Seeing Udaipur: Tourist Images and Practices as Agents of Space Election

Guidebooks often represent the approaches to the city of Udaipur as a pleasing and aesthetic experience. From Ahmadabad in the south, the traveller sees endless mountains, valleys and twisted geological formations. From New Delhi in the north, the railway to southern Rajasthan goes via Ajmer and Nathdwara, through wild and rugged country, taking one of the few narrow passes through the Aravalli mountains. This route is largely followed by the major conduit National Highway 8, which similarly approaches the city through narrow, winding roads. Approaching Udaipur at the end of the journey, the traveller sees an increasing number of billboards lining the track and roadway, announcing the traveller's imminent arrival in this tourist site. Billboards advertise marble companies near Udaipur, a major industry, the hotels in and around the town, and the region's tourist attractions. Tourism-related billboards mostly depict the ancient royal city and its natural environment in lush colours that belie the brown, deforested hills around the city and often-dried up condition of the lakes. These billboards highlight the same images and attractions as those promoted by tour operators. The traveller is left in no doubt that she or he is entering a tourist destination.

The actual entry into Udaipur is a dramatic contrast to the journey and to travellers' expectations, provoking a certain reserve, even among the most enthusiastic visitors. Heavy traffic, air pollution, and the whole urban landscape appear to have fallen to the effects of a recent and uncontrolled development. But as soon as visitors go through the somewhat battered gates to the city *intra muros*, they are surrounded by the anticipated sights, and now can usually ignore the problems facing its half-million inhabitants. Narrow, winding roads lined with temples and typical Rajasthan houses, a palace on top of a hill, *ghats* (steps) leading down to a lake, the town laid out along its shores and climbing up into the surrounding hills are attractive views. These confirm the images in the tourist brochures and in the visitor's imagination. The preconceived map in the tourist's mind comes to life, as noted by Mentzos[2] when he or she sees it on the ground.

Although these marketing images of Udaipur are not the only factors influencing tourist activities and determining the sites the tourists visit, such perspectives play an important role in the system as a whole. In effect, the images substitute for the actual sites and build reputations – often leading to world-wide notoriety. The 'imaginary' Udaipur acts as catalyst in its economic development and, on occasion, as obstacle to development and change. In fact, my data show that the symbolically charged nature of these sites created by words and visual media largely conditions tourism in the region.

Urban tourism in Rajasthan depends on a number of evocative places that particular writers have defined as outstanding sites.[3] They comprise Rajasthan's crucial symbolic sites, in that they have been associated with key moments in

---

2   Quoted by Travlou, P. (2002) 'Go Athens: A Journey to the Centre of the City', Coleman, Simon and Mike Crang (2002). *Tourism:Between Place and Performance*. (New York: Oxford: Berghahn Books).

3   'Outstanding sites', *hauts-lieux* have been defined in several ways. For this chapter I have used that of Debarbieux, (1995: 95), 'an element of a system of expressions territorially materialized of a system of values.'

Figure 5.1 Vista looking east showing Lake Palace hotel (in lake, foreground), City Palace Complex (centre left) and in background development of industrial and residential suburbs of Udaipur. *Photo courtesy of Jorge Reverter.*

the region's history. The tourist imagination of the state is one of outstanding and authentic heritage sites. Udaipur shares in these images (Agrawal 1979).

Points of interest within the tourism destination (Chambers 2002, 31) of Udaipur city itself offer a certain exotic fascination, described in detail in tourist guides, in travel agency advertisements world-wide, in newspaper and magazine articles and, most recently, on the Internet (see chapter by Henderson). These tourism sites within Udaipur are developed and promoted *in situ* by one or more economic and/or political agents. Synergy between marketing and consumption patterns – the promotion of these points of interest in brochures produced by local tourist industry organizations and reinforcement by the complimentary remarks made by foreign tourists on their return home – tends to promote these same sites' selection for development by particular actors in Udaipur. This in turn reinforces the ways in which tourists explore and use the city.

Udaipur is one of a number of places in the world that is marketed to tourists through the language of chivalry and romance (Ramusack 1998). This is in part due to the nature of the site, in a valley surrounded by high hills, with several man-made lakes and ponds skirting the edges of the city that provide a setting for some of its grandest palaces. The tourist literature has long called Udaipur the 'Venice of the East' because of this similarity to the famous Italian city, thus adding to its romantic appeal.[4] This view of Udaipur relies on earlier travellers' imaginative descriptions, which have been enhanced by the tourist industry in the town and elsewhere. In reality, Udaipur has a number of problems: buildings are in disrepair, there is visible air and water pollution, and its famous lakes contain sewage, if they are not bone dry most of the year, due to recurrent droughts. The often-dry lakebeds are being subjected to land fill and encroachment for housing and agricultural purposes. Nevertheless, the impression that visitors have of the city is positive. The descriptions and images provided by the tourism-oriented media have not yet been seriously challenged by any account of the actual state of the city.

Images produced by the tourist industry and the media are almost invariably based on the role Udaipur played in history, and on traces of this history visible in the city landscape. These accounts refer to Udaipur's physical characteristics, geographical situation, and more often than not, its hills and lakes. These images of Udaipur merge into those of Rajasthan, 'the abode of princes', thus complementing and strengthening the area's regional identity.

Udaipur's history as presented to tourists is that of a kingdom. Udaipur both identifies itself with the history of the kingdom of Mewar, for the city was its last capital, and represents itself, through the kingdom's rejection of marital alliances with the Mughals, as the exemplar of the purest Rajasthan culture as a whole (Manakekar 1976). This history emphasizes the royal aspects of Rajput heritage as its major tourist attraction and the basis of the local tourist sites that have come to symbolize the territory, while other sites are under represented or receive no mention in this tourism-driven historical chronicle.

---

4   See, for example, E. Fodor and W. Curtis (eds.) (1974), Murray (1949); Singh and Cox (1999).

In Udaipur, as is frequently the case with medieval cities, spatial exclusion is apparent in the town's physical layout. Principles and ideas derived from Hindu texts define the ancient city centre as the most sacred area. All aspects of the town's administration and life lead there. As one leaves the symbolic centre of the city, one enters a contrasting zone of spiritual danger (Malamoud 1989, Cadène 1998). This way of seeing the town – based on ancient texts – does not account for today's organization of urban space, although tourism appears to have accentuated the classical divide between centre and periphery. The tourist industry looks for symbolic sites, and has mostly found them in the historic city centre,[5] what Micoud (1991) defines as the process of recognition as the social construction of exemplary models. The complexity of the urban territory, in terms of its layout and the many forms of social interaction this represents, is obscured and replaced by a single image dominated by the Rajputs and their identity as rulers, not that of other groups who also live here, such as priests or merchants. Visitors from different backgrounds select a minute part of an urban area as representative of the town as a whole, to the exclusion of others. This principle, it turned out, applied regardless of the site on which the interviews were carried out.[6]

Constructing Udaipur: Tourists and the Tourist District

The Lake Palace Hotel on Jag Niwas, an island in the middle of Lake Pichola is most frequently chosen by the tourist literature and other media as the quintessential representative monument of Udaipur. Most tourists referred to this group of buildings and the surrounding lake, when asked to describe the city and what best represented their stay there. This result was further confirmed when I asked tourists to cite the particular aspect or site that best symbolized the town itself, or the site most often mentioned prior to their visit to Rajasthan. In these interviews, 129 out of 140 persons mentioned the Lake Palace, an overwhelming response.

An examination of these replies suggests that both Indian and Western tourists most often associated Udaipur as a whole with this particular palace. They consider it to be one of the remaining visible parts of the built heritage that reflects the wealth of the former Mewar kingdom. Ironically, other buildings in the city palace environs have a longer history than the palace on Jag Niwas island, whose construction dates to 1760, roughly 200 years after Udaipur's founding. This island structure

---

5   The prehistoric (ca. 1700 BCE) Ahar archaeological complex which also includes the site of the cenotaphs of the former kings of Mewar since the founding of Udaipur, is a good example of an outstanding site. Few tourists visit the site on account of its geographical situation, three miles from the historic city centre. This calls into question the nature of tourists' usual behaviour in urban areas, so-called cultural tourism, and its superficiality.

6   The place where interviews are carried out plays a determining role in the places cited. This needs to be corrected by the survey methodology. In this instance, a number of sites were chosen to correct possible bias under influence of the specific site where the questions were asked.

served as the ruler's summer palace until it was transformed into a hotel for wealthy Western tourists in 1963. Today, despite the development of tourism infrastructure and the construction of many other luxury hotels in Udaipur, the Lake Palace most often cited. It has become what Debarbieux (1995) calls *lieu-attribut*, a territory's 'outstanding representative site.'

The second site most often cited by tourists in my survey was the complex of structures and compounds that comprise the former centre of royal power. Known locally as the City Palace, this includes the earliest royal structure, the ca. 1571 *Rai Angan* or 'royal courtyard.' The complex as a whole embodies the eventful history of the Sisodia dynasty and the Mewar kingdom of which it was the last capital. The City Palace's role in history has become an essential part of the general tourist presentation of the city. In addition to the important role that the City Palace plays in the tourists' imagination, this complex of monuments also draws tourists on account of its location in the centre of the ancient capital, on a hill overlooking the rest of the town and Pichola Lake, with magnificent city and lake views. The size of the site also has a significant impact: it consists of several buildings separated by *chowks,* courtyards with hanging gardens. Seen from the outside, the arches, crenellations, domes, and walls with their vast façade, are in stark contrast to the interior: two luxury hotels, Shiv Niwas and Fatehprakash, that now occupy the royal complex The complex's ca. 1620 Dilkhusha Mahal ('Palace of Joy'), Moti Mahal ('Palace of Pearls'), and ca. 1716 Sheesh Mahal, ('Palace of Mirrors and Glass',), and early nineteenth-century Chhoti Chitre-Shali ('Residence of the Little Pictures'), with its glass peacock designs, evoke the wealth and beauty of the former kingdom.

The vast collection of buildings forms a self-contained urban unit within the town, called in one proposal prepared by its managers, the 'City within the City' (MMCF n.d.). The City Palace tends to attract and retain tourists, given its sheer size and the range of services it offers (a post office, a bank, travel agency, numerous craft shops, even a World Wide Fund for Nature India boutique). The City Palace's historic buildings are owned by the Mewar royal family, whose representative manages them personally, and through a series of charitable trusts. The site includes part of Pichola Lake, the Lake Palace island itself, and the island called Jag Mandir, named for the mid-eighteenth century Maharana Jagat Singh. The City Within a City project also claims two additional sites, although they are outside the city's boundaries: the temple of Shri Eklingji, a manifestation of the Hindu deity Lord Shiva, in the small town known by that name, and the memorials to royal ancestors of the Mewar kingdom, located at the Ahar site, a short distance outside Udaipur (MMCF n.d., 15).

Most tourist activities in Udaipur take place within the walls of this ancient centre of power. All Udaipur's most important heritage symbols, as far as tourists are concerned, are located there. The collection of various magnificent buildings at the City Palace site strike the imagination and have a direct impact on the nature of the tourism activities in their vicinity. This central area attracts a stream of tourists, thanks to its special place in the collective imagination and several more practical aspects (such as access to a post office), which provide form and content for Udaipur's tourist image.

Tourist discourse also presents a large part of the historic centre of the Udaipur as closely linked to Rajput history. The medieval city with gates at each cardinal point is the area most frequented by tourists, although tourism is not its dominant economic activity. From the royal palace enclosure, the tourist district radiates outward from the City Palace as far as the main temple, Jagdish *Mandir* (temple) (c. 1640), a temple that honours the Hindu deity Lord Vishnu in his form of Jaganath, as well as along the roads fanning out in all directions from Jagdish Temple Square, as far as Lake Pichola and the city gates. The main feature in the layout of the old city is Jagdish Chowk. This is a public square that has long been the site of religious, political and everyday social functions. Today, Jagdish Chowk is much frequented by groups of tourists, innumerable rickshaw drivers, and tourist guides.

The socio-spatial disparities, at least partially created by tourism, can be seen in the degree of economic specialization and relative dynamism of the various businesses in nearby streets. Shops directly involved in tourism appear to be successful both on account of their original activities and of their proximity to areas that interest tourists; however, their proximity to the most popular tourist sites appears decisive. Facing Tripolia Gate, (ca. 1725), which marks the northern entrance to the City Palace complex, the shops lining City Palace Road are mostly held by craftsmen, book-binders, miniature painters, textile dealers and antiques shops. This is one of the city's main commercial thoroughfares, and it leads to the nearby bazaars. This street is lined with numerous small stands selling snacks, fruit juice and tea, and bustles with informal sector[7] hawkers selling a variety of items to tourists. This street is the centre of the tourist industry in Udaipur.

Heading north, City Palace Road leads to the Hathi Pol ('Elephant Gate') neighbourhood, which is less frequented by tourists, and where the shops are less tourist oriented than at the City Palace and Jagdish Chowk. One reason for the falloff in tourists here is that they usually explore the town on foot, and this district is some distance from the centre.

Near the colonial era Clock Tower, symbolizing commerce and trade, the tourist industry is more intense and more specialized. Numerous jewellery shops cater to the tourist trade, while other shops produce and sell articles for local consumption. Rajasthanis travelling to Udaipur on business or for personal reasons make a point of visiting these shops, too. The present-day nature of businesses in the district is a relic from the past. These shops belong to the members of merchant communities, whose houses, often in the form of a *haveli* (an urban mansion built around an inner courtyard), are nearby. In this district, tourism gives shopkeepers the possibility of diversifying beyond their main market, which is local.

---

7   The informal sector, sometimes called the non-organized sector, comprises all economic activities that are not declared under the Law of 1948. With the rapid growth in subcontracting and industrial diversification, the boundaries between the organized and non-organized sectors have become vague. By the 1990s, the non-organized sector appeared to cover 90 percent of total production. For more on the subject see Heuzé, (1992).

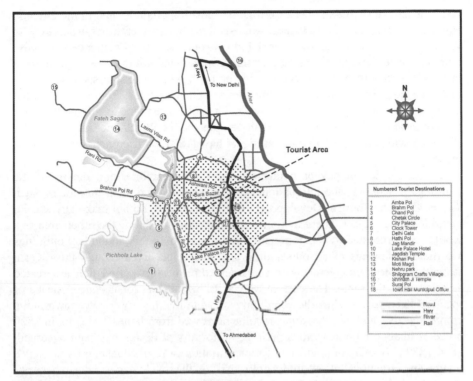

Map 5.1   Tourist locations in Udaipur

Lake Palace Road goes south from Jagdish Chowk to an entrance to the royal complex that leads to the hotels and the lake. Along here, the street has a number of shops selling textiles and craft-goods, craft workshops, painting and decorating cooperatives, travel agencies, shops renting bicycles, and small storefronts selling various items to tourists such as bottled mineral water, books, and camera film. Gangaur Ghat Road runs west from Jagdish Chowk to Chand Pol ('Moon Gate'), then along the shores of the lake on the edge of the Brahmpuri (or Brahmpol), district. The street is popular with tourists as far as the Badi Pol ('Great Gate'), even if there are fewer shops here catering to their interests. The nearby lakefront is lined with hotels, and these constitute the main economic activity in the area.

Tourists and the Urban Landscape

In the tourist district of Udaipur, interestingly, the tourists do not appear to be particularly aware of the characteristics of individual buildings lining the streets. According to my survey, not many tourists visit the district's temples, for example. Only 76 out of the 140 tourists surveyed, both Indian and non-Indian, entered a temple in the city centre. Most of these – 52 – visited Jagdish Mandir. Tourists visit this temple essentially because it is the most important temple in the city and conveniently near to the City Palace. Almost all the Indian tourists in my survey who visited a temple during their stay were Hindu (49 out of 64 survey respondents). These tourists visited these buildings as tourists, however, and not in order to participate in religious rites of *darshan*[8] ceremonies or for a *puja.*[9] The tourists also did not really consider the tourist city's architecture as of much interest. Tourists singled out only its main buildings as targets to visit. The sole exceptions to this indifference to individual buildings were the Jagdish Temple and the West Zone Cultural Centre (WZCC), which occupies a large traditional haveli that has been transformed into a museum.

If tourists do not pay particular attention to the architectural details of the buildings in Udaipur, the international tourist agencies and local promoters, such as the Rajasthan Tourism Development Corporation, also do not make any special mention of the subject. These institutions concentrate on selling the urban area as a whole, as represented by the dominant royal narrative. In this, individual buildings are merely elements of an outstanding city landscape. Even though the diverse structures at these sites were constructed over a three century period, they are treated as essentially the same. The current Mewar Encyclopedia, for instance, speaks of the 'architectural unity' of these buildings despite this history (www.mewarindia. com/ency/city), a phrase that appears to be borrowed from James Tod who, in 1829 noted 'Although built at various periods, uniformity of design has been observed' (Tod 1829: 276). These practices of representation raise the question of the city's image, and virtually all these guidebooks insist on the royal image, at the expense of the cultural diversity actually found on many sites in the tourism district.

The historic city centre as a whole benefits from this royal image, above all because tourism discourse associates the entire town with the power of the Sisodia Rajputs: Udaipur would not exist without the dynasty that founded it in the middle of the sixteenth century. The conversion of many old buildings into hotels, following along the lines of the palace, further consolidates the image retained by tourists. Both these conversions and newly built hotels are bundled together in the tourist imagination, and are considered to be part of the local Rajput heritage, whether or not this is the case.

As seen above, the study's questions, interviews and other field work established the main images representing Udaipur. The results of the study strongly confirmed that the development of tourism goes hand in hand with the selection of particular target areas. This trend is similar to those observed elsewhere in the world. The targeting of particular areas as the tourist centre, in turn encourages the specialization of nearby zones and competition among zones for tourist income. Tourist specialization is both

---

8   Darshan: In Hinduism, it is a glimpse of a God or an idol. It can also be, in the context of a kingdom, a public function of a king giving his appearance to people.

9   *Puja* is the act of showing reverence to a god. It generally includes offerings of flowers and food, and retrieving the blessed food and consuming it. This act aims to create a relationship with the divine.

economic and social, as the people and groups concerned often play significant roles in other ways and on other levels. This process highlights and accentuates existing spatial divisions, creating new disparities that have a significant impact on the social changes taking place.

The heavy selling of particular areas leads to others being excluded and to various different types of exclusion in the areas selected. Shifts in the built environment can promote or inhibit certain developments, and particularly those based on perceptions of heritage.[10] This process can be seen in the locally produced tourist information, which omits large areas of the town and the activities there, so as better to target a cultural tourism whose criteria are geared to precise overall objectives.

Local tourist organizations tend to follow the latest trends in international tourist advertising to sell their heritage. In this instance, the tourist information unwittingly reveals the difference between the proposed urban developments and what is actually happening on the ground. This process tends to increase, rather than to reduce, this exclusion. Many businesses and tourist organizations are also active in other ways that affect the urban management of the town as a whole. The tourist district is thus the key area in the city, and as will be seen, is subject to a continuous struggle for its control.

Exclusion, Territorial Management and the Decision-making Process

Scholars generally accept that control of space is a major issue in relations between social groups.[11] Control over spatial relations is the main factor determining the way territory is managed. This process is more than obvious in Udaipur. Since the 1980s, tourism has been one of the most dynamic sectors in the local economy. Tourism's rapid growth can be seen in the numerous services and products now available for tourists. Certain districts in the city have specialized in entrepreneurship linked to tourism.[12]

Only a very small portion of the urban territory of Udaipur is actually concerned with these changes. A large part of Udaipur city and its region are effectively excluded from the tourist trade, and thus from the sector that has for many years been seen as the best way of earning money. In general, this exclusion appears to result from the role heritage-linked real estate plays in Udaipur's territorial dynamics. On top of this imbalance in the spatial development of tourism, the tourist district suffers from the effects of the growth in tourists and tourism services which have had very real negative, and seemingly ignored, impacts.

---

10 Also see Molotch, Freudenburg, and Paulsen (2000). See also Berque (1993).

11 For details on the work of these major French scholars, see for example Brunet, Roger. 1991. *Le territoire dans les turbulences*. Montpellier: R.E.C.L.U.S., Kayser, Bernard. (1990). *Géographie: entre espace et développement*. Toulouse: Presses Universitaires du Mirail. and Touraine, Alain. (1965) *Sociologie de l'action*. Paris: Editions du Seuil. See also Knafou and Bruston (1997), Levy and Lussault (2000), Scott (1999); Gentele (1995); and Durand-Dastes.

12 For more details on actors involved in tourism entrepreneurship see Bautès (2003).

This complex situation, the end product of a number of contradictory forces, has accentuated the subdivision of Udaipur urban space into 'tourist' and 'non-tourist' zones.

At the same time that the tourist districts have been developing, they have been, and are likely to be, affected by a number of dramatic changes. No major transformation has occurred in the physical layout of the historic centre since the early nineteenth-century, and this has put a definite brake on its economic development. This development has been and will above all be limited by its physical layout and the

Figure 5.2   This view of Udaipur looking west towards the Palace City Complex, from the 'Old City' residential neighbourhood illustrates high density of settlement, including the proliferation of tourist accommodations. *Photo courtesy of Jeffrey Snodgrass. All rights reserved.*

high population density of the area. The lack of vacant plots suitable for development seriously limits the potential for redevelopment and other improvement schemes that are essential to avoid the public areas becoming saturated.

That emphasis on certain points of interest to tourists involves the exclusion of others can be seen in the physical appearance of the city. This in turn restricts both physical change and business dynamics in the area, inasmuch as the only business activities that development planners here consider viable are those satisfying the demand for heritage-linked products. As noted above, the concept of heritage drives the narrative of tourism and its development. This process occurs in a general context in which tourism is one of the few sectors creating jobs in the city for most of Udaipur's population. More and more people are drawn into tourist-related activities on a number of different levels.

The tourist area itself suffers from specialization, which inhibits innovation by restricting production to specific product types. This apparently all-pervasive heritage, in fact a combination of sites and products, is not equally shared by all the inhabitants of Udaipur. It has not been *'developed by all, for all'* (Lassave and Querrien 2002), but is on the contrary, a heritage owned by a fortunate few. The monopolization over the definition of this heritage, as I discuss subsequently, negatively affects the city as a whole. There is no real examination or discussion of the role to be played by this heritage and of the best options and related policies on what should be preserved and enhanced for the tourists, or what might be developed for other uses. The area in which tourism and tourist activities are omnipresent thus tends to specialize even more in this single activity. As this process continues, thinking about development in the city is likely to be confronted by two conflicting objectives: whether to encourage further economic development to satisfy tourism's future needs, thus requiring the preservation of the historic urban layout and the structures within this, or whether to concentrate on urban redevelopment and to create innovative business activities and new uses of the urban space.

The City Within a City Project

The development of tourism in Udaipaur is part of a set of complex dynamics, within which the territory has evolved rapidly as a result of changes in its economy. This dynamic, in turn, is influenced by the way tourists actually use the space and urban amenities within it, along with such town planning measures as have already been implemented. Several protagonists seem to have been influential in these changes. Their initiatives have an impact far beyond their own local environment, and are veritable and rather extensive urban projects that will determine how the whole territory evolves in the future.

A development project agenda originally proposed in 1991 by the Maharana Mewar Charitable Foundation basically splits off the royal palace complex from the historic city centre and thus from the rest of Udaipur. Through the Maharana Mewar Charitable Foundation, Shri Arvind Singh Mewar, second son of the former Maharana and the Foundation's trustee-in-chief, hopes to achieve what he has titled 'the renaissance of Udaipur' (Maharana Mewar Charitable Foundation 2002).[13] Fully aware of the development potential of the royal family's heritage, and with a sophisticated command of the various techniques of communication on an international level, Arvind Singhji, to use the polite form of his name in Rajasthan,

---

13 In a lawsuit over the succession to the throne of Mewar, Arvind Singhji was awarded management of the historic properties over the claims of his elder brother. Although Westerners often refer to Arvind Singhji as the Maharana, because of his energetic and leading role in the Maharana Mewar Charitable Foundation, he himself is very careful in his official documents and statements, not to claim the title 'Maharana.' Strictly speaking, his title would be 'Maharaj Arvind Singhji', as a son of the former Maharana. Today, of course, these titles strictly speaking are honorifics, and have no governmental role.

has implemented a vast project to restore the ancient royal palace complex. The project, begun in 1991, is financed by a partnership consisting of several trusts managed by Arvind Singhji and his external partners, who periodically issue calls for proposals. The work has already started to restore certain buildings, preserve the Mewar State Archives, and revitalize the museums and art galleries in the City Palace complex. All the work planned for what the project's proponents present as a new phase in the history of Udaipur, will be limited to the royal palace complex, as this is defined by the MMCF.

Arvind Singhji's view of the goal of ensuring a balanced development of the territory, in a project that clearly separates the complex from the rest of the city, is not set out in any of his speeches or project-related documents. However, the title of the project, 'The City Within a City' is evocative of a narrowing of vision. The plan for the development of the royal city excludes the rest of Udaipur, which is run by a municipal corporation, elected officials, and government civil servants.

The City Within a City series of projects, backed by large financial resources, is based on a kind of auto-legitimization on historical grounds and on Arvind Singhji's real ability to mobilize both private and public organizations in support of his cause. The project emphasizes the 'preservation of our heritage', 'sustainable development', 'the protection of our ancient heritage', 'the continuity of our architectural heritage', 'the establishment and continuous revitalization of a number of centres of excellence', 'the promotion of local arts and craftsmen', 'environmental and ecological management', and the 'development of safe tourism.' These terms suggests a comprehensive and inclusive purview for the project, but when examined closely, the City Within a City project clearly envisages establishment of a private tourism zone which will, on its own, represent Udaipur. Project reports note that this is to be a 'self-sufficient' zone (Maharana Mewar Charitable Foundation n.d., 14). This zone already has its own water and sewage treatment plants, independent of municipal facilities (Maharana Mewar Charitable Foundation n.d., 14).

Concentration of tourism in the 'City Within a City' complex institutionalizes the Sisodia dynasty representative's control over Udaipur's image. The City Within a City project includes the majority of Udaipur's heritage tourism assets, making this a formidable player in urban development. Successful implementation of all the plan's provisions will enable Arvind Singhji to reinforce his economic power and position at the top of the local social hierarchy. Seen in large perspective, it appears that enduring control over urban space, which includes previous powerholders under the pre-Independence former social system are retaking power through the subdivision of Udaipur into two sectors: one vibrant and growing (tourism-related) and one stagnant (non-tourism related). Given the envisaged scope of the 'City Within a City' project, this will effectively determine Udaipur's future and consolidation, perhaps, into a 'company town.'

Exclusion Processes, Imagination, and the Control over the Heritage Destination

During the period of my fieldwork, no local representatives of the national, state, district, or municipal governments responded publicly to the 'City Within A City' proposal. These authorities have not mounted any complementary project, nor for that matter any other project in response to those proposed by the Maharana Mewar Charitable Foundation. In my interviews with senior officials in local town planning services, who included town planners of the Urban Improvement Trust, municipal officials at various levels of governance, and particularly with those responsible for the development of tourism in the town and the surrounding region including the Rajasthan Tourism Development Corporation Tourist Officer in the Udaipur office, I was unable to obtain from them any analysis covering the local area as a whole. They did not, for me, even identify ways in which their agencies collaborate – a very basic requirement – with the entities which were managing the town's heritage or, more generally, the urban territory.

The main reason for this gap in discourse and action, on the governmental level, appears to be the lack of financial resources for such large-scale projects. Additionally, the imprecise allocation of governmental and civic responsibility for tourism and town planning, public authorities' failures to address real estate shortage in the city, and what in my view is to a habit of bowing to major private players' interests, inhibit government actors' and public civic groups' ability to realize even the smallest rehabilitation or development project. Presently, the municipality, in partnership with the Rajasthan Urban Infrastructure Development Project (n.d.), has embarked on ambitious water supply, sewage, and street widening projects, which are currently under construction. Publicly accessible documents do not appear to include discussion of how these projects intersect with the tourism sector of the urban economy. The absence of public debate about the tourism-linked urban planning issues, on a public level at the time of my fieldwork, was glaring.

Even modest proposals for improvements, such as sign-posting tourist sites and marking tourist routes in the city, have been stymied. The plastering over of the tourist district with advertising billboards, posters, and signs – practices which provoke highly negative reactions from tourists and many local inhabitants as inimical to the heritage site – also continues unabated. It would be a fairly simple matter for municipal authorities to enact or enforce existing standards regarding such signage, and to encourage pride in, and voluntary adherence to, heritage standards, as practiced in other world tourism destinations. Shopkeepers and tourist guides, deeply involved in this part of the town that provides their major source of income, do not appear ready to join forces to make general improvements to enhance the tourists' access to and use of the area. This is true, even though a number of them stated in interviews that they were concerned about social life in the historic districts, and appeared to be aware of the issues raised and the possible future impact of the proposed developments on their professional lives.

Udaipur city's vacuum in urban planning for tourism has meant that this function of city government is *de facto* vested in its most powerful groups and citizens. The absence of official reflection or planning in the city's tourism centre has left the way free for independent individual actions. However well-intended, these actions tend further to subdivide urban space into 'tourist' and 'non-tourist' sectors, and had not produced, as of the time of this writing, city-wide civic discourse about the nature and meaning of Udaipur's future development as a tourism destination. In the case of the 'City Within a City' project, discourse supporting the project emphatically legitimizes this division using local history and what its proponents have understood to be the organization of urban space at the time of Udaipur's founding.

Specialization in tourism – here as elsewhere at many other tourism destinations – inhibits the development of other economic sectors and jobs. Tourists have specific needs. Their much greater purchasing power, relative to the local cost and demand structure, drives out urban amenities pitched to the local market and acts to exclude city inhabitants' access to services, or to the prices for goods and services that are available in non-tourist districts. Local residents may be 'priced out' of their own neighbourhoods by tourists' far greater purchasing power. Unsurprisingly, many of the entertainers who work in the tourism business, live in semi-legal settlements on the city's fringes (see chapter by Snodgrass).

The emphasis placed on Rajput cultural heritage has encouraged the town's inhabitants to see themselves as legitimate heirs to a magnificent past that it is their duty to perpetuate. More and more local inhabitants, whether or not they are Rajputs themselves, consider that they have an obligation to pass on this heritage. However, this identification appears mainly to have a purely economic objective: heritage tourism is the best way of earning a living. At the same time, assertions of closeness to this heritage legitimize these actors' role in society's Sisodia Rajput discourse dominated sector. Udaipur's other traditions – which might be incorporated into tourist narratives and prove vibrant additions to these – are overlooked.

Competition is fierce on the tourism job market, such that the majority of those who work in the industry are in unstable, if not precarious situations. As noted above, during the late 1990s competition in the tourist sector intensified. Jobs are often part-time and low-paid, without any fixed amount or a salary of 50 rupees a day only, or around US $1 per day at current exchange rates according to a survey of 150 tourist shop employees that I conducted in 2000. The situation is just as difficult for local businessmen in the tourist sector who suffer from dramatic swings in demand and growing competition. In 2000, 325 people under the age of 30 identified during the tourist shop survey, who were associated with these shops as marketers, did not have regular jobs. In most cases their only income was their markup on products they sold to tourists in the boutiques, for the transport they provided, and occasionally as tourist guides.

Tourism often has been lauded as the answer to long-standing economic problems, for it appears to be a short-cut to economic development. Actors involved in tourism construct specific ways of seeing themselves and of managing tourist space. They adopt specific attitudes related to modernity and economic development. But in a sense, tourist areas are also social exclusion zones. While tourists are obviously not directly responsible for the situation, they consume the local products and look for a certain aesthetic approach. In doing so, they exclude other styles, business activities, and types of behaviour. Exclusion thus appears to be a complex and local process linked to the strategies of, and actions by, the dominant actors in Udaipur's tourism sector.

References

Agarwal, B.D. (1979), *Udaipur* Rajasthan District Gazetteers (Jaipur: Directorate of District Gazetteers, Government of Rajasthan).

Bautès, N. (2003), 'Forms and Expressions of a Local Heritage: The Case of Udaipur City', in Surjit Singh and Varsha Joshi (eds.), *Institutions and Social Change* (Jaipur: Rawat Publications,106–126).

Berque, Augustin (1993), *Du geste à la cité. Formes urbaines et lien social au Japon* (Paris: NRF Gallimard).

Brunet R., Ferras R., and Théry H. (1993), *Les mots de la géographie, dictionnaire critique,* (Montpellier: Reclus Paris: La documentation Française),

Cadène, P. (2001), 'Le développement du tourisme au Rajasthan. Usage ou abandon d'un patrimoine fragmenté', in A. Montaut (ed.), *Rajasthan: Hommage au Dr. N. Joshi* (Paris: Kailash)

Cadène, P. (1998), 'Le génie du propre', in Bailly, Antoine (director), *Terres d'exclusion, terres d'espérances* (Paris: Economica).

Chambers, E. (2002), *Native Tours: The Anthropology of Travel and Tourism* (Prospect Heights, IL: Waveland Press, Inc).

Debarbieux, B. (1995), 'Le lieu, le territoire et trois figures de rhétorique', *L'espace géographique* 2, 97–112.

Durand-Dastès, F. (1996), 'La mémoire de Gaïa', Groupe DUPONT, *Espace et nature dans la géographie aujourd'hui,* Géopoint 96 (Avignon: Université d'Avignon et des Pays de Vaucluse).

Fodor, E. and W. Curtis (eds.) (1974), *Fodor's India* (New York: David McKay Company).

Gentelle, P. (1995), 'Haut-lieu', *L'espace Géographique* 2, 135–138.

Lévy, J. and M. Lussault (2000), *Logiques de l'espace, esprit des lieux* (Paris: Belin).

Knafou, R. and M. Bruston (1997), 'Une approche géographique du tourisme', *L'espace Géographique* 3 (Paris: Belin).

Lassave, P. and A. Querrien (2002), 'La demeure du temps', *Annales de la Recherche Urbaine* 92, *Ce qui demeure,* 3–5.

Maharana Mewar Charitable Foundation (2002), 'Udaipur Renaissance. A partnership proposal with the House of Mewar for the sustainable development of palaces, museums, educational institutes in the City-palace Complex', Udaipur.

Malamoud, C. (1989), *Cuire le monde. Rites et pensée dans l'Inde ancienne* (Paris: La Découverte).

Manakekar, R. (1976), *Mewar Saga* (Delhi: Vikas Publishing House).

Micoud, A.(ed.) (1991), *Des hauts-lieux: la construction sociale de l'exemplarité* (Paris: CNRS).

Molotch, H., W. Freudenburg, and K.E. Paulsen (2000), 'History Repeats Itself, but How? City Character, Urban Tradition, and the Accomplishment of Place', *American Sociological Review* 65:6, 791–823.

Montaut, A. (ed.) (2001), *Rajasthan. Hommage au Dr. N. Joshi* (Paris: Kailash).

Murray, J. (1949), *A Handbook for Travellers in India and Pakistan, Burma and Ceylon* (London: John Murray).

Ramusack, B. (1998), 'The Indian Princes as Fantasy', in C. Breckenridge (ed.) (1998), *Consuming Modernity. Public Culture in a South Asian World* (Minneapolis/London: University of Minnesota Press).

Rajasthan Urban Infrastructure Development Project (n.d.), Web Page www.ruidp. org/project-cities/CityStatusList. Accessed 15 August 2006.

Scott, A.J. (1999), 'L'économie culturelle des villes', *Espace, Economie, Société*, 1:1, 25–47.

Singh, S. and M. Cox (1999), *Rajasthan,* 2nd Edition (Melbourne: Lonely Planet).

Tod, J. (1997), [first ed. 1829 and 1832] *Annals and Antiquities of Rajast'han*, vols. I, II. (London: South Asia Books)

Travlou, P. (2002), 'Go Athens: A Journey to the Centre of the City', in Coleman, S. and M. Crang (2002), *Tourism: Between Place and Performance* (New York/ Oxford: Berghahn Books).

Internet Resources

www.unescodelhi.nic.in: Website of the UNESCO representation in India.

www.indiagov.in: Website of the Government of India. Provide links with other gouvernemental websites.

www.indiatourism.org: Indian Ministry of Tourism.

www.investrajasthan.com: Website of the Government of Rajasthan, providing information about economic trends of the State, Main objectives of development and investment potential.

www.mewarindia.com: Mewar Group.

www.ucciudaipur.com: Website of the Udaipur Chamber of Commerce and Industry.

Chapter 6

Names, but not Homes, of Stone: Tourism Heritage and the Play of Memory in a Bhat Funeral Feast

Jeffrey G. Snodgrass

Years ago, according to the tale, the king of Mewar[1] wagered half his holdings against the skill of a beautiful dancer from the Nat community. The young Natni, as Rajasthanis refer to women of this group, had but to tightrope walk across a lake bordering the royal palace, and half the kingdom would be hers. The king's servants stretched a rope from the palace to a hamlet on the lake's opposite shore. Encouraged by shouts from a crowd that had gathered to watch, the Natni nearly reached the palace grounds. With success almost within the Natni's grasp, one of the king's barbers emerged from the shadows and sliced the rope with his razor. Injured and drowning in the water below, the dancer cried out before sinking to her death, 'I care neither about the kingdom nor the money! Only let my deed be remembered! Only let my name live forever!'[2]

Honouring the request, the king ordered that a stone memorial commemorating the Natni's demise be placed on an island in the middle of the lake. Bansilal, the narrator of this story, clearly identified with the Natni's effort to improve her status. He is a Bhat – but he is descended from Nats who today use the name 'Bhat' to suggest a higher social status for themselves than before. The tale of the Natni expresses metaphorically the Bhat dream of moving from the margins of society to its centre. The tourist industry has fuelled such a dream, as it has seemed to offer the means by which Bhats might overturn their lowly social status and construct a new 'heritage' of, and for, themselves.

Many Bhats are now darlings in Rajasthan's folk art circuit and have travelled as far afield as Europe. Bhats have had the opportunity to amass small fortunes and, Natni-like, win the kingdom, so to speak. Despite these earnings, most Bhats

---

1   Centred around present-day Udaipur district, Rajasthan.

2   The current Mewar Encyclopedia identifies the king as Maharana Jawan Singh (r. 1828–1838) and the memorial with a chabutra (raised stone platform) on one of the islands in Pichola Lake). However, this version ends differently than that collected from the Nats. In the Mewar Encyclopedia version, the Natni curses the Maharana's family to have no heirs. In fact, six out of the next seven Maharanas were adopted. See www.mewarindia.com/ency/nat .

inhabit urban slums. Many of my informants remained uneducated with relatively few material possessions and irregular access to modern amenities such as electricity and running, or even clean, water. Some Bhats blame their continued poverty and failure to advance in contemporary India on the corruption of those in power – not barbers, as in the Natni's tale, but middlemen in the tourist industry, be they hotel managers, restaurateurs, folklore festival organizers, or moneylenders, who skim profits from Bhat performances and sales.

This complaint does not tell the whole story. In Bansilal's version of events, the Natni claims that she is more concerned with her immortal name than she is with attaining the wealth and station of kings. As the tourism industry began its boom in the 1990s, I discovered that Bhats similarly sought to ensure that their name – their fame – would be memorialized forever. Rather than saving their tourism earnings or using them to accumulate possessions, Bhats, and especially the older generation who were centrally involved in my research in the 1990s, poured most of their earnings into a single ritualized funeral feast for their father, termed a *mosar*.[3] Most Rajasthanis commemorate death with feasts reminiscent of the mosar. Each Bhat family, I was told, must spend on a mosar before other essentials like food, clothing and shelter. The extravagant feast can and does send Bhat families into debt. The Bhat version of this fête was particularly extravagant and featured, as they acknowledged, *pagal* ('lunatic') destructions of wealth. One man told me, 'Only we spray alcohol all over each other at the mosar, no other caste group does this!'

Despite the fact that Bhats themselves characterize the mosar as an 'upside-down' and 'backward' tradition, the mosar is the central ritual, even the central activity, of Bhat life. As such, the mosar feast provides a point of entry to examine the Bhat encounter with tourism, and how the practices and identities associated with tourism reinforce the Bhat community's concern with memory and the past. In the early to late 1990s, tourist income provided both the material resources as well as the social circumstances that allowed the mosar feast, as well as the particular status and poetic concerns it nourishes, to flourish and even expand. Tourism has encouraged Bhats to conceptualize and present themselves to others, as 'traditional' performers who remember the past and preserve the old ways: that this is their heritage. This identity story has helped Bhats prosper in the modern tourist industry, as has the mosar rite itself, which my informants use, along with other performance traditions, to build their case for being 'traditional.' I therefore hope this chapter will contribute to the larger discussion of tourism's impact on social expenditures, the display of social status, performance standards, and identity (see for example Chambers 2000, Edensor 1998, and Smith 1998).

This chapter draws from a larger project on the Bhats, for which I conducted three years of fieldwork between 1991 and 1998. I returned to Rajasthan in the summers of 2003 and 2004 to study state and local tribal forest management in southern Rajasthan. Though not directly investigating social change in the Bhat community,

---

3   Also referred to as a *nukta* as well as a *marto bhojan* ('banquet of the dead') and a *mela* ('festival' or 'carnival').

I stopped whenever I had a free moment in Udaipur in order to catch up with my Bhat friends. The details of this chapter are drawn from inhabitants of the Jaipur and Udaipur urban Bhat settlements, and especially from about fifteen closely related nuclear families that in the mid-1990s inhabited tents on the outskirts of the town of Udaipur. Data included in-depth interviews with key individuals, historical research, and participant observation of Bhat daily life, performance, and life cycle rituals. In the following sections of this chapter, I shall first summarize the recent past and current situation of Bhats. Second, I examine the mosar feast itself, and thirdly, look at the most recent changes in the ways in which Rajasthanis and Bhats in particular have transformed their display of social status.

Of Bhats and Nats, Heritage and Performance

Bhats originate from the region of Rajasthan referred to as Marwar, an area rich in traditions of poetic and narrative composition. Though the Bhats claim descent from the bards of kings, Bansilal, along with most of his kin, eventually told me that this was a ruse used in an attempt to elevate their status. The name 'Bhat,' I was told, was a post-Independence appropriation meant to associate themselves with the royal Rajasthani bards of yore. In actuality, Bansilal and his kin were descended from the lowly Nat community that features in this tale of the acrobat's death. Once upon a time, my informants too were camel-jumpers, sword-balancers, tumblers, tightrope walkers, and rope dancers.[4] Most Indians think of Nats as acrobats. Though the term '*nat*' literally translates as 'Dancer', Nats also worked as praise-singers for village patrons. Bansilal's Nat ancestors kept the genealogies and histories of a formerly untouchable, or Dalit, caste of leather-workers often referred to by others as 'Bhambhis' or, more politely, as Meghwals. My informants still do this work at these patrons' weddings. Nats also performed acrobatics.[5] Despite the name change and other like-minded schemes, my informants are Dalits – former untouchables on the Indian state's list of Scheduled Castes.

Nevertheless, like the Natni who features at the start of this chapter, my Bhat informants – I will refer to them as 'Bhats' given their preference for this title and to the Bhambhis as 'Meghwals' in line with *their* preferences – have tried to use their artistic skills to help them escape their traditionally degraded social status. Shortly after the princely state of Mewar became part of independent India, Bhats began performing local myths and legends for Rajasthani merchants and military officers who had migrated to Delhi, Calcutta, and Mumbai. Today's conversion of Rajasthan's former nobles and rulers' mansions, palaces, and forts into hotels and restaurants provide settings where Bhats stage five-to fifteen minute puppet dramas in hotel lobbies next to gift shops, or in hotel restaurants as dinner entertainment.

---

4   For more on this aspect of Nats and recent changes in their occupational status, see Swarankar, 2001.

5   See Bharucha, 2003, chapter 9 for a discussion of naming practices related to social groups.

Most tourists are likely to encounter Bhats in their work as puppeteers. These puppet dramas typically celebrate the exploits of knights from Rajasthan's medieval period. The Bhats' signature character is Amar Singh Rathore – a minor seventeenth-century noble from their home district of Nagaur, who is said to have served under the Mughal emperor, Shah Jahan. Because of their work, many people now refer to Bhats, not as either 'Nats' or 'Bhats', but instead as *kathputli-wale* or 'puppeteers' – literally, 'those of the wooden figures.'

Figure 6.1   Bhat puppeteers demonstrate their art for villagers as part of a state-wide gathering of Rajasthani performing artists sponsored by a non-governmental organization. Meetings such as this one address changing performance conditions including overseas travel. *Photo courtesy of Carol E. Henderson. *

In recent years, Bhats have settled in urban areas throughout Rajasthan to take advantage of the new opportunities offered by the state's tourist industry. Many Bhats reside in three slum neighbourhoods in Jaipur, the state's capital, and on the north side of Udaipur, the capital of Mewar when this was a princely state, and today capital of the district of that name. Here, Bhats live in a mixed neighbourhood of tribals (mostly Bhils), Dalits, and members of other economically 'backward' groups.

In Udaipur, Bhat puppeteers frequently entertain tourists in the very same palace that features in the tale of the Natni – the Udaipur City Palace. Likewise, Bansilal Bhat, the narrator of the Natni's tale, said he won the favour of the Maharana of Udaipur with a puppet drama performed in the Lake Palace Hotel about Maharana

Pratap, Mewar's ruler who heroically resisted the Mughals. More extended discussion of other venues for performance and of the shifts in economic livelihood affecting the members of this community will follow after a description of the mosar ritual.

The Mosar

The mosar is a round-robin feasting cycle in which, as my informants say, 'Each Bhat who has eaten must in turn feed others.' At the heart of the mosar is an extreme form of competition and an attempt to distinguish oneself hierarchically from other Bhats. Bhats, to put it bluntly, sponsor mosars for name and reputation, much as the potlatch on the northwest coast of North America functioned for Native American groups there in the late nineteenth century (Rosman and Rubel 1971). The mosar feast resonates with many other traditions documented by anthropologists which demonstrate a similar use of money, property, gift transactions, and ritualistic spending both to promote selfish-individualistic interests as well as to domesticate impersonal cash and commodities in order to build social 'capital' and relations of various kinds (Appadurai 1986; Gregory 1982; Mauss 1990; Munn 1986; Parry and Bloch 1989; Strathern 1988; Taussig 1980). It is also implicated in how the Bhats conceive history and heritage.

Normatively, the mosar feast is performed on the twelfth day following the death of a father, and it should take place in his natal village. On this day, his sons are responsible for financing this feast. 'Honour only grows from great expense', my informants fondly recounted. Plying hundreds of guests for weeks at a time with buffalo and goat meat, whiskey, countless *rotis* (unleavened, flat bread), and sugary tea takes a big bite out of a Bhat family's budget. It is thus not surprising that Bhats refer to the term 'mosar' as equivalent to the more common Hindi word for expense, *kharch*.

The sponsors of a mosar must make elaborate offerings to each guest, such as grain, sugar, *ghee*, (clarified butter) and sweets. In the key moment in the mosar ritual, these foods are carefully weighed and distributed to each guest. In recent times, however, Bhats have tended to substitute cash equivalents for food items and to distribute the cash from a *thali* (large round metal rimmed plate). In this way, Bhats say, the host can symbolically 'feed' his guests despite the fact that real foodstuffs are not being distributed.

'Feeding' guests from the thali can come at any time during the mosar, though it usually occurs days after the feast has begun. Just before this dispersal of cash, the host and his family members forcibly detach the principal guests – by now quite drunk – from their small islands of discussion and dispute that fan out haphazardly from the host's house. They drag the guests to a central point where a large cloth, known as the *mehfil* (a word more often used in conjunction with formal courtly and religious events, which denotes an assembly), has been spread on the ground. The hosts press the men down to the cloth in a rough circle, while the women hover on the wings. My informants explain that the circle testifies to Bhat unity. The guests tend to wander off as rapidly as they have been collected and must be hauled back by their hosts amidst taunts, flattery, and shots of whiskey. Bhats sometimes describe this process as trying to collect sand in a wide-thatched basket.

When the party of guests is more or less assembled, aggressive debates frequently arise over the relative merit of by-gone mosars as memories of beloved ancestors return. The men sob, clutch their – and others' – chests, shout, and yank their rivals' moustaches. The hosts shove spiced chunks of goat and alcohol shots at them, force-feeding the group willy-nilly. Finally, the host announces the monetary amount that he plans to give to each guest. A medley of 'oohs', 'ahhs', challenges, shouts, nods of approval, shrugs, toasts, and even derisive showers of ill-aimed rocks, follow. Much of this is play-acting. Over half the fun of these occasions, according to Bhats, is creating an illusion of high drama.

Guests usually know the host's intentions in advance. Some guests may even have helped him to decide the monetary figure. The Bhat caste councils often discuss setting limits on these sums or suggesting an acceptable level for the gift, mindful as they are of sustaining the Bhats' standing among other groups. On occasion, I saw a feast's maestro adjust the announced amount because of an unexpectedly flat audience response, even borrowing money at this very moment in order to increase his bid. The last-minute upping of the ante, and especially given that no one knows exactly how many rupees are hidden under the cloth which covers the thali, provides great suspense.

Now the sponsor adjusts the total in the stack of rupees in the covered plate, and begins the cash distribution to guests. Each guest collects not just his own share, but also that for his family members. The host multiplies the sum by the number of family members in the guest's family. A literate attendee may be pressed into service to carefully write down the sum given. Before accepting the money, each guest echoes the host's words as he accepts the money and repeats the family members who will be receiving the gift. He loudly and tediously counts out the family members: paternal uncles, brothers and their wives, sons, and unmarried daughters. Bhats representing large families count more brazenly as there is pride in numbers ('We are strong!').

After the distribution, which can drag on from early afternoon into the late evening, the sponsor is crowned with a symbolically significant 'white turban', which his son binds tightly to his head. Only Bhats who have held the mosar can safely don such a turban or sit with the other white turban wearers at a formal event. During the mosar ceremony, the other Bhats now lift the host to their shoulders. Amidst jubilant laughter, friendly banter, hugging, and testaments of devotion, the Bhats carry the host to a swing. Plastering him with coloured dyes, just as at the Holi festival, they push him high into the air. Occasionally, they stop the swing and force-feed their host sweets and shots of alcohol, and put marks of blessing (*tilak*) on his forehead. At this 'beautiful' moment at which a Bhat proves himself a 'true Bhat', my informants say that the cool evening air brushes against a host's face and all his worries simply melt away.

After this figuratively and literally uplifting moment, Bhats gather up the man, this time high upon their shoulders, and perform what they call 'circle wandering.' They place him high in a cart pulled by a camel, buffalo, or team of oxen and parade him around their village. Men and women dance behind the cart in abandon during this tour of the village. The cart weaves past the homes of Meghwals, Rajputs, and members of other castes. Patrons and friends alike may shower the procession with money and gifts, especially if they are pleased with the colourful dancing. The host also flings shards of coconut, peanuts, and vegetables prepared just for this occasion over dancing crowd. Children rush to pick up the goodies hurled over the heads of the dancers. The celebration escalates as the host and guests spray bottles of alcohol over the crowd and fling the empty bottles aside so that they shatter noisily. The host throws cash over the entourage, demonstrating that he can even let his money 'fly' without thinking about it.

On one occasion, one man shredded and burned 500 rupees' worth of notes, one 20-rupee note at a time. The notes had been specially withdrawn from the bank for this moment. The festivities, which invariably do not end with sunset, generally continue for many days and, on rare occasions, for several months. The host's status rises as the feast lengthens into several days of celebrations.

A Bhat, in sponsoring a mosar, tries to out-feast his rivals and to become a 'king for a day;' and thus, 'a man with no equal.' As one man commented, 'We do it for pride. We do it because we want to fight, clash, and collide with others.' In fact, those who do not hold mosars, or who sponsor feasts of little grandeur, are referred to as 'children', 'self-spenders', or 'dogs', who think only of their own hungers and stomachs.

Why such fighting? Another Bhat explained, 'You see, they think that no one is their equal. They feel like kings. And as a king, they think they can do anything. 'I can kill others, who cares? I am outside the law! There is no one who rules me!''

Such is the competitive nature of these feasts that Bhats resort to any trick, ruse, or insult in order to sabotage another man's mosar. Once the sponsor sets a date for a feast he must call in person to invite the guests, even though the Bhats are now spread to the four corners of India. There are substantial Bhat communities in West Bengal, Bihar, Madhya Pradesh, and Rajasthan (Swarankar 2001, 2). If a host, for example, relied on the telephone, then guests potentially would be insulted and refuse to attend.

Protocol requires that guests have to be begged to come to a mosar. Hosts plead with guests to come and enjoy a days-long feast and take away a good sum of money! Indeed, an entire week of activity, which includes flattery and innumerable bottles of alcohol, might be needed to ensure the attendance of one important guest, one who will draw in or represent other invitees. A stubborn guest can throw a sponsor's plans into disarray and necessitate resetting the date and restarting the entire invitation process. And such guests often did so.

Many Bhats purposely did not attend their rivals' feasts, hoping that these would be nullified by the caste council as not representative, thus not really a mosar. Most invitees would eventually stagger drunk into the host's village at well-spaced intervals, thus assuring that key ritual moments such as putting the money in the thali were endlessly postponed and that likewise the host's expenses were endlessly increased. At other times, Bhats would threaten to leave a mosar early and thus dramatically humiliate their host.

After the completion of a mosar, a sponsor, no matter how expensive the feast, joins the community of Bhat mosar givers. His brethren 'beg' him to come and sit and drink with them, chanting, 'Come brother, the doer of the mosar! Come brother, the doer of the mosar! Come brother, the doer of the mosar!' When he sits next to his brethren, the other Bhats pat him on the back and offer him a drink. He now has the right to sit in proximity to other Bhats who held mosars, and the white turban he wears does not differ in appearance from other white turbans – as I was told, 'The amount given on the occasion of the mosar is not written there.'

Changing Status Displays

Many groups in Rajasthan have recently cut back on mosar-like feasts, though individuals often spend extravagantly on events such as weddings.[6] The development discourse of the Indian state has for decades roundly condemned such social displays as irrational and wasteful spending that contribute to the continued 'backwardness' and poverty of Indians by reducing their investment in new capital improvements, particularly in agriculture. Despite official denunciation of these expenditures, in the 1990s my informants had not curtailed their mosar spending. In fact, most Bhats described the mosar as growing explosively. Some mosar expenditures, at the time of my fieldwork in the early- to mid-nineties, topped 100,000 rupees, an unheard of sum for such an impoverished community where 100 rupees a day is considered princely. Bhats struggled to spend, minimally, a year's salary on the mosars of their fathers – ideally, two to three years' salary. Weddings, by contrast, consumed less than a full year's salary.[7]

In an intensification of this process, in the 1990s some Bhats began celebrating *jivat mosars* ('living mosars'). In these events, Bhats orchestrated feasts commemorating their own deaths. In doing so, a man presumably had already thrown his father's mosar and was thus upping the ante in these competitive displays of spending. Some

---

6   I often heard weddings defended as investments in their children's futures, as opposed to 'wasteful' spending on the dead. Even dowries were defended to me in similar terms, as transfers of wealth from parents to their daughters akin to a form of inheritance.

7   The exchange rate while I was in India in the 1990s averaged 30 rupees / 1 U.S. dollar. A mosar that could still bring honour to the family cost between Rs. 40,000 to 60,000. A mosar that would not embarrass a family cost between Rs. 20,000 to 40,000. Anything less than Rs. 20,000 was described as 'nothing.' Bhats of Udaipur, based on informal polls, earn on the average about Rs. 24,000 a year in the tourist industry; In contrast, Rs. 36,000 was considered to be a good middle-class salary at this time. Bhat weddings seemed to average between Rs. 10,000–15,000 each.

Figure 6.2   **Many Bhat performers use new wealth derived from tourism in part to replace old mud-and-tent homes (top) with mortar and stone, such as this one currently under construction (bottom).**
Photos courtesy of Jeffrey Snodgrass. All rights reserved.

Bhat men even spoke of planning to throw their sons' funeral feasts, though I never personally witnessed such a display of financial and funereal bravado.

On return trips to Rajasthan in the summers of 2003 and 2004, in contrast, I was stunned by how much had changed in the five years since my last visit. In the late nineties, one stone house sat on the slope just outside of Udaipur that was home to the Bhat tent colony that was my primary field site. Now, every Bhat household had built a home of stone. Virtually every household had – or was soon to have – an electric fan, a television, and, in many cases, a motor scooter. All these families were also thinking more carefully about how best to 'make their children's future', and one of these households sent their children to a private school, using their earnings from puppet performances in Scotland.

Unlike my informants in the early nineties who were in their early thirties and older, this new cohort of young men and householders had not sponsored mosar feasts. Or, at the least, they had sponsored minimally acceptable, even perfunctory, ones. These new spending practices were, in turn, fed by a host of other new factors. Although sustained discussion of these factors is outside the scope of this chapter, several shifts relating to Bhats' legal status and relationship to other groups seem to have occurred.

In many cases, Bhats are no longer beholden to local strongmen for rights of occupancy. A number of my Udaipur informants now have legal certification of their plots of land on which their homes sit. They gained such rights either through direct purchase or government regularization of squatter settlements. The growing security of land and property ownership enjoyed by Bhats encourages investment in durable homes. The growth of literacy in the Bhat community enhances this trend, which allows my informants to defend their property rights in a more successful fashion than in earlier times. The falling cost of house construction relative to earnings is also an important factor.

Underlying these trends is the growth of income in the tourist industry. The proliferation of sponsored trips to international folklore festivals outside India is of special significance. Earnings from these trips today are typically earmarked for house construction. Likewise, Bhats participate in a state-sponsored 'living museum' called Shilpgram ('Craft Village') situated on the outskirts of Udaipur. Shilpgram's purpose extends beyond the exhibition of traditional cultures of western India to tourists, to display and instill pride in regional arts and crafts among locals as well. There is always one family of Bhat puppeteers in this setting. In the 1990s, each family would earn about 1500 rupees per stint in this museum (100 rupees per day for each 15-day engagement). This was a significant amount of money for my informants. This work provides a steady source of income and also brings Bhats into contact with educated Indians and employees of non-governmental organizations (NGOs) who likewise encourage Bhats to invest in durable forms of property (for more data, see Snodgrass 2004, and 2006).

Bhats now sometimes seem more interested in impressing their urban neighbours as opposed to their caste mates. Once upon a time, a mosar host normatively invited Bhats from a territorial unit known as a *khera* ('circle'), consisting of twelve contiguous villages, that is, the eleven villages closest to one's home village. As a Bhat ideal, all fourteen Bhat clans would be in one's *khera*, and thus witness the event. This territorial unit has long since been 'broken.' In recent mosars, Bhats, who are no longer as interested in these local relationships, began limiting invitations primarily to the members of their own or their in-laws' clans. But now, even this seems to have changed: Bhats invite outsiders to the feast. Or, instead of holding a mosar feast, young Bhats simply try to impress their peers and neighbours in the alternative idiom of modern consumerism: houses and durable consumer goods.

Once upon a time, if a Bhat were to build a house before sponsoring his father's mosar, others within the community would ask, 'What is this? Get out of my presence! Have you no respect for your parents? You should die of hunger before you fail to do your father's mosar!' The moral economy represented by the mosar, however, seems to be passing. It is being overtaken, for better of worse, by urban anonymity and an idea of success measured in televisions, VCRs (and lately DVD players), motorized vehicles, and diplomas.

To date, this new movement is not without its critics. As Bansilal put it, pointing to big houses across the street facing his own abode:

> To me, those homes are nothing but "latrines". All the money I made and spent in my life on *mosars* and feeding guests adds up to how many of those houses? How many I ask you? How rich would I be if I hadn't spent my money in this way?! My neighbours look at me and see a poor man..... They think themselves so superior. They judge me in the language of cars and scooters and nice clothes. But I have honour I tell you! I feed others all the time. You've seen it. One doesn't fill one's stomach by giving, but one certainly does build honour! This is why my near kin and I are "forwards", because we keep the old ways alive. This is why they are "backwards" because they forget them.

Tourism, Puppetry and Heritage

Mosars are memory machines in a way that stone houses are not. Mosars construct images that freeze the dead into a perfect and durable form. This seemingly impossible task fuels the excitement of this rite. Mosars bring to mind the same representational issues that lie at the heart of the Bhat profession as genealogists and praise-singers. And, likewise, recently Bhats have cunningly deployed these skills and sensibilities to cement and market an identity as traditional artists. The mosar feast, then, mirrors the central dilemmas and aspirations of Bhat society, past and present. The mosar, following Geertz's (1973) classic essay on the Balinese cockfight, is a story Bhats tell themselves about themselves, a theatre in miniature of the Bhat community. The Bhats' traditional profession as genealogists and praise-singers for Meghwals was realized in a language of economic generosity drawn from the ideology of kingship. Traditionally, generous patrons are lauded as high and good because they support and sustain their dependent clients, such as the Bhats. Meghwals, of course, are not kings or nobles, nor are they even traditionally landlords – but they are patrons. Bhat praise poems suggest that in imitating kingly models of generosity, Meghwals take on some of the characteristics of real kings and even potentially of the generous and god-like kings of the past.

These details help make sense of why Bhats in the 1990s found feasts such as the mosar compelling social drama, and why it may re-emerge in yet a new form in the near future. Despite their new work and residence in urban areas, Bhats return periodically to their natal villages to provide praise-singing services to Meghwals and other patrons, especially during those summer months in which the tourist season grinds to a standstill. As such, Bhats are still immersed in a rural gift economy that is somewhat intact. Thus as praise-singers, Bhats strive to create simplified images of their patrons, a few verses of poetry perhaps, that stand in the place of the more intractable lived reality of this relationship.

In celebrating their own mosars in the manner described above, Bhats construct an ideal model of hierarchy and social relations that continues to be of great economic as well as cultural relevance – that of the generous, and thus virtuous, patron-lord, which is a highly prized element of cultural heritage broadly shared by all social groups in Rajasthan (see chapter by Jhala). Likewise, in staging a lavishly unforgettable feast of death, a Bhat dreams that he will create a glorious and perfect image of his father: 'What a feast, what a man!' Now, if a dead man's name should arise in conversation, fixing their minds and mouths to the days of this feast, Bhats respond laconically, *'Accha kiya'*, 'It was done well'.

Or they simply cite the cash placed in the thali, '51 rupees, 101 rupees.' Returning from a mosar, I was seldom asked more than, 'How much?' implying, 'How much money was placed in the thali?' The mosar, then, is not so different from the Bhat art of praise-singing. It serves as much a poetic as a competitive end, and participates in a similar 'linguistic ideology' (Robbins 2001) related to the Bhats' belief in their own poetic power over memory.

Outside local relationships within the Bhat community and links of Bhats to Rajasthani patrons lies the increasingly global tourism industry, with its demand for purveyors of traditional entertainments. These performers face many challenges in adapting to this new environment. New performance niches have opened up to some subaltern groups as the result of other performers' abandonment of these professions for the more highly rewarded, secure, and lucrative professions of medicine, law, journalism, and politics. However, this upward mobility is limited to just a few individuals in each group.

In their work for Meghwals, Bhats are curators of memory and the past. From this perspective, tourism is perfectly continuous with the Bhat preoccupations characteristic of the mosar – death, memory, and heritage. Yet in the tourist industry, foreign and domestic tourists are the chief consumers of the Bhat puppet dramas. Most of these will not understand one word of the dialogue, even if they might follow a line of action. My Bhat informants realize that there is still a demand, in everything from the tourist sector to nationalist politics to development, for those who can forge compelling stories about what tourists consume about traditional Rajasthani society.

Some Bhats earn thousands of rupees a month selling puppets to tourists, many times what they might garner elsewhere. Tourism, not praise-singing, finances the Bhats' extravagant mosar feasts and their new stone homes. The connection between tourism and mosars goes deeper than this. As such, this industry does not merely provide the financial capital that leads to the expansion of this feast. Rather, it promotes an entire way of life that references the imagined Rajasthani past.

Rajasthan's palace hotels, signalling as they do a bygone era of kings, cater to nostalgia and exoticism (see chapter by Henderson). Bhats would seem to meld seamlessly into these settings in their guise as traditional artists. Bhats consciously cultivate this identity, even when it involves innovation. Bhats exploit the romantic fantasies of tourists and folklore organizers by posing as the once glorious, though now fallen, bards of royalty. Their presentations feature kings, queens, and nobles and seemingly extend a connection between themselves and these exalted personages. This last is a fiction. Royals were never Bhat patrons in traditional times, but royals may become patrons, for they are now hoteliers who must ensure a steady stream of 'traditional' entertainment for their guests.

Bhats first presented themselves to me, and present themselves to most tourists, as puppeteers with an art dating back thousands of years. As I note at the start of this chapter, I learned that Bhat ancestors learned to dance puppets about seventy years ago from a nomadic troupe originating from a region in what is now Pakistan. Not only is this work tradition not thousands of years old, as sometimes claimed by Bhats, but also it was adopted from a Muslim community – ironic, given Bhat plays celebrate Hindu warrior struggles against Muslim invaders. Likewise, to bolster the myth of the great age of their puppets, Bhats sometimes clothe them in tattered *saris* picked up from rag vendors and bury their puppets' wooden heads in the ground with lye, so that they decay more rapidly.

Do these strategies matter? Tourism research indicates that the tourists' perception of authenticity is what counts. Further, arguably the Bhats embody live cultural traditions in their making and remaking of themselves. The mosar itself is best thought of as a continuously reinvented tradition, capable of forming a part of the Bhat public identity, a new identity self-consciously promoted by my informants. That Bhats, who are traditionally untouchables, may host a public ceremonial even in front of the homes of high-caste families, might scarcely have been permitted decades ago. The annals of conflicts between members of scheduled castes and tribes and elites are filled with resistance by the latter to public displays by the former. In some areas, before independence, it was unheard of for an untouchable to build a stone house. Today, Bhats want others to see the wealth they have amassed in their new urban homes, and thus to bear witness to the fact that these formerly untouchable persons have 'made it.'

But, there is more to the current public nature of Bhat mosar performances, as revealed in the following Bhat observations about the passers-by gaping at a mosar: 'Look, all these people are looking at us artists. Yes, we are 'artists', we are different, we have the old traditions. This is what they are saying to themselves. The mosar is an 'old thing', a part of 'old culture.' Just like our puppet art, it is tied to the old village traditions.'

In part, the Bhats' ability to possess, temporarily, public spaces rests upon well-publicized Indian Supreme Court decision barring upper-caste groups from preventing low-caste groups' public celebrations. In part, the withdrawal by other groups from the enactment of these traditions and migration of status into new markers opens a niche to Bhats as the constructors, creators and containers of tradition. As Udaipur's middle classes perceive themselves as 'modern', the Bhat's self-representation is less of a point of confrontation than, perhaps, in the past. This opens symbolic space for the Bhats to claim meaningful difference from the members of other caste groups: one that expresses a positive identity – as great king, as gift-giver – rather than the negative identity of untouchability and social ostracism.

Conclusion

It is a commonplace in the social science of tourism that the industry leads to an Orientalist construction of an exotic India that responds to the needs and fantasies of modern elites longing for adventure and difference. I hope that this essay has shown that not all Indians passively tolerate and embody the fantasies of the West. Bhats, as has been seen, utilize traditional skills of narrative and poetic composition, honed on the occasion of mosar feasts as well as in ritual performances for village patrons, to play such fantasies for all they are worth.

Scholars also often point to the transformative force of tourism on local economies and identities (e.g., Chambers 2000, Edensor 1998, and Smith 1998). I hope that this essay has illuminated such a presence; the way tourism encourages, first, the expansion and then the potential demise of this Bhat rite, and the rise of new forms of social display. In fact, the mosar has always concerned death and the fleeting beauty of life, a beauty that is magnified through acts of economic sacrifice that in turn fuel a wondrous feast. As such, it is perhaps fitting, or at least not surprising, that the mosar feast itself would eventually die.

It is also fitting that such a looming death, that I would point out is not yet a certainty, would follow the expansive burst of renewed life in this rite alluded to in this paper; after all, the dynamic tension between human energy and death lies at the heart of this feast itself. Nevertheless, as in the Bhat relationship to tourists' fantasies, we should never assume that tourism's power in this context exists in itself, above and beyond Bhat lives.

I hope this essay makes clear that changes in Bhat society are mediated by my informants' changing desires and agendas, even if Bhats only partly control the contexts that fuel and energize these desires and agendas. Bansilal reversed the state's definition of the meaning of progress, finding advance not in renouncing the old ways but in remembering them. I heard many Bhats echo Bansilal's sentiments, though the meaning of the mosar unstably fluctuated between its social-communal and individualistic-competitive facets. As one young Bhat told me during my fieldwork, 'Whenever we get money we think to the mosar, 'Can we do it now?' 'Is it the right time?''

Citing the example of his neighbour, who had just landed a lucrative contract worth tens of thousands of rupees for performing puppet dramas for a local bank, this young man continued: 'He will spend this all on the mosar. He has been thinking about it for the past five years. He will not save this money. He will not spend it on a television or a car, like you. He will finally do such a large mosar that no one will be his equal.'

The mosar always offered a contradictory promise. On the one hand, it promised immortal names that stood still like stone monuments. On the other hand, the mosar only offered only fleeting moments of grace and fame. As one Bhat put it, 'For two hours your name is big. After that, no one remembers you. Your name is gone forever.' Perhaps it is the tourist industry, in the way it brings Bhats into contact with an alternative view of wealth and status that has led Bhats to see in their mosars not a tension between immortality and momentary grace, but between financial insecurity and the status derived from public consumption.

In Bansilal's version of the story told at the beginning of this chapter, the Natni renounced the wealth of the kingdom of Mewar for an immortality etched in stone. In a sense powerless, in the Bhat telling of this tale, the Natni nevertheless asserted herself and forged a name and place for herself in the annals of Mewar. Bhats too, for a while, were ready to renounce the dreams and aspirations of mainstream Indian society, and preferred instead to concentrate on wars of reputation in 'mad' attempts to forge their immortal names. As Bhat wealth has grown, however, they seem less eager to follow in the path of ancestors who placed more value on the praise of living men, than in the new way of valuing the security of stone homes. Like the Natni, Bhats demonstrate wilfulness and agency. In pointing to the power of tourism, either in the pervasive Western fantasies it fuels or in its economic heft pure and simple, we should not forget the Bhats' own power, if partial, to engage and rework these fantasies and resources as they see fit.

References

Appadurai, A. (ed.) (1986), *The Social Life of Things: Commodities in a Cultural Perspective* (Cambridge: Cambridge University Press).

Bharucha, R. (2003), *Rajasthan: An Oral History: Conversations with Komal Kothari* (New Delhi: Penguin Books).

Chambers, E. (2000), *Native Tours: The Anthropology of Travel and Tourism* (Prospect Heights, IL: Waveland Press).

Edensor, T. (1998), *Tourists at the Taj: Performance and Meaning at a Symbolic Site* (New York: Routledge).

Geertz, C. (1973), 'Deep Play: Notes on the Balinese Cockfight', in *The Interpretation of Cultures* (New York: Basic Books, 412–453).

Gregory, C. (1982), *Gifts and Commodities* (London: Academic Press).

Mauss, M. (1990), *The Gift: The Form and Reason for Exchange in Archaic Societies,* trans. W. D. Halls (New York: Norton).

Munn, N. (1990), *The Fame of Gawa: A Symbolic Study of Value Transformation in a Massim (Papua New Guinea) Society* (New York: Cambridge University Press).

Parry, J. and M. Bloch. (1989), *Money and the Morality of Exchange* (Cambridge: Cambridge University Press).

Robbins, J. (2001), 'Ritual Communication and Linguistic Ideology: A Reading and Partial Reformulation of Rappaport's Theory of Ritual', *Current Anthropology* 42:5, 591–614.

Rosman, A. and P. Rubel (1971), *Feasting with Mine Enemy: Rank and Exchange Among Northwest Coast Societies* (New York: Columbia University Press).

Smith, V. (ed.) (1998), *Hosts and Guests: The Anthropology of Tourism* (Philadelphia: University of Pennsylvania Press).

Snodgrass, J.G. (2004), 'The Future is not Ours to See: Puppetry and Modernity in Rajasthan', *Ethnos* 69:1, 63–88.

—— (2006), *Casting Kings: Bards and Indian Modernity* (New York: Oxford University Press).

Strathern, M. (1988), *The Gender of the Gift: Problems with Women and Problems with Society in Melanesia* (Berkeley: University of California Press).

Swarankar, R.C. (2001), '"Nat" Women in Rajasthan: from Rope Dancers to Sex Workers', Paper Presented at the *Fourth International Conference on Rajasthan in the New Millennium: Religion, Culture, History, Society, Polity and Economy.* 28–30 December (Jaipur: Institute of Rajasthan Studies).

Taussig, M. (1980), *The Devil and Commodity Fetishism in South America* (Chapel Hill: The University of North Carolina Press).

Chapter 7

Sickly Men and Voracious Women: Erotic Constructions of Tourist Identity

Maxine Weisgrau

Introduction

English-language guidebooks routinely advise Western women travelling in India to avoid dress and behaviour that will be interpreted by Indian men as communicating sexual availability and inviting unwanted sexual advances. Advice to women tourists draws on simplistic renderings of cultural Indian norms referencing family, gender, appropriate behaviours and modest dress. The authors of these guidebooks presume that female European American tourists, particularly those travelling alone, are likely to challenge many gendered social norms, and therefore, be subject to harassment. Tour books on India in general and Rajasthan in particular published over the past two decades repeat verbatim advice about modest dress and behaviour. Recently, the Internet has become a ubiquitous source for the perpetuation of this advice, which has obtained the status of 'master narrative' in tourism discourse, naturalized as indisputable in its authority and veracity (see chapter by Karatchkova this volume).

This narrative's closest companion in India seems to be the widely reported and sometimes violent harassment of women walking in public or travelling on public transportation – a phenomenon that Indians call 'Eve teasing.' Guidebooks routinely add comments about Eve-teasing in their warnings to women tourists. As opposed to the advice addressed specifically to Western women tourists, this discourse makes no distinction among women based on country of origin, but does argue that violation of expectations of feminine modesty and demeanour, *i.e.*, gendered cultured norms, may result in harassment or violence.

I argue that this simplistic cultural explanation for the harassment of women ignores complex ideas about male and female gender and sexuality.[1] The culturally-based argument of the guidebooks relies on a one-sided reading of gender construction and social behaviour that embodies a vision of the travelling woman as innocent, naïve, and sexually vulnerable to the advances of predatory men. In the case of European

1   This discussion derives from fieldwork supported by research grants from the American Institute of Indian Studies and the MacArthur Foundation for which I am extremely grateful. I also thank, most heartily, co-editor, colleague and friend Carol Henderson for invaluable suggestions made on multiple drafts of this chapter.

American tourists, the culturally-based argument overlooks the complex ways in which contemporary tourism is implicated in a process of mutual construction of the other, particularly through imagined visions of sexuality and gender.

During the course of research trips to Rajasthan between 1988 and 1995 (Udaipur district) and related travel in Northern India, I encountered several tourism-based narratives. Some were descriptions of harassment and attempted harassment of women travellers that were consistent with the tourist guide master narrative. However, I also encountered many stories that ran counter to the guidebooks' (and Internet travel guides') advice: stories authored by Rajasthani men about women travelling in Rajasthan; foreign women's tales of initiating sexual and financial relationships with Indian men; and Rajasthani women's stories about these relationships. Only the master narrative imagines a victimized European American tourist. The rest of these narratives all present a European American woman who initiates sexual adventures with local men. These stories collectively present a group of voices rarely heard in the discourses around the sexual behaviour of European American women travelling in India: a local construction of the tourist not as the reluctant victim of unwanted sexual attention, but as an active pursuer of sexual activity.

This chapter focuses on adult erotic constructions of identity in the tourism encounter as revealed in diverse forms of narratives. In this, I attempt to disentangle the multiple forms of representation of the 'Other' contained in these different narratives. This discussion also suggests significant gaps in the growing scholarly literature on gender, sexuality, and tourism in India. Considering the ubiquity of the theme of the harassed European American tourist in the master narrative of tourism in India in general and in Rajasthan in particular, the scant scholarship on sexual encounters in the tourism experience is inadequate to understand this highly complex phenomenon.

In thinking about these four competing narratives, I suggest that a significant component of the process of their production is vested in the intersection of multiple gazes and related contexts that occur within the institutionalized sexualization of tourism in Rajasthan and other Asian destinations. These different contexts range from the use of gendered and sexualized imagery (see Oppermann and McKinley 1996) in the marketing of tourism destinations (see Henderson this volume), to narratives of sex workers. These contexts encompass a diverse array of personnel with widely divergent and contingent relationships to sex tourism.

In the present work I therefore stress the necessity of exploring multiple voices on sexuality and tourism in Rajasthan, with particular attention to the version of a contemporary, or urban, legend that is transmitted by and among male workers in the tourist industry. The tourism encounter is a lens onto a mutually constituted and constantly changing discourse of identity in Rajasthan that reflects elements of the state's evolving relationship to globalizing forces, shifting politics, and a growing yet uncertain economy. This is an encounter where the gazes of tourist and of locals intersect and in which new assumptions of identity may be forged.

My discussion of the local male-authored contemporary legend referred to in this chapter derives from six separate discussions: one informal discussion in Jodhpur in which the legend was mentioned, and five follow-up open-ended interviews with taxi drivers/tour guides in Udaipur. As described below, the subject stemmed from the context of multiple research trips to Udaipur district in the late 1980s to mid-1990s. The frequency with which the issue of sexual advances arose in informal discussions with travelling European American women suggests that the perception of being sexually propositioned or harassed is widespread among women travellers in India. And the frequency with which texts aimed at tourists address these issues demonstrates its presence as a continuous theme in the western construction of the tourism encounter in northern India.

This discussion will not address factuality or veracity of the events narrated or facts claimed in these stories. Some of the particular stories that I relate bear all the hallmarks of what folklore scholars term variously an 'urban legend' or 'contemporary legend.' These are stories that are *told as if they are true* and they relate events that supposedly happened to a *friend of a friend of the narrator* [emphasis added] (Georges 1981 cited in Fine 1992). Whatley and Henken (2000, 2) note that, 'Located as they are in contemporary society, [urban legends] reflect with particular clarity the current fears and anxieties of a group and serve as warnings about potentially dangerous situations, behaviours, and assumptions.'

I start this chapter with a description of how this topic intersected with my research in India, for it is important to understand that narratives of tourism intertwined with my work, even when this explicitly was not part of the anthropological practices which I (and others) constituted as research. I follow this discussion with a brief background to the study of sexuality and tourism as a global phenomenon. I then suggest some historical continuity in the gendered construction of female tourists by making reference to colonial-era narratives about European female sexuality in India and their relationship to gendered modes of contemporary travel writing. I examine the four narratives of tourist encounters as embodied in tourist discourses, and link them to suggestions for further research and discussion.

Methodology: Sex, Lies, Tourism, and Anthropology

The contemporary legends about a sexually predatory woman and her passive husband/partner are stories told to me, and were repeated orally to me in conversation with Rajasthani men involved in the tourism industry. This is a legend of a sexually insatiable and predatory European American woman, and her initiation of sexual encounters with an at first reluctant Rajasthani man, observed by and with the tacit approval of, a passive and sickly European American male partner. These three key individuals and motifs recurred in each version of the legend. I have never encountered this legend in writing or elsewhere. It appears to belong to a male oral folklore tradition, although, as I will discuss, some of the themes expressed in this contemporary legend have colonial counterparts. The narrators of these stories do not claim first-hand knowledge, but they do assert personal knowledge of another person who was a participant in the events, the classic 'friend of a friend' (FOAF) distinctive of the urban or contemporary legend.

European American women participants who told me narratives about sexual relationships described these first-person accounts as 'romantic encounters' with Rajasthani men. These women are tourists, travelling alone and unaccompanied by husbands or male companions. They are women in their 30s–50s, and they establish, through their sexual encounters with local men, what they construct to be romantic relationships that, they envision, will result in on-going contact with their male partners. One of the dominant themes in these stories is the woman's assumption of the role of financial and social benefactress to the Indian man. These narratives also create a vision of a sexually experienced and wealthy European American woman who dispenses various forms of capital and critiques Rajasthani gender norms. As in the romance novel genre, 'love' creates the relationship; and as in missionary narratives, an unequal moral and financial calculus powers the woman's efforts to rescue her partner from what she perceives as the oppressive practices of his culture.

The fourth set of narratives I will discuss are also oral tales. Rajasthani women told stories about the sexual/romantic encounters between Rajasthani men and European American women tourists. These women's stories commented on, and provided an incisive critique of the economic relationships and inherently unequal power relations embedded in the encounter between local persons and international tourists. Rather than demonstrating the power of romantic love, as valorized in the Western women's stories, these stories might be akin to a treasure story, in which male labour magically endows his wife and family with security.

These four narratives exist side by side in different genres and multiple forms of tourism discourse. Printed guidebooks and Internet sources arm foreign women with advice for avoiding the sexual encounter. Internet blogs and on-line travel diaries document the inclusion of references to eroticism in the marketing of Rajasthan as a tourism destination. A subgroup of travelling women of all ages seeks sexual and romantic connection with local men. Men relay the contemporary legend to one another. Their wives and sisters observe events, from a different vantage point. Situated somewhere in this multivocalic set of narratives is what appears to be the increasing sexualization of tourism in Rajasthan, an obvious but under examined social fact 'hidden in plain sight' (Di Leonardo 1998, 10) suggested by guidebooks, Internet sites, and the self-promotion of Rajasthani tourist locations.

I distinctly recall my first conversation about tourism as a field researcher in Rajasthan. It took place in early 1990. I was in the midst of dissertation fieldwork on non-governmental organizations in Udaipur district. While most of my time during this field trip was spent in rural communities outside of the city of Udaipur, I kept a room in a small guest house in Udaipur, about 50 kilometres (35 miles) from my primary field site in Gogunda subdistrict. I returned to this guest house regularly to transcribe field notes, to contact relatives at home by phone and fax, and to enjoy the relative comforts of running water, a toilet, and electricity, none of which were readily accessible in the villages where I was conducting my primary research.

At this time in my research agenda in Udaipur I ignored connections with the tourism around me (Crick 1989, 309). In retrospect this was a serious lapse in scholarly imagination: Udaipur is one of Rajasthan's major tourist attractions. In 2001 Udaipur attracted 57,000 foreign tourists and 663,000 domestic tourists.[2] Over tea one morning, I shared a conversation with an Australian traveller who, like most of the other tourists I encountered, asked me why I was spending so much time in Udaipur. He sarcastically asked me, before I started describing my work, 'What are you doing, studying tourism?' I promptly and defensively denied the charge, and went on to explain the subject of my 'real' research, what I then considered to be the 'more serious' pursuit of the complexities of economic development discourse and its local interpretations (Weisgrau 1993, 1997).

This conversation, however, stimulated me to think about the tourism economy around my field site, and to begin trying to understand the connections between development, tourism, and the local political economy (see the chapter by Snodgrass). By the mid-1990s when I returned to Udaipur, this connection was impossible to ignore. My entry point into thinking systematically about tourism came by my paying more careful attention to the ubiquitous casual conversations I had with travelling European and American women around the theme of sexual advances. I found, embedded in my field notes, documentation of scores of conversations with women tourists, students, scholars, and references to my personal experiences. These conversations were very easy to have with travelling European American women like myself. Every woman, no matter what her reason for being in Rajasthan, or the duration of her stay, had a story to add to my growing collection of travelling women's narratives. I also discussed these encounters with Rajasthani women. Some of these individuals were the sisters, mothers, and wives of my male informants, and were also directly or indirectly involved in tourism, primarily because their families owned and managed guest houses in *havelis,* converted traditional courtyard mansions, within Udaipur's tourist zone (see the chapter by Bautès). These conversations took place in Rajasthan over the entire span of my research trips, and are supplemented by similar conversations that I had with individuals on my return to the United States.

My introduction to the male legend that I describe at the start of this chapter came about unexpectedly. It is complicated to understand why any Rajasthani man would discuss sexual encounters, even those involving others, with me. It is highly unlikely that these young men (between the ages of 20 and 30, younger than myself) would talk about any aspect of sexuality with a woman under any circumstances – particularly an unrelated woman who stood, as I thought I did with my male informants, in the status of 'Didi' or older sister. This was obviously a fictive relationship in many different ways. Probably more in the forefront of everyone's minds was my liminal,

---

2   Source: Indiastat.com (2006 statistic cited is for 2002). It is important to note that the number of foreign tourists in Udaipur reported for 2001 is the lowest figure in the preceding four years. The high of foreign tourist arrivals in Udaipur in this four year period was in 1997, when over 84,000 foreign tourists visited the city. Total number of foreign visitors to Rajasthan in 2001 was 608,000; (Government of Rajasthan 2002) in 2005 1.1 million (Indiastat.com).

'neither-nor' status as a foreign, but long-term, resident who was incompletely integrated into local identities. Perhaps there was also the unfamiliar thrill of sharing stories about sex with a woman. Although the intentions and motivations of my male informants remain unclear, I feel it is legitimate to view their stories as part of a local narrative tradition, not just personal idiosyncrasy. This male narrative was repeated to me on several occasions, with only minor variations.

Theorizing the Sexual Encounter in Tourism

This chapter argues that discourses of tourism are a powerful force in contemporary Rajasthan related to the shaping of identity by tourists and by Rajasthanis, by women and by men, all of whom, to a greater extent than previously, think about themselves as both local and global actors. This topic has not been explored extensively in literature on either Rajasthan or India, more generally (exceptions are Hottola 2002a and b). Studies of sexuality, tourism, and gender have focused on the phenomenon of sex tourism and its impact on local communities in Asia and increasingly, the Caribbean and Central America. Studies of guidebooks indicate that for travel in Asia, at least, the tourism encounter is highly scripted by gender expectations about sexuality and its expression. These ideologies of gender and sexuality are not new. Studies of travel writing indicate that the constructions of sexuality and travel described for contemporary Rajasthan have their counterpoints in colonial history. This chapter attempts to put these perspectives into conversation with each other, as a starting point for uncovering their histories and contradictions.

Although this chapter's subject is a contemporary legend about a consensual adult sexual encounter, it is important to reference the trajectories of sexual tourism economies elsewhere, and the dire consequences of a sex-dependent tourism economy in India. The term 'sex tourism' evokes images of men from developed countries travelling to lesser developed countries in Asia, Africa, Latin America and the Caribbean to engage in 'sexual pleasures generally not available, at least not for the same price, in their home country' (Oppermann 1999, 251). Often the services are not legal in these men's home countries. Demand for sexual services may generate a prostitution and related-service economy dependent upon the flow of tourists (Ryan 2000, 23. See also Clift and Carter 2000).

The nexus of sex tourism – prostitution and child abuse – is widely documented throughout Asia and other areas (Clift and Carter 2000; Ryan and Hall 2001). The added spectre of AIDS and other sexually transmitted diseases creates a social crisis of major proportions. India recently has been identified as the new 'ground zero' for sex tourism, with the largest number of child prostitutes in Asia despite the efforts of journalists, social activists, politicians, and non-governmental organizations (NGOs) (e.g. SANLAAP 2003, Bedi 1996). Scholars identify the specific political and social environments that foster sex tourism, particularly '...[the] peculiar and unstable combination of sexuality, nationalism, and economic power' (Leheny 1995: 369) in which the trade, often illegal, nevertheless flourishes. India is facing a medical and social crisis due to its increased rates of HIV/AIDS infection (Waldman 2005). The epidemic is well documented in the American media for the major cities of Rajasthan (e.g. Russel 2004); but judging from the content of tourism 'blogs' and tour guides, this issue is not widely discussed or referenced by either male or female travellers.

Until recently, scholarship on sex tourism focused on the male tourist seeking sexual partners as a component of tourism (see, for example, Kinnaird and Hall eds. 1994; Edensor and Kothari 1994; Pritchard and Morgan 2000). A second strand of research, as yet much smaller, has begun to study women's agency as sex workers, and their manipulation of gender roles and expectations in order to exploit the limited potentials of sexual liaisons with European and American men (e.g. Brennan 2004, Kempadoo 2004). These studies suggest the complexity of women sex workers' understanding of the economic and political relationships linking themselves, their families, and the globalized realm of tourism and sex work. These studies also foreground the transition in gender roles in sex tourism economies, and how local participants reconstruct their ideas about race, masculinity and femininity under the influence of an emerging sexualized tourism economy.

A much smaller body of literature discusses the topic of women travellers as sexual consumers, as the obvious fact that women have sex when travelling makes its way into scholarship. Pruitt and LaFont (1995) have categorized encounters between European American travellers and Jamaican men as 'romance tourism', as opposed to the male activity of 'sex tourism.' The term romance tourism distinguishes these sexual relationships from those of sex tourism, these authors argue, because the women consumers constitute these relationships as products of a discourse of romance, rather than physical sexuality (Pruit and LaFont 1995, 423). De Albuquerque (1998) and Herold and DeMoya (2001) question the value of this analytic distinction, showing that, for the men involved in these sexual encounters with European American women, this is work, not romance. To the local male partner, the European American woman is one of a sequence of clients who are targeted and managed in a fairly standardized fashion (see also Samarasuriya 1997).

In contrast with the tourism literature on the Caribbean and Southeast Asia, scholarly discussion on contemporary travelling women in India in general, and Rajasthan in particular, is notable for its absence of analysis of sexuality and the tourism encounter. Most writing on tourism sexuality is from the advocacy and health worker perspective. Writing on sexuality in India, as a much more general topic emphasizes the social construction of gender and its transformations under colonialist regimes – not contemporary tourist practice.

A genre of scholarly writing that touches on issues of sexuality and tourism is the study of guidebooks, both print and on the Internet. Guidebooks, tourist websites, and travel magazines become authoritative voices for tourists that preconfigure and mediate their experience of India, its geography, and its people (Mohanty 2003). The guidebook has been most significant for what it describes and the claims of authority inherent in those descriptions. The guidebook is equally significant for what is edited out of its content and omitted from the authoritative narrative on travelling in India (Bhattacharyya 1997).

For the contemporary traveller, additional sources of prefiguring the experience of Rajasthan include Internet sites and tourism industry contacts. Tour guides, airlines, tour attendants, hotel service staff, and destination guides (official and un-official) all narrate a highly selective and specific vision of the history and present context of the tourism destination.

Guidebooks – at least those aimed at the mainstream travelling American audience, where prostitution and/or its promotion is illegal in nearly all jurisdictions – say almost nothing on the topic of sex tourism and its companions, sexually transmitted diseases and HIV/AIDS infection. The closest any guidebook appears to get to the issue is to include a brief injunction to use a condom and '[h]ave safe responsible sex' (journeymart.com 2006). Most 'advice' is directed at warning the woman tourist to dress and behave modestly.

Advice to 'lone women travellers' now appears regularly in tourist guides, warning of potential dangers and providing encouraging advice designed to avoid harassment (e.g. Abram *et al.* 2003: 80). Specific advice for the woman travelling alone in Rajasthan, contained in a guidebook popular with budget travellers states:

> India is generally perfectly safe for women travellers, even for those travelling alone. Having said that, foreign women have been hassled, stared at, spied on in hotel rooms and often groped, although the situation was rarely threatening. Rajasthan is, unfortunately, no exception, and *women travelling alone will find themselves constantly the centre of unsolicited male attention* [emphasis added] (Singh and Coxall 1999, 98).

On-line travel guides single out Rajasthan, viewed as particularly conservative (and hence attractive to tourists as an authentically 'traditional' destination), as a place where women must exercise particular caution (see www.insightguides.com/ig2/places/india/travel_tips.asp; http://india.journeymart.com/jaisalmer/need.asp).

In her excellent analysis of guidebooks on India, Bhattacharyya (1997) notes three characteristics of this genre of travel writing: different ethical standards applied to the implied European American readership than are applied to Indians; its tolerance for certain activities that European Americans might enjoy specifically during their time in India; and different advice to European American women than to European American men.

> ...[T]he behaviour of the traveller is not evaluated ethically...the behaviour of local Indian inhabitants are subject to moral judgments in several important ways. .... The focus is to provide a warning about the potential for sexual harassment and unwanted sexual attention from Indian men (although not from fellow Western tourists... (Bhattacharyya 1997, 376–377).

This writing emphasizes the need of women to protect themselves, by modest dress and behaviour, from the dangers of the Indian male gaze. This moralistic warning clearly echoes the colonial anxiety of the late nineteenth- and early twentieth-centuries expressed in part through fiction, as well as British efforts to censor film depictions of European American women after the introduction of this new media (Arora 1995).

Indian authors writing in their own languages in the same period paint a very different picture of European American women, one that includes the idea of the sexually available European American woman. Indigenous Indian literature therefore provides a resource for understanding local constructions of gendered foreign identity. V. B. Tharakeshwar (2003) for example discusses the representation of travelling 'white women' in the Kannada language travel diary of the author V. K. Gokak in *Samudradaacheyinda* ('From the Other Side of the Ocean'). The diary entries indicate the writer's astonishment at encountering a white woman travelling alone on the ship that carries him to England in 1936 to pursue graduate studies at Oxford University (Minajagi 1999, 14).

In his travel diary recording his experiences sailing from India to England Gokak 1988 [1938]) expresses shock at the dress and behaviour of the women he encounters on board: 'The behaviour of English women on the ship draws our attention. [Following men] these women are ready to travel even to the North Pole. They can swim, jump, laugh, smoke like men. Sometimes they dress like men, too! This is not civilization. "The Empire" has created this new model' (in Tharakeshwar 2003, 140).

The diary continues with Gokak's observations recorded while in England, in which he comments on a debate he observes at Oxford on liberalizing divorce; one of the debaters is a woman, who is speaking in support of the proposed measures. He describes her as follows: 'This girl is a reformist, what we call as *"Gondu Rami"* (i.e. a Kannda word equivalent to tomboy)...Her dress has reached the height of a joke. We already know that the English dress is half-naked. But her dress was sky naked...Her lips had the red colour of a chilly [sic]...A *queer* person. Even the clouded moon won't be as faded as her face! This *animal* stood up and spoke belligerently' [emphasis in original] (in Tharakeshwar 2003, 140–141).

Tharakeshwar (the translator of the diary) summarizes Gokak's discussion impressions of women in England as follows: 'Western women are generally represented as of immoral character, being ever ready to seduce men at any time, and to squeeze Indian men of their last penny...' (2003, 141).

The sexually voracious American woman appears in print in India in the late 1920s. A comic play entitled 'Miss American' by Pandit Badrinath Bhatt, a professor of Hindi at Lucknow University describes an Indian poet 'who loves obscenity and vulgarity. ...depicted as falling in love with a "Miss American", the epitome of the stereotypical Western woman' (Gupta 2001, 45). In conversation with the poet about erotic Sanskrit and vernacular language poetry, '"Miss American" states in the play: "I cannot digest my food till I've seen some lewd pictures printed in Paris, though the government is now tending to ban such things. What a terrible move!"' (Gupta 2001, 45).[3]

---

3   Deanna Heath makes the following observation on such images: 'By the end of the nineteenth century, postcards of naked white women, for example, could and did circulate

A wide body of literature on nineteenth- and early twentieth-century European and American women travellers in colonial India provides an analytical basis for discussing the contemporary discourse around and about female tourist sexuality (see for example Mills 1991, Burton 1998). In Ghose (1998), a key question asked is, 'how does travel writing constitute the Other?'

> Poststructuralist theories of cognition…postulate that reality is not given but is produced in discourses. These discourses shape perception….. the texts produced by travellers do not simply reflect a pre-given reality, but create the world they purport to describe. Knowledge is not produced from a transcendent position at all, but is a product of social and 'sensuous interaction' (Ghose 1998, 7).

The diverse politics informing the constructions of male and female in their roles as tourist and 'toured.' are the stories that these actors tell *about each other* therefore are rooted in the politics of those relationships, in inequality and differences. According to Ghose, '…the politics of knowledge implies that the gaze is linked to a specific political agenda: it effaces itself from the situation of perception. This enables it both to distance itself from the object of observation and, as a technology of power, to monitor and thus control the other' (Ghose 1998, 7).

The contemporary legends and stories I analyse are evidence of a complex set of ideas expressed by tourism workers and tourists in Rajasthan. These stories go to the heart of a historically informed vision of ideas about the sexuality of foreign women and men. Analysis of these stories requires shifting the framework from a simplistic discussion of local norms about women's behaviour into a much larger arena of ideas about Indian and non-Indian perceptions of race and sexuality, strength and weakness, masculinity and femininity.

These stories also point out the dynamic processes involved in the construction of an 'other', and of the inadequacy of Rajasthani norms alone as explanations for complex behaviour. I argue that it is necessary to situate the tourist encounter in contemporary Rajasthan as an arena within which such social constructions may be created and played out. Contemporary tourism in Rajasthan is itself in flux. The nature of the encounter, the various participants, and the ideas they bring to the encounter are not fixed into some unchanging set of cultural norms. As this encounter changes, so too must those participating it in transform their frameworks for understanding and the discourses in which they participate. The stories told by male tourism workers in Rajasthan are, like the stories told by women travellers, productions of discourse about the other.

---

fairly freely in India with little official intervention. So the image of the sexually available white woman has been prevalent in India for over a century' (Heath 2002).

The Voracious Woman Legend

The narrator of this story is a Rajasthani male between the ages of 20 and 30. He is reporting events told to him by 'a cousin' or related to him by someone else who was told the story by the participant. It is a classic 'friend of a friend' story. The reported original source of the story is the driver of an automobile taxi (not a smaller rickshaw). A foreign tourist couple, male and female, engages the driver. The legend refers to these simply as the 'husband' and the 'wife.' The couple has hired the driver, in either Jodhpur or Udaipur, to drive to Jaisalmer, a distant location in the Thar desert prized by tourists because of its golden sandstone castle, the nearby spectacular sand dunes, and beautiful carved architecture. En route to Jaisalmer the husband becomes ill. Also en route, the wife makes sexual advances to the driver. The driver and the wife have sex, either in view of the husband or with the clear knowledge of and consent of the husband. The trip continues, the outing ends, and the participants go their respective ways.

When I asked if this happens every time a driver takes a couple to Jaisalmer the response was no, of course not. Does it happen often? Well, the story-tellers say, drivers report that this does happen 'often.' The storyteller retails the encounter as a normalized series of events that are part of the practice of tourism in western Rajasthan.

After telling me the taxi-driver story in one conversation in Jodhpur, the narrator shifted his discussion to the 'well-known' fact of Western women's sexual promiscuity He supported this representation of the wanton sexuality of the travelling Western woman by referencing what he stated was the 'fact' that European and American women routinely walk around in public bare-breasted. When I asked how he knew that, he reported with a great deal of confidence that he had 'seen pictures of it in *Life* Magazine.'[4]

In these stories, one necessary condition for the sexual encounter is the illness of the husband. His physical weakness transforms into sexual inability, and sexual powerlessness. The wife's voracious sexual drive is an unstated given, as is the contrasted sexual potency of the driver. The encounter demonstrates what is already 'known' about European American men and women: white men are sexually weak, white women are sexually available and demanding, and Rajasthani taxi drivers are merely accommodating the situation.

These stories make it obvious that the contemporary tourism encounter is the occasion for the telling of narratives that embody ideas about masculinity, femininity, and sexuality. The legend is that of a male Rajasthani voice, from the local perspective (although in the conversations about the tourism encounters these stories were told to

---

4   *Life* magazine, published only sporadically in the United States since 1972. Its wide availability in India in the 1990s was questionable, although there is a probability that back issues continue to circulate informally.

me in English). This is a discourse that articulates a vision of Indian sexual potency that contrasts dramatically with the impotence of the European American man.[5]

Rumours of Romance and Tourism: Romantic Encounters and Local Commentary

Gossip and other forms of knowledge reveal the construction of knowledge about the European and Indian gendered 'others' embodied within the sexual encounter between European American women and Rajasthani men. Throughout my stays in Udaipur, Rajasthani women told me stories of what they described as 'rich' European and American women, who engaged in sexual liaisons with local younger men while on extended stays in Udaipur. The Rajasthani women's construction of these encounters, not surprisingly, converges and diverges in interesting fashion with how the European American women narrated their romantic encounters.

The European American women's stories envisaged the sexual encounter as the beginning of a romantic connection to a Rajasthani man. In some of these stories, the sexuality of the encounter is ambiguous. Whether or not man and woman engage in sex, the European American narrator projects the encounter as a romantic one. These narratives follow a pattern that constructs the Rajasthani social landscape from the European American story-teller's perspective. She is a woman who has travelled to Rajasthan independently. Her lover is an Indian man who is younger than herself, occasionally by as much as half her age. In these narratives the man is either engaged or married; in some of the stories his marital status is left ambiguous.

The Western women's narratives always contain a social critique: she will save her lover from oppressive, retrograde social practices that stifle his upward social and financial mobility. The narrator scorns the man's engagement or marriage on the basis of its having been 'arranged.' The man, she states, complains about his impending or current marriage. It conflicts with his desire for self-improvement through travel abroad, or to better himself through education or business opportunity in India. Seen as a motif, the engagement embodies, in shorthand fashion, the European American narrator's negative construction of Indian social norms. The woman articulates her scorn for arranged marriages, and suggests that the romantic liaison rescues him from an oppressive social practice. She envisions herself as patroness, pays for his travel, and gives him what local people regard as large sums of money.

In this role, the European American woman tourist constructs her encounter as innocent, blameless, and beyond the critique of adultery or impropriety which would apply were her partner an engaged or married European American man, or if the encounter were taking place in her home country. This female narrator constitutes as absent, or irrelevant, her Rajasthani partner's wife and children, or, if mentioned, brushes them aside as impediments to his economic future. The western moral taboo

---

5   This narrative dramatically reverses the nineteenth century British colonial vision of 'the manly Englishman and the effeminate Bengali' the history and analysis of which is discussed in Sinha 1995.

or, at least illicit thrill of romantic and/or sexual relationship with a married or engaged man is not part of the narrative. The European American woman's distance from home seemingly renders these issues irrelevant.

To the local gaze, this encounter may be envisioned, at least by some, as a form of social capital that pays returns over time. Udaipur women's commentaries on these sexual relationships always noted the 'wealth' of the European American woman traveller. This is consistent with local understandings; Udaipur tourist workers generally assume all tourists are rich. The workers' knowledge of the cost of hotel accommodations and restaurant meals in tourist sites, compared with their earnings, and the obvious fact that travellers are on extended holidays and not working, affirms this perception.[6]

Indian women (and a few men) commented on the fact that the European American women travellers' sexual partners were men who worked, sometimes marginally, in the tourism industry. These informants' critique of the relationship is articulated through the violations of local social norms assumed about relationships between men and women, based on class, age, and other social categories. For example, on many different occasions, one woman in Udaipur described to me the details of a relationship she claimed close knowledge of, between a Western woman and a rickshaw (not automobile) driver. According to one informant, an American woman engaged in a two-week sexual affair with a rickshaw driver, during which time 'she brought him' to stay with her in a five-star luxury hotel. When it was time for her to leave, according to my informant, she gave the young man an amount of money that enabled him to purchase his own vehicle. My informant told me that the driver named the rickshaw after his American patroness and decorated it with photographs of the two of them together.

In the telling of this story, my informant expressed moral outrage only at the part of the narrative that involved the bringing of the young man by the woman to her hotel for an extended stay. She commented on the age difference. She repeatedly referred to the rickshaw driver as 'the boy' (this story was told to me in English). She also commented that he was a 'Muslim boy.' These statements indicted her perception of the social distance between the driver and his patroness, and also perhaps, that between the narrator and any rickshaw driver. The storyteller's most vocal objection was to the transgression of locally significant barriers of class and space. She was most shocked that the European American woman brought her young lover into the tourist enclave space of the five-star hotel.

---

6   The cost of a luxury five-star hotel room in Rajasthan over the past 15 years has escalated from approximately US$80–$100 to the 2005 level of approximately three to four times that, depending on location, with the possibility of spending US$1,000 to $1,500 per night in luxurious 'villas' in palace hotels in Udaipur. Middle range hotels charge approximately US$50–$100; even 'budget' accommodations for the presumably younger, less well heeled traveller, US$10–20 per night, converts to the rupee equivalent for many hospitality industry employees, of a month's salary.

Other informants narrated tales of on-going relationships with women that began as encounters in Udaipur, between European American woman travellers and either employees of the hotels where they resided or, in one case, the son of a Rajput guest house operator. This last relationship continued over several years. The narrator of this story, a friend of the young man's mother, described his taking several trips to Europe where the woman resided, and her lavishing him with money, gifts, and opportunities for travel.

This story was related without any moral commentary, and without the suggestion of transgression. The status of the European woman as benefactress was accepted without comment. What seemed most relevant to the narrator was the young man's travel abroad, and the opportunities the relationship presented to him. The visits took place in Europe, not in Udaipur. The visits did not disrupt the family's social life and norms.

During one of my extended visits in Udaipur in 1995 I found that I was the subject of a similar form of gossip. A British scholar residing in a guest house adjacent to the one in which I was staying told me that one of the employees in that hotel, a Dalit (Scheduled Caste) boy of about 14, had announced to her that 'Maxine is going to take me home with her when she returns to America.' This came as quite a surprise to me, as I had never had any conversations with this young man other than to greet him on occasion.

What seems significant to me about all these narratives linking older European American women and younger Indian men is how these encounters are viewed locally as forms of access to money and travel. They are generally not cautionary tales of breaches of immorality. They are stories of the possibilities of financial and social windfalls that result from romantic encounters with women travellers. The narrators of the stories, Indian women, are not for the most part offended by the women's behaviours. The stories document evidence that these relationships are productive for the young men and boys' families. They are stories of unexpected and prized access to overseas travel, and of on-going contact with foreigners. As the case of the young Dalit boy employed in the guesthouse suggests, his imagining of the tourism encounter provides what would otherwise be impossible in his world.

Conclusion

My goal in relating these rumours, legends, and stories is to suggest the multiple ways in which different participants in the tourism encounter imagine and construct themselves and others. As stated at the outset of this discussion, the truth of the claims made by these multiple voices is irrelevant. The only truth embedded in these narratives is the vision of self and other they describe.

Stories about sexual encounters between Indian men and Western female travellers in Rajasthan reveal evolving cultural constructions of female eroticism. Analysis of these stories suggests the connections between tourism interactions and globalized media with the Indian-authored construction of an eroticized 'other' that contrasts dramatically with the ways in which Western female travellers and Western guidebooks present the female as reluctant victim of a harassing, predatory male. But the European American women tourists' stories about continuing relationships with Rajasthani men add the singular dimensions of financial support from a benefactress, who, while dispensing wealth to her lover, also critiques local social norms. These narratives are seemingly descendants of the nineteenth-century conception of 'moral uplift' as the responsibility of the European American, as constituted against a non-Western other. In contrast, the Rajasthani women's stories present a different critique, one embedded in the local constructions of class, gender, and family. These women's narratives present family as central, for the family benefits from the wealth acquired from the foreign tourist, not the individual man. These women's stories critique the limited possibilities for social advancement, in the economic climate of Udaipur (see chapter by Bautès), as well as the differential between the West's wealth and the relative lack of this for tourism workers, as opposed to upper class owners and entrepreneurs, in Udaipur. The motif of the disjuncture between the social status of the woman and that of the man, of her bringing him into settings inappropriate to his status, underscores this parable of global difference.

Tourism does not create ideas without context. Tourism is an arena within which ideas are reshaped drawing on histories of encounters with others. These encounters importantly implicate a rich and complex set of ideas shaped in interaction among the experience of participants of differing perspectives. The economic and social inequities inherent in contemporary practices of international tourism in Rajasthan are founded on the vast differential in purchasing power between the Western – usually European American – tourist and the local Rajasthani participant. Yet this reality does not mean that there cannot or should not be any intrinsically Rajasthani discourse, or that this discourse can only be derivative of European American visions.

References

Abram, D. *et al.* (2003), *India,* 5th Edition (New York: Rough Guides).

Arora, P. (1995), 'Imperiling the Prestige of the White Woman: Colonial Anxiety and Film Censorship in British India', *Visual Anthropology Review* 11:2, 36–50.

Bedi, R. (1996), 'Bid to Protect Children as Sex Tourism Spreads, *News-Scan International Ltd.* 19 March, 1996.

Bhattacharyya, P. (1997), 'Mediating India: An Analysis of a Guidebook', *Annals of Tourism Research* 24:2, 371–389.

Brennan, D. (2004), *What's Love Got To Do With It? Transnational Desires and Sex Tourism in the Dominican Republic* (Durham: Duke University Press).

Burton, A. (1998), *At the Heart of the Empire: Indians and the Colonial Encounter in Late-Victorian Britain* (Berkeley: University of California Press).

Clift, S. and S. Carter (eds.) (2000), *Tourism and Sex: Culture, Commerce and Coercion* (London: Pinter).

Crick, M. (1989), 'Representations of International Tourism in the Social Sciences: Sun, Sex, Sights, Savings, and Servility', *Annual Review of Anthropology* 18, 307–344.

de Albuquerque, K. (1998), 'Sex, Beach Boys, and Female Tourists in the Caribbean', *Sexuality and Culture* 2, 87–111.

Di Leonardo, M. (1998), *Exotics at Home: Anthropologies, Others, American Modernity* (Chicago: University of Chicago Press).

Edensor, T. and U. Kothari (1994), 'The Masculinisation of Stirling's Heritage', in V. Kinnaird and D. Hall (eds.) *Tourism: A Gender Analysis* (NY: John Wiley & Sons).

Fine, G.A. (1992), *Manufacturing Tales: Sex and Money in Contemporary Legends* (Knoxville: The University of Tennessee Press).

Georges, R. (1981), 'Do Narrators Really Digress?' *Western Folklore* 40, 245–42.

Ghose, I. (1998), *Women Travellers in Colonial India: The Power of the Female Gaze* (Delhi: Oxford University Press).

Gokak, V. K. (1988) [1938], *Samudradaacheyinda (From the Other Side of the Ocean), Pravasa Studies* (Bangalore: IBH Prakashana).

Gupta, C. (2001), *Sexuality, Obscenity, Community: Women, Muslims, and the Hindu Public in Colonial India* (Delhi: Permanent Black).

Heath, D. (2002), Personal communication.

Herold, E.R.G. and T. DeMoya (2001), 'Female Tourists and Beach Boys: Romance or Sex Tourism?' *Annals of Tourism Research* 28:4, 978–997.

Hottola, P. (2002a), 'Amoral and Available? Western Women Travellers in South Asia', in *Gender/Tourism/Fun?* M. Swain and J. Momsen (eds.), pp. 165–172. Emsford: Cognizant.

—— (2002b), 'Touristic Encounters with the Exotic West: Blondes on the Screens and Streets of India', *Tourism Recreation Research* 27, 83–90.

Indiastat.com (2006), Table 'Foreign Tourists: Centrewise Number of Foreign Tourist Arrival in Rajasthan'. www.indiastat.com.

Journeymart.com (2006), 'Need to know facts', *Destination Explorer* http://india.journeymart.com/jaisalmer/need.asp, accessed 8/26/2006.

Kempadoo, K. (2004), *Sexing the Caribbean: Gender, Race, and Sexual Labor* (New York: Routledge).

Kinnaird, V. and D. Hall (eds.) (1994), *Tourism: A Gender Analysis* (NY: John Wiley & Sons).

Leheny, D. (1995), 'A Political Economy of Asian Sex Tourism', *Annals of Tourism Research* 22: 2, 367–384.

Mills, S. (1991), *Discourses of Difference: An Analysis of Women's Travel Writing and Colonialism* (London: Routledge).

Minajagi, S. (1999), *Vinayaka Kishna Gokak (Vinayaka)* (New Delhi: Sahitya Akademi).

Mohanty, S. (ed.) (2003), *Travel Writing and the Empire* (New Delhi: Katha).

Opperman, M. (1999), 'Sex Tourism', *Annals of Tourism Research* 26:2, 251–266.

Opperman, M. and S. McKinley (1996), 'Sex and Image: Marketing of Tourism Destinations', in M. Opperman (ed.) 'Pacific Rim Tourism 2000: Issues, Interrelations, Inhibitors', Conference Proceedings, Centre for Tourism Studies, Waiariki Polytechnic, Rotorua, New Zealand.

Pritchard, A. and N. Morgan. (2000), 'Privileging the Male Gaze: Gendered Tourism Landscapes', *Annals of Tourism Research* 27:4, 884–905.

Pruitt, D. and S. LaFont. (1995), 'For Love and Money Romance Tourism in Jamaica', *Annals of Tourism Research* 2:2, 422–440.

Russel, S. (2004), 'AIDS in India: South Asia's Smoldering Threat', *San Francisco Chronicle*, 4 July, 2004.

Ryan, C. (2000), 'Sex Tourism: Paradigms of Confusion?' in S. Clift and S. Carter (eds.) *Tourism and Sex: Culture, Commerce and Coercion* (London: Pinter).

Ryan, C. and C. Michael Hall (2001), *Sex Tourism: Marginal People and Liminalities* (Routledge: London).

Samarasuriya, S. (1997), 'Sun-Surf-Sex Tourism', *Samar* 7, winter.

SANLAAP (2003) 'A Situational Analysis of Child Text Tourism in India (Agra, Delhi, Jaipur)' (Bangkok: ECPAT).

Singh, S. and M. Coxall (1999), *Lonely Planet Rajasthan*, 2nd Edition (Melbourne: Lonely Planet Publications).

Sinha, M. (1995), *Colonial Masculinity: The 'Manly Englishman' and the 'Effeminate Bengali' in the Nineteenth Century* (Manchester: Manchester University Press).

Tharakeswar, V. B. (2003), 'Empire Writes Back? Kannada Travel Fiction and Nationalist Discourse', in S. Mohanty (ed.) *Travel Writing and the Empire* (New Delhi: Katha).

Waldman, A. (2005), 'On India's Roads, Cargo and a Deadly Passenger', *The New York Times* 5 December, 2005.

Weisgrau, M. (1993), 'Social and Political Relations of Development: NGOs and Adivasi Bhils in Rural Rajasthan', PhD. dissertation, Department of Anthropology, Columbia University.

—— (1997), *Interpreting Development: Local Histories, Local Strategies* (Lanham, MD.: University Press of America).

Whatley, M. and E. Henken (2000), *Did you Hear About the Girl Who...? Contemporary Legends, Folklore, and Human Sexuality* (New York: New York University Press).

Chapter 8

From Privy Purse to Global Purse: Maharaja Gaj Singh's Role in the Marketing of Heritage and Philanthropy

Jayasinhji Jhala

Introduction

The rituals and events at the 1996 birthday celebrations of Maharaja Gaj Singh II of Jodhpur clearly illustrate heritage tourism's strategies of engagement in Rajasthan.[1] By compartmentalizing and distributing himself as *Kuladhipati* (as lineage head to his Rathore clan), as kinsman to his Jhala relatives, as friend and businessman to international and business visitors, and as father figure to the Jodhpur poor, Maharaja Gaj Singh II of Jodhpur, one of India's former princely states, constitutes himself as a modern leader and citizen king (see also Appadurai 1991). His legitimacy, derived from inherited pedigree, is repackaged with a new charisma in light of his personal career as diplomat, social worker, and champion of heritage crafts and tourism. Maharaja Gaj Singh II hereinafter referred to as 'Bapji', the term used by locals, uses his influence to advance the interests of the cultural region of Marwar – broadly consonant with modern-day Jodhpur District – and Jodhpur city (pop. 800,000). In the process, Bapji accrues new prestige, stature, and wealth for himself as an hotelier and tourism entrepreneur. His personal example and his operating principles provide a model for many other heritage hospitality markets in the tourism industry in Rajasthan.

Jodhpur's ex-princely ruler is, like other former royals around the world, reconstructing the symbols and meanings associated with royalty (Cohn 1983; Galey 1989). The Japanese monarchy, for example, radically transformed its ritual significance in the wake of World War II. Among the European royals, the British monarchy has led in its explicit concern with producing a public image suited to its goals and, not incidentally, stimulating tourist visits to Great Britain (Cannadine 1983).

In India and particularly in Rajasthan, former royals have heavily invested in the tourism industry, for a number of reasons. Democratic reforms, land redistribution, and the 1971 abolition of the 'Privy Purses', payments by the Indian government to

---

1   I thank His Highness Gaj Singhji of Jodhpur for his support and access, and Dr. Kenneth X. Robbins for his support of the film and research project.

compensate rulers for their lost income sources, forced Bapji and his peers across India to face a crisis of how to salvage their lives, maintain their properties, and retain some'measure of their former stature in India's late twentieth-century social and political environment. The concurrent growth of a viable mass tourism industry has become the means by which these goals may be sustained for many Rajputs, the caste category of Rajasthanis of, or related to, aristocratic descent (Ramusack 1994).

Many of these ex-royals have pioneered a distinctive form of 'hands-on' hospitality in which a significant appeal to tourists is the opportunity to meet and mix with Indian royalty, in their forts and palaces now refurbished as hotels (Sugich 1992). A stream of news and magazine articles, books, and websites promotes this central fact, supported by the ex-royals-dominated heritage-oriented marketing association, the Heritage Hotels Association of India. The image of a hands-on host is one of the most striking symbols of today's social construction of 'traditional Marwari hospitality' by Jodhpur's former royals – Marwar is the alternative name for Jodhpur state and its cultural region, who encouraged visitors to think of themselves not as 'tourists', but as valued 'guests.'

Prior to 1947 hospitality and entertainment were important diplomatic instruments of royal statecraft. 'Hosting' and 'guesting' were expressions of concession and acquiescence (Raheja 1988). Revenue from the Maharaja's extensive land holdings and those of subordinate nobles was expended to generate symbolic capital to enhance the ruler's stature. Now, the objective is not the conversion of land revenue into symbolic capital that is useful for political ends – as this income stream became limited following land reform, but rather the pursuit of tourism earnings. Hospitality revenue in turn allows these individuals to maintain, in part, their former prestige and stature as dominant social and political players, to play a leading role in Rajasthani elite society and even, in some respects, to continue to constitute this society hegemonically as a Rajput-identified domain.

This chapter examines the events of Bapji's fiftieth birthday celebration to understand hospitality strategies and practices that make up the conduct of persons and institutions associated with the royal tourism industry in Rajasthan today. I discuss the genealogy of hospitality in Rajasthan as practiced by royalty and the local aristocracy, to demonstrate how present-day practice descends directly from earlier norms of hospitality and courtesy. Second, I propose – in an argument little noted in writing about royal tourism in Rajasthan – that the performative aspects of royal hospitality are replicated on a smaller scale at all levels of Marwari society (Dumont 1970; Dirks 1987; Fuller 1985; Jhala 1991; Mayer 1981, 1985; Srinivas 1987; see also the chapter by Snodgrass, this volume).

I have chosen an extraordinary event rather than an annual event for analysis in this paper, for an important reason. At extraordinary events, it is possible to identify the full range of the different sets of guests hosted by the Maharaja. It is possible to document how guests are treated as special constituencies, and to find out what kinds of meaning and significance these guests claim to derive from this event. The ways in which the event is organized creates the overall framework of understanding and of interaction among these different sets of guests and their hosts.

Why is the celebration of a single person important for Rajasthan tourism, it might be asked? It is because, in the position of Maharaja, Bapji remains centrally positioned in Rajasthani culture and cultural expression. This centrality is so today, despite the emergence of the Government of Rajasthan and private groups as sponsors and supporters for cultural heritage preservation. Dance, music, painting, architecture and sporting activities such as polo find enduring patronage by Bapji and those closest to him. Recognition and usage at today's court underscores the court's claims of historical authenticity for these colourful artistic expressions even when, as candidly admitted by Bapji, these are invented traditions such as the recently established 'Desert Kite Festival' (see also Chambers 2003).

The fact that there is still a court and a nominal king is vitally useful for the performer and for the legitimacy of performance in the tourist arenas of entertainment. The Maharaja energizes the event with his presence and patronage. He re-establishes the traditional ties and longevity of the tradition. He provides a role model for other patrons of lesser rank to hold such events in smaller and more remote locations in town and country.

The evidence that I bring to this analysis comes from personal experiences of my childhood in the 1950s and 1960s. In my childhood conversations of my elders, members of royal families and the aristocracy, who lost their kingdoms, power and much of their estates, reflected their serious concern about the future. Bapji is my first cousin; his father and my mother are siblings, as are his mother and my father.

The fiftieth birthday celebrations held at the end of 1996 were an extended affair designed to last several months and to be marked by several different events in different locations of the former kingdom of Jodhpur. I was invited, along with a team of five graduate students from Temple University to attend this event and to document it on video over a two-week period. This work resulted in a corpus of over 120 hours of spectacle and interviews that provided data for this chapter.

The four ceremonies discussed in this paper took place over two days, the birthday itself and the activities held on the next day. Many other ceremonies were held on these days as well. These four events each showcased a particular constituency or audience. The events described and analysed are presented in the sequence in which they occurred: the Darbar (court reception); the *Asva Bhet* (horse gift); the official banquet in the palace; and fourth, the *Tula Dan* (weighing gift ceremony).

Constituencies for 'Royal' Tourism

Immediately after independence in 1947, the central government of India was not enthusiastic about the development of tourism in Rajasthan. National leaders viewed Rajasthan as a feudal state filled with hostile and backward-looking local kings and aristocrats. The new central government swiftly stripped the rulers of their remaining political, administrative, and judicial roles. Legislation designed to eradicate feudal institutions compromised the former rulers' ability to sustain their royal levels of consumption. Many palaces and big homes crumbled as their owners lacked resources to sustain them (Gold and Gujar 2002). Yet some entrepreneurs recognized the potential these properties represented, as substantial forms of capital that might be shifted to new uses.

Jaipur's Ram Bagh Palace came in first for development, followed by Udaipur's Lake Palace. Jodhpur and the other princely states located in the western part of Rajasthan faced the lack of transportation links. As these problems gradually were solved, particularly after economic liberalization in air and road transport in the 1990s, the tourism industry in Western Rajasthan experienced significant growth.

For purposes of this analysis I identify four major tourist constituencies for Jodhpur that are associated with distinctive Marwari cultural framings of this experience. Local domestic tourists, residents of nearby villages and towns wish to see and know the *Patnagar* (capital city). They want to see the temples, the fort, the palaces, the museum and if possible, Bapji himself. Their journey is often taken as a quasi-pilgrimage: it may be conceived as a kind of duty, and an obligation. It seeks union and self-identification with the objects of the journey.

Diaspora Marwaris who have left Marwar to make lives elsewhere in India or further afield seek to reestablish connections with their roots (see chapters by Hardgrove and by Cort). They visit town and temple for personal and spiritual rejuvenation. Their journey is anchored in memory and locality and combines in many cases with an effort to conserve Marwari identity in the younger generation.

A very important and growing group of tourists includes the newly economically-empowered non-resident Indian middle-class, including those who live in other countries, such as the United States. They come to Rajasthan as part of a *Bharat darshan* ('India Viewing') in which the object is to affirm their historical and religious heritage. Many were schooled in identifying Rajasthan as the land of heroes, and can recite the legends of Rana Pratap, hero of Udaipur sovereignty; and Marwar's Durga Das, who resisted the Mughal rule in medieval Rajasthan.

Foreign tourists not of Indian descent include persons who come from the United Kingdom or the Commonwealth countries, with historic connections to the British Raj. All foreign tourists may be drawn to India by its projected and self-promoted 'otherness.' For these visitors, India is a land spiritual and mystic, with naked holy men, burning corpses, snake charmers, wandering cows, temple bells, and Maharajas.

Each of these tourist groups was represented among the constituencies present at the Maharaja's birthday celebration. The event organizers placed guests into one of four broad categories that overlap generally with traditional social distinctions. The 'domestic' guests here comprise members of the ruler's own Rathore clan and his traditional prebendal nobles, those whose families prior to 1947 received income from lands granted to them by the then-Maharaja or his forebears (Jhala 1991). The second group, diaspora Marwaris, consists of members of clans that are linked to the Rathores through marriage, or affines. The third group of visitors is the ruler's religious functionaries. Lastly, the fourth group, seen from the traditional Marwari perspective, is everyone else, those who are 'foreign.'

'Domestic' hospitality can be understood to be that historical set of hospitality exchanges that, prior to 1947, occurred between the Maharaja and his subjects within the confines of his kingdom. The Maharaja was explicitly styled as the father to his people. These hospitality events occurred in the capital city and at different locations on events such as royal tours, inspections, pilgrimages, hunts and marriages and diverse events in the religious calendar. These events were convened to restate and reaffirm the centrality of the ruler and the court to the kingdom and its governance.

Alongside these events were a class of progresses and processions wherein the ruler opened fairs and festivals, and conducted local pilgrimages to important religious shrines within the kingdom. These events expressed a culture of hospitality that was very mindful of local political and religious hierarchy. Gender, age, seniority and socioeconomic ranking of participants were immediately recognizable to local domestic guests.

The category of affines, relatives-by-marriage, was associated with visiting relatives and neighbour kings and their courts, since these might supply brides to the Rathore men, or accept Rathore daughters in marriage. Precise protocol set by the precedents prevailing between those royal families was the benchmark on which the most recent meeting would be based. These relationships of marriage remain important today.

The third category, the religious, is associated with the visits of religious leaders of all religions to the kingdoms as well as the visits of Hindu deities to the kingdom, brought in procession from their temples elsewhere. The deference paid to and protocol maintained by Rajput kingdoms with regard to such visitations was quite different than that paid to the first two constituencies, and was marked by the ruler's multiple expressions of gravity, formality and humility.

The fourth category of visitors resonates with the historical categories of overlords, Mughals, Marathas, and the British. In colonial India, inspections, processions and formal Darbars or gatherings were regularly held where loyalty to the overlord was expressed. The opening of hospitals, educational institutions, railways, industrial complexes and other development projects went alongside polo, organized hunts and duck shoots as occasions to host and impress the outsider. Here too, very precise norms governed how and where persons of varied rank were to be seated and housed, along with a very well articulated regime of dress and costume worn by all participants at these events (Cohn 1983).

The Darbar

The birthday celebration Darbar, a formal court, took place in a huge white tent set up in the parade ground inside and under the western ramparts of Jodhpur's Mehrangarh fort. The Darbar incorporated three main events: first, the gifting of Brahmans, members of a specialized, hereditary priestly caste group who provide religious services to the royal family; second, the receiving of homage from kinsmen and members of the traditional multi-caste and multi-religious leadership of Jodhpur; third, the awarding of honours to persons who had achieved a mark of distinction in Rajasthan, the country or in international affairs – and who, in doing so make Jodhpuris proud. The seating arrangement at this all-male event is of special significance, as it underlines the type of relationships each group in attendance had with the king, as well as the hierarchy that obtained between various sections.

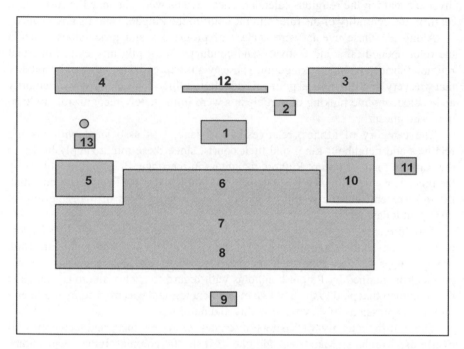

Figure 8.1   Seating chart of royal birthday Darbar

All members of the various sections were seated on the floor on carpets well before the arrival of the Maharaja. Section 1 contained the throne and chair for the heir-apparent, along with space behind it where the officials holding the insignia of office would stand. Section 2 was occupied by the nearest kin, such as Bapji's father's brothers. Section 3 held members of the senior cadet lines of the Rathore clan and holders of long-standing hereditary posts. Section 4 included Bapji's family members and those associated with him through marriage. Sections 5 and 6 are really one grouping, being made up of important local town folk. Section 7 was seating for male foreigners. Lastly, in section 12, four small groups of individuals, official staff and standard bearers were located directly behind the throne. These included, importantly, the religious head of the Chidiyanath sect (section 13), a Hindu group that has been closely associated with Jodhpur's ruling family since the founding of the fort; the official Brahmans, who carried out the religious rituals during the event; and the musicians who performed at this event.

Members of only two sections did not approach the royal seat: the head of the Chidiyanath sect and the foreigners. All other sections would in the course of the court approach Bapji in the order of hierarchical seniority. Section 2 began, and Section 6 ended, the parade of persons to the royal seat.

The Darbar formally began with Bapji's arrival along with a retinue of insignia bearers, holding the symbols of royalty and the royal umbrella over him. Bapji's son and heir accompanied him. All wore formal court dress, including brightly coloured turbans and long coats. The Maharaja and his son carried swords to which were tied scarves in token of peace, while the officers accompanying them carried bare swords. The assembly rose as a body with the Maharaja's entry.

Figure 8.2   **Maharaja Gaj Singh II (in dark glasses, centre) arriving at the darbar, attended by relatives and the media. The author, the Maharaja's maternal first cousin, is seen at extreme left foreground.** *Photo courtesy of Jayasinhji Jhala. All rights reserved.*

The Chopdar, the court official who fulfils the role of major-domo, announced Bapji's arrival with a recitation of his titles. Bapji immediately walked to the only seated figure in the assembly, the head of the Chidiyanath sect. Assisted by an aide, Bapji presented the Chidiyanath sect head with a tray of gifts including cloth, fruits, nuts and cash. The religious leader accepted the gifts and blessed Bapji. After this rite, the Maharaja walked to the throne and sat. The throne was backed with a display of the royal coat of arms presented by Queen Victoria to one of his ancestors. The insignia and standard bearers and officers formed a line behind Bapji. His son and heir Yuvraj Shivraj Singhji, now sat down on his father's left.

At this signal, the entire gathering took their seats. A contingent of Brahman priests stationed on the right, who had been conducting a series of rituals on Bapji's behalf for him as well as worshipping his new horoscope – cast especially for his birthday, approached him as a group. They recited mantras, prayers, and performed the *arati*, the fire framing ritual (for description see chapter by Cort). At the end of this ritual, the priests returned to their section, making sure as they did so that they did not turn their backs to Bapji, but rather they withdrew walking backwards.

A moment after these rituals concluded, at a signal from an aide, the heir-apparent approached his father. He is the senior-most person present in the line of succession, and as such had the privilege of being the first to offer his obeisance and allegiance. Two rituals were the core of this obeisance. First, the heir apparent performed *nazar*, the offering of a gift to the Maharaja. The heir took a silk square and on it a bag full of gold coins. He offered this to his father as a token of allegiance and subordination. The father accepted the bag and handed it to an aide.

Figure 8.3   **Maharaja Gaj Singh II (centre) attended by royal retainer (left in white) accepts *nazar*, an auspicious offering, from his son and heir Yuvraj Shivraj Singhji during the darbar ceremony**
Photo courtesy of Jayasinhji Jhala. All rights reserved.

Second, the heir performed a ritual known as *nicharwarl,* or *ghor.* Holding an auspicious sum of money (a number ending in 'one', such as 21, 101, etc.*)* in his right hand, the heir rotated this in a circular clockwise gesture that began at Bapji's waist and proceeded in a spiral clockwise and above his head and then back down to his waist or knee. At this low point, the heir released the cash at his father's feet. He touched his father's feet and knees, and when the heir apparent straightened up, his father embraced him. Released from the embrace, the heir moved backwards several steps before returning to his seat. Ghor is an act of worship and of protection, done in this instance by an inferior to a superior.

I have described these two rituals in some detail because they are the central and most potent acts of the entire Darbar. Every man who approached the Maharaja repeated these gestures. The Maharaja reacted differently to each person according to his rank and status. To certain members of the immediate Jodhpur royal family and nobility, he would rise; some he would embrace; and others he would not. These statuses are governed by historical precedence of past service and proximity. The Maharaja's maternal kinsmen and kinsmen by marriage would not give nazar, because they are not tied in service and filial loyalty and allegiance to him. They would perform ghor, however.

The key feature of this ritual is the personal contact each male participant has with the person of the Maharaja. All who have approached single file return to their seats and witness this repeated performance by the others who follow. The whole event takes several hours before the last person has completed the last act of nazar and ghor-nichraval.

At the conclusion of the nazar-ghor ceremony, other officers of the court came forward and sought permission to announce the awards. These awards combined privileges, titles and gifts, along with one lifetime award, granted to an individual in recognition of his service to the people of Jodhpur and the Maharaja. At the announcement of their names, each approached Bapji and stood before him while the citation was read aloud. This concluded when the Maharaja gave him a scroll containing the citation, after which the honoree returned to his seat. Awards were announced in a hierarchical order beginning with recognition of nationally-known politicians, Rajasthani politicians and professionals, and ending with individuals recognized for their personal service to the city of Jodhpur and the royal family's various enterprises. The end of the awards ceremony signalled the end of the Darbar.

A moment after the last honours recipient returned to his seat, the standard bearers of the royal insignia moved out from behind the royal seat, and the chief officer requested that the Maharaja rise. The whole assembly stood as he did so. As Bapji moved towards the exit, his son and relatives converged around him and, as Bapji emerged from the tent, the state brass band struck up again. The assembly within broke up, the attendees formed informal groups and moved out from various exits.

Very clearly, the Darbar centred on four sections of attendees. They were the (1) the Maharaja, his family, and his immediate family of Rathores; (2) the head of houses of the Rathore clan and other prebendal nobles; (3) prominent citizens whose families were long associated with the royal house; and (4) finally, specialists attached to the court, such as the Brahman priests. Their interactions constitute the event. The foreign male guests and male relatives by marriage were primarily witnesses and spectators to this bonding ritual. They simply observed, while the other participants enacted.

Many of the participants in the Darbar rites reported to me that it was the actual act of paying allegiance and of being recognized by the Maharaja that was the most significant aspect of the ceremony. It was not just the fact of *darshan*, of the ritualized mutual sight of subject and sovereign, but of *lagan,* or the sense of personal connection, that was the transforming experience. This act emphasized membership in a special fellowship of blood, descent and service.

The *Asva Bhet*, the Horse Gift Ceremony

The horse gift event occurred immediately after the Darbar. The announcer, who stated that a purebred Marwari mare, a highly regarded horse breed of Rajasthan, was to be presented to the Maharaja by his Jhala relatives, made proclamation of this event repeatedly. Bapji's mother and his brother-in-law are members of the Jhala royal family of the former princely state of Dhrangadhra in Saurashtra, Gujarat. The horse gift ceremony was to occur outside the fort palace's entrance to the *Zenana* (women's quarters) Darbar courtyard, the formal setting for women's court events. This black and white piebald mare had been dressed in red and gold Rajput trappings and was stationed near the approach to the Darbar events for all to admire throughout the morning.

During this announcement, Bapji, flanked by his mother's brother's son JiBava, the heir-apparent of Dhrangadhra, on one side and Bapji's brother-in-law, the Raja of Lambagam, on the other side, emerged from the Darbar tent. Accompanied by the umbrella bearer and other attendants, kinsmen, clansmen, staff and personal friends, a few hundred persons in all, he proceeded towards the zenana courtyard, which is overlooked by windows from which the court ladies and their female friends watched the ceremony. The brass band struck up the *Dusso*, the solemn march that is the Jodhpur state anthem. The mare faced the entrance to the zenana, held by her groom. Beside her stood the two Brahman priests who would assist with the ceremony and two bards.

As Bapji approached the mare, the bards began to recite his genealogy and that of his mother's father's patriline, the descent from father to son since time immemorial, of the Jhalas of Dhrangadhra. The bards recalled the different occasions when these families were united in marriage over the past centuries. One of the bards recited the merits of the Jhala clan and its many acts of bravery and sacrifice in the defence of Hindu religion and duty, and the clan's upholding of the values of *Rajputai,* or right Rajput conduct, over the past five hundred years.

This praise song was followed by another about the place of the horse in the Rajput imagination. This song also recalled a seventeenth century occasion when a Jhala ruler had, at that very spot, gifted a lucky number of 141 horses to the bards on the occasion of his marriage to a Jodhpur princess. The qualities of the Rajput warhorse, and especially the Marwari breed were stated, with special emphasis being placed on its bravery and loyalty in battle.

As this recitation ended, the mare was led towards Bapji and JiBava. JiBava began the formal greeting of the mare with the assistance of the two priests, who recited verses in Sanskrit. From an array of ritual substances on a silver tray held by the priest, JiBava anointed the mare's forehead with red kumkum powder in the same manner that an important guest might be greeted. JiBava then placed a garland of flowers on the horse's neck and finally offered it several lumps of brown sugar. The ritual and the mantras were identical with the ritual of greeting that was made by the women of the zenana earlier that morning, when they welcomed Bapji to their midst.

After JiBava completed his honouring of the mare, he took her by the reins, brought her to his cousin Bapji, and handed over the reins in the act of gift giving. Bapji passed the reins to his son, who now stood beside him on his left. The heir-apparent welcomed the mare in exactly the same manner as previously, though in a somewhat shortened form. After this greeting, the cousins embraced in front of the horse. This sealed the gift.

Thereafter Bapji embraced his other Jhala cousins and they in turn embraced a wide number of persons. This action solidifies the gift as one between two persons, two families, and two Rajput clans. The brass band struck up another number and as the gathering began to break up, Bapji and his Jhala cousins with others entered the zenana to meet and seek the blessings of the two queens, the mothers of the gift-giver and the gift-receiver. The horse gift concluded with group photographs of all the participants.

The horse gift ceremony was, as the local papers reported next day, a ritual associated with the Rajmata (queen mother) and her paternal relatives. Everyone else was witness. In the horse, the Jhala relations gave a traditional and very potent symbol associated with Rajput identity. The horse was a gift between royal families, between the head of the Jhala clan and the head of the Rathore clan. It was a gift by extension between two Rajput clans, the Jhalas and the Rathores; and finally, the horse was a gift between two historical regions, Jhalavad in Saurashtra and Marwar in Rajasthan.

All the other male and female attendees, citizens of Jodhpur, Rathore clansmen, foreign visitors and Indians from elsewhere, were spectators and witnesses to this event. The ritual was significant for the Jhalas as it was a prized form of proclamation, in culturally significant terms, of the Jhala daughter who had given the Rathores their present and, they felt, internationally renowned, leader.

The gift of a horse is probably the most precious of Rajput gifts: the horse and the Rajput are inseparable in history. The horse highlights the continuity of the Rajput code of conduct and honour. Finally, by Bapji acknowledging the place of non-

Rathores in this important personal event, he signaled to other Rajputs a pan-Rajput sentiment of solidarity.

This ritual as a theatre of the past reimagines that past in the present. The pains taken in staging and authenticating costume combine to reconstruct a past reality that allows for an assertion of personal identity in the present. The horse gift becomes a rite of renewal and of agency. Occurring on the very historical stage of the zenana courtyard where similar acts were once routine, allows for a great associative power to attach to this event, and to vest it with authenticity, legitimacy and continuity between past and present.

Cocktails, the Zenana Mehfil, Dinner, and the Disco

That evening, after an open-air rally and reception at the city centre with Jodhpur's elected mayor, civic authorities, and the general public, the Maharaja and his family retired to Umaid Bhavan Palace, across town and on a hill facing the fort. Umaid Bhavan is a large twentieth-century palace built in the syncretic Imperial style, which in this case combines indigenous and Art Deco elements. It is the perfect stage, symbolically constituted, for the evening's events. Most of the foreign visitors and those from major cities of India invited for this event were housed in this palace hotel.

The evening was organized in large part so that these guests could participate in this birthday's celebration as friends of the Maharaja, something they could not do at the formal, public events of the day. The evening began segregated by gender. The women went to a large hall for the Zenana Mehfil, (women's private gathering), which consisted of an evening of traditional Rajasthani dance and song. The men congregated in groups in a large adjacent hall where a classical Kathak dancer and her troupe of musicians entertained. There were seats near the dancer for those men who wished to watch, while others stood off to the side in small groups as waiters laden with drinks and snacks moved among them.

The Zenana Mehfil was a more formal and traditional affair than the men's event. The Indian women wore brightly coloured saris or traditional Marwari dress of silk or chiffon, decorated with gold and silver embroidery or brocade. All were adorned with masses of exquisite Indian or western jewellery. The event was presided over by Bapji's wife, Maharani Hemlata Rajye, who sat on a traditional brocade cushion seat with round bolsters. On one side of her sat her mother-in-law, Rajmata Krishna Kumari, and on her other side, Maharaj Kumari Shivranjani Rajye, wife of the heir-apparent. Other ladies of the family and aristocracy were seated in accordance with rank, as were the women guests.

The Maharani welcomed the company. Then ensued a session of traditional dancing and singing, accompanied by women artists from the Dholani and Langa groups, who are traditional Rajasthani musicians. The women guests danced – sometimes one, sometimes two and sometimes more, would rise up and enter the open space at the centre of the room, and begin the 'Marwari *ghomad*', the dance known to all women in Marwar. From time to time, one or more persons from the audience would rise, some cash in hand, approach the dancers and circle their heads with the cash in a gesture before dropping the money on the floor. This is a simplified version of the ghor ritual seen earlier in the day at the Darbar. Alternately, these persons would move towards the seated musicians and gracefully drop the money before them. In time, some of the non-Rajasthani guests, including a few foreigners, also came up and did the ghor. The event progressed from its formal beginning to become a lighthearted party as the evening passed.

Towards the end of the mehfil, Bapji entered and took his seat beside his wife. It was close to midnight when this event ended. Now, the women and men came together in the large banquet room for the birthday dinner. There was an enormous cake with fifty candles. Some of the Maharaja's friends from the University of Oxford, along with Senator Patrick Moynihan of the United States Senate and other special guests, gathered around Bapji, who with his son and daughter approached the massed candles and proceeded to blow them out amidst much merriment. Dinner was over by one o'clock in the morning and the gathering broke up. Most of the elders retired to their rooms or drove to their homes in the city.

The remaining guests proceeded to the final event of the evening, a discotheque dance party. A huge tent had been set up in an adjacent courtyard. An entirely different sort of dancing to recorded music now began that resembled a night club event in any locale in the cosmopolitan world – but for the liveried and turbaned staff and the bejewelled women in their traditional dress. Hosted by the heir apparent, this event continued until four a.m.

These evening activities were designed, it would appear, to accommodate and to draw in the non-Marwari visitors. This provided them a point of privileged access and also to underline the fact that many of these guests were the Maharaja's personal friends. The event also showcased the Maharaja and his family's multiple identities, one being their membership in the cosmopolitan world, even as they were part of a traditional world, which they had so carefully enacted during the day's events.

The evening events stressed the common experience of education, travel, business, diplomacy, and language that existed between the Maharaja and his many outside guests. The food, the variety of alcoholic drinks, the immense birthday cake, and male-female social interaction referenced cosmopolitan mores in the western world and in the big commercial cities of India.

For the tourist, this taming of the exotic event by including within it strains of the familiar and the nostalgic, allows a circumstance whereby they are brought into the celebration as co-celebrants, rather than as spectators. It also allows for the familiarization and domestication of the exotic – experienced all day in a sensory overload. The hotel becomes a home, a haven of the familiar in terms of language (English), décor (Art Deco), dress (formal Western attire alongside Rajasthani clothing), cocktails (Western and Indian liquors), and time: the familiar progression through cocktails, a formal sit-down dinner, birthday cake, and club-like music and dancing.

The evening events provided a feeling of stability and assurance to the foreign guests. The Darbar and horse gift during the day, with their unfamiliar rituals, the puzzles associated with the unexplained, the physical discomforts as well as the delights are mulled over safely and now can be recalled and placed into familiar categories of significant experience. In time, these form personal memories for the guest, who has safely embarked and returned to a familiar Western ambience.

The *Tula Dan*, or the Weighing Ceremony

I end with the weighing ceremony, for this distinctly calls into play an important local constituency, which is more or less separate from those who participated in the previous day's events. The weighing ceremony took place in a poor slum section of Jodhpur city. The chief organizer of this event was an elder resident of this area who had made good in the munitions business as a trader in the explosives produced and used by Rajasthan's mining industry. In line with cultural expectations of those more fortunate, he was now able to support various good works. The weighing ceremony came about because this individual came to the birthday celebration planning committee with a proposal for a Tula Dan. This traditional ceremony was often performed on the occasion of an important event in the life of a monarch. Weighing Bapji with silver coins would be appropriate for the occasion and a continuation of tradition. The money would be given to charity. The organizer promised that members of his community would raise the requisite handsome sum for the Tula Dan, and requested Bapji for a matching contribution of his own from his own resources. The combined amount would then be distributed among the poor.

A crossroads in the poor neighbourhood was cordoned off to form a square in which was constructed a raised platform. Several chairs were placed on top of this. In the centre there was one chair more ornate than the others. A large weighing scale was erected next to these chairs, making a large 'T' with two trays on either side held up by chains. The whole structure was decorated with flowers, and in one tray, a large red cushion was placed.

At the appointed hour in the morning, Bapji arrived with his entourage in a Mercedes-Benz accompanied by pilot and follow cars and other vehicles, just as important officials travel when on government business. This morning, Bapji was bare headed and wore a white kurta and pyjama outfit (a loose tunic with long sleeves worn over baggy matching pants), the now-standard uniform worn by most politicians, and not the elaborate Marwari turban and court dress of the previous day. Bapji wore over the plain kurta a vest made from the easily recognizable, rough hand spun and woven woollen fabric used for blankets and shawls by the local cattle herding communities. People in Bapji's entourage were also bareheaded and wore the traditional closed collar coat, which Westerners would recognize as a 'Nehru' jacket.

On alighting from the car, Bapji was garlanded and seated in the ornate chair. Next followed a number of welcoming speeches. Certain themes emerged. The speakers repeatedly mentioned the fact that Bapji was acting in the traditions of his forefathers, as a protector of the poor. They noted how Bapji was working to pacify Hindu-Muslim tensions in Jodhpur, an issue of some local importance at the time of the celebration. The speakers honoured Bapji's work in promoting Jodhpur in the field of crafts and tourism, and in supporting initiatives to improve the local economy.

Bapji in turn stated his commitment to work to secure more jobs, and signed off with his signature phrase, '*Meh tumse dur nahi*' ('I am not distant from you'). His late father used this phrase and its usage by Bapji signalled that his service to the people of Jodhpur was part of a continuing family tradition.

After the speeches, Bapji was led to the flower decorated balance and seated on the cushioned tray. Open bags of silver coins were placed in the other tray, until a balance was achieved. At that moment, a shout of appreciation went up. The main organizer thanked Bapji and publicly requested that he personally decide how the collected money had best be spent – also making some negative comments about how some of today's corrupt politicians handle public responsibility when charged with such tasks.

Bapji replied that he was glad to help, but insisted that the concerned citizens who organized this event should constitute a committee to decide such issues. They know best what was needed in the immediate community. Bapji would certainly listen to their views. The meeting broke up amid shouts of '*Bapji amar rahe, Maharaja Gajsinhji amar rahe*' ('Long live Bapji, long live Maharaja Gaj Singhji').

The Darbar was held on the grounds of the medieval fort, the horse gift was held inside the palace within the fort, and the evening events were held in the modern Umaid Bhavan Palace – three private, elite spaces – but the weighing took place at a public crossroads in a poor section of Jodhpur. Here, the king and his entourage did not wear royal or formal dress, but the dress of the local politician, social worker and person on the street.

They used local and easily recognized fabrics and props. The selection of spoken phrases used was in the local Marwari language, not in the Hindi, English, Sanskrit, or Gujarati spoken at the other. The key participants and audience at the weighing ceremony were the poor. Their needs are for support now and, in this context, they have little concern with distant history or the presence of foreigners. Bapji's role was as a bringer of resources and relief.

In fact, Bapji is careful how he articulates his participation in their affairs. He says nothing against any politician or political party, and only states that he is near to the people and will hear their complaints. He is light and informal in his manner, dress and speech, so that he can draw the persons closer to him.

Conclusion

Examining these rituals of the fiftieth birthday celebration provides us a window to appreciate how Bapji and his staff handle the varied constituencies that participate in these events. The customizing of rituals draws in these constituencies as guests to participate as co-architects of events, rather than as mere consumers of the spectacle. This property of the event allows for a closer relationship between Bapji and the guest, who is thereby provided with a sense of involvement and a personalizing of privilege.

All these separate constituencies are central at some point in each of the above-described ritual events. Bringing them into the spotlight for certain ceremonies and later providing them a duly honoured spectator's place deliberately moves them into different positions within the event. This dual role helps drive home the appreciation of their dual status as both central and peripheral. They learn and appreciate that it is the many constituencies that make up the event – yet Bapji is the central pivot that allows for this visibility of association.

This highly visible, stratified, and compartmentalized event is a blueprint of similar events and similar treatment afforded to the constituencies of the tourist. What Bapji does for the tourist in Jodhpur is replicated by the Rajput hierarchy that is involved in tourism down the line from city to town and to the village. Tourists who travel for religious or recreational purposes meet with a set of experiences and opportunities where they are in turn participants and spectators. This combination, embedded in a vocabulary of hosts and guests, is a particular draw for more and more tourists.

Persons and constituencies are accorded their appropriate status in this Rajput display of hospitality. An effort is made to treat visitors in certain ways and to engage them in spaces that are congruous with these requirements. The villager or urban slum dweller is not made uncomfortable by bringing him to a western style banquet. Being asked to pay homage to the Maharaja at a formal court does not embarrass the foreigner. At all times, the effort is made to make guests feel somewhat familiar about their situation and contribution to the event. Their position constructs them as glad to be with their hosts, to feel welcomed in their midst, and to feel privileged by the particular proximity and access they have to Rajasthani royalty.

References

Appadurai, A. (1991), 'Global Ethnoscapes', in R.G. Fox (ed.) *Recapturing Anthropology: Working in the Present* (Santa Fe, N.M.: School of American Research Press).

Cannadine, D. (1983), 'The Context, Performance, and Meaning of Ritual: The British Monarchy and the 'Invention of Tradition', c. 1820–1977', in Eric Hobsbawm and Terence Ranger (eds.), *The Invention of Tradition* (Cambridge: Cambridge University Press, 101–164).

Chambers, E. (2003), *Native Tours: The Anthropology of Travel and Tourism* (Prospect Heights, IL: Waveland Press).

Cohn, B.S. (1983), 'Representing Authority in Victorian India', in Eric Hobsbawm and Terence Ranger (eds.), *The Invention of Tradition* (Cambridge: Cambridge University Press, 165–209).

Dirks, N.B. (1987), *The Hollow Crown: Ethnohistory of an Indian Kingdom* (Cambridge: Cambridge University Press).

Dumont, L. (1970), *Homo Hierarchicus: The Caste System and Its Implications* (London: Weidenfeld and Nicholson).

Fuller, C.J. (1985), 'Royal Divinity and Human Kingship in the Festivals of a South Indian Temple', *South Asian Social Scientist* 1: 3–43.

Galey, J.C. (1989), 'Reconsidering Kingship in India: An Ethnological Perspective', *History and Anthropology* 4: 2, 123–87

Gold, A.G. and B. R. Gujar (2002), *In the Time of Trees and Sorrows: Nature, Power, and Memory in Rajsathan* (Durham, NC: Duke University Press).

Jhala. J. (1991), 'Marriage, Hierarchy and Identity in Ideology and Practice: An Anthropological Study of Rajput Society in Western India, against a historical background. 1090–1990 A.D.', PhD. Thesis, Harvard University.

Mayer, A.C. (1981a), 'Perceptions of Princely Rule: Perspectives From a Biography', *Contributions to Indian Sociology*, 15, 127–54.

—— (1985), 'The King's Two Thrones', *Man*, n.s. 20, 205 21

Raheja, G.G. (1988), *The Poison in the Gift: Ritual Prestation, and the Dominant Caste in a North Indian Village* (Chicago: University of Chicago Press).

Ramusack, D. (1994), 'Tourism and Icons: The Packaging of Princely States in Rajasthan', in *Perceptions of South Asia's Visual Past*, C.B. Asher and T.R. Metcalf (eds.) (New Delhi: Oxford & IBH Publishing Co).

Srinivas, M.N. (1987), *The Dominant Caste and Other Essays* (Delhi: Oxford University Press).

Sugich, M. (1992), *Palaces of India: a Travellers Companion Featuring the Palace Hotels* (London: Pavilion).

Part 3
Tourism and Spiritual Spaces

Introduction to Part 3

Carol E. Henderson and Maxine Weisgrau

Visitors are generally welcome at nearly all spiritual sites in India, whether these are tiny local shrines, or great religious complexes. Tourists will find themselves advised in nearly all cases, like all visitors, to remove their shoes, and in some cases, for women and occasionally, men, to cover their heads. The observant and sensitive tourist will notice that it is a very good idea to present oneself at the shrine freshly bathed and clothed in crisp clean clothes – as will be many of the persons arriving there for purposes of worship: bare feet and cleanliness signal respect for this sacred place's ritual purity. Sometimes there will be guides eager to conduct the visitor about the shrine. The visitor may also notice mendicants, to whom giving is an act of piety and good luck; vendors selling auspicious bags of sweets or special foods to be presented to the deity; and a special schedule for viewing of the deity or the saint's space.

India's diverse religious spaces have long drawn visitors, pilgrims, devotees, and tourists. Many Westerners firmly – and wrongly – believe that in India, 'everything is religious' – by which they mean religion is the preeminent, if not sole, motivation for human behaviour. Others believe that somehow Indian religion possesses all the characteristics that they feel are absent or underemphasized in Western religious practice. The view of India as a repository of religion, with important historical monuments associated with it, motivates many tourists. Great movements of Western tourism, such as the 1960s youth fad for travel to India as spiritual seekers – spearheaded by the Beatles' highly publicized visit – have been inspired in part by the vision of India's all-pervasive spirituality. Simultaneously, persons of faith travel within and to India in order to visit shrines, to fulfil personal vows, or to mark significant life events: the birth of a child, a marriage, or a death.

Today religion in India is enacted in part within the frameworks of globalization of communication networks, conservative identity politics, and the rise of new wealth. The chapters in this section take the reader inside temples and saint's complexes along with pilgrims from far and not-so-far places. We meet local people and supporters of these sites. We emphasize, however, that this section's discussions of religious sites is embedded within a much larger societal context. Religion rises importantly in questions of heritage: though this might seem a self-evident relationship, these chapters document how members of various groups present and position their religious resources. These chapters all discuss how religious identity interacts with other forms of identity in religious settings, especially if one of the key issues in a religious site also involves the management of visitors whose primary interests are less devotional than historical and architectural.

Cort unpacks the diverse constituencies of a temple complex at Osian, located in the Rajasthan desert north of Jodhpur. This diversity is an important characteristic of religious sites: that there will be different groups simultaneously present within a site, focused on different elements and different deities within the complex. Some groups live near by; others, including the tourists, most likely come from farther afield. Perception that a deity or saint associated with a religious space is actively engaged and helping all those who come to the shrine, despite their religious affiliation, expands its constituency.

A site's appeal to these different constituencies affects its governance. Usually, there is a board or a committee that oversees the maintenance of the site, sometimes local, and sometimes located where members of the community live and work. For example, the Jain temple complex of Ranakpur in central Rajasthan, a major tourist destination for all visitors to the area around Udaipur, is managed in part by a temple trust located in Ahmedabad, Gujarat, several hundred miles away. Different constituencies may also support special events, such as a fund for a festival associated with the site, or construction and renovation of specific spaces within the complex. When a constituency gains wealth, endowments rise. Individual status display focuses on donations, volunteer work, and sponsorship of important ritual occasions. Here, any discourse of heritage blends with personal and local-regional sociopolitical ties.

Tourist arrivals at Osian are few in number and are not separately tabulated in statistics compiled by the Government of Rajasthan. Osian is usually a stop for travellers who are en route, by car, from Jodhpur to Jaisalmer. Efforts to promote the site have focused on creation of a 'camel camp' which treats tourists to camel rides and scenic vistas of the temples. In contrast to the devotees and pilgrims' interests in the religious life of the temples and shrines, tourism marketing of Osian emphasizes that this is a historical site. Marketing points tourists' attention toward the oldest temples as archaeological relics of the past.

Sanyal shows how the great shrine of a Sufi saint – also attracting multiple constituencies – has been represented over time, and how today the shrine constructs its appeal as an ecumenical centre welcoming Muslims from around the world, as well as people of all faiths. The history of this shrine, as Sanyal shows, illustrates the distinct characteristics of Indian Islam and its evolving relationship with regional and local cultural religious sensibilities. This documentation challenges many of the stereotypes associated with Muslim religious sites both in India and abroad. Sanyal traces shifting representations of the shrine over time and shows how its political relationships evolved through the Mughal period, when it was patronized by rulers, to the present day, when it reckons with the rise of Hindu fundamentalist political movements. The current challenges to Muslim minorities within India pose particular issues for the shrine's managers, who must mediate the interests of these quite distinct interest groups. Rather than seeking identity as a specific heritage interest such as

Indian Sufism, these mediators emphasize universal, general religious values and ecumenicalism at the shrine of the saint as its distinctive heritage contribution.

Joseph's paper examines what happens when one of the multiple constituencies (foreign tourists) of a religious site is accused of transgressions. The site in question, Pushkar, is holy to Hindus as the focus of local pilgrimage cycles, and as a central location within the great traditions of Hinduism, particularly associated with the god Brahma. Almost twenty times as many domestic tourists and pilgrims come to Pushkar as do foreign tourists, but anti-tourism discourse here has focused on a small subgroup of foreigners whose sexual behaviour threatens the sacred purity of the site. Religious leaders in Pushkar are responding to global pressures, as the Indian economy expands and encourages more foreign tourism. But local reactions to tourism also include the conservative voices of various factions among the Hindu nationalist political parties which have made strong showings in recent elections in Rajasthan.

Pushkar reflects global, national, and local pressures. Growing numbers of tourist visits encourage efforts of groups previously uninvolved in tourism entrepreneurship in Pushkar to enter the industry. This sparks resistance by those already dominating the industry, resistance that is articulated in both political and religious discourses. Improvement of the national highway linking Jaipur and Ajmer, just around the corner from Pushkar, has cut travel times and improved access, as will the planned construction of a regional airport here. Although Pushkar's rather substantial (one out of five residents) Scheduled Caste (former untouchable) community is not usually heard from in tourist discourse, this group's potential as a voting bloc – not to mention that Pushkar and Ajmer are linked within a larger district administration (Ajmer) dilutes the possibilities of sustaining the tourism monopoly of its dominant community. Thus, there are many cross-cutting claims of legitimacy and illegitimacy linked to visions of Pushkar; these conflicts, however, are submerged within the dominant rhetoric focused on 'foreign' (i.e., Western) tourist transgressions of ritual purity, gender norms, and sexuality.

Foreign tourists, for their part, may imagine that they are behaving in accordance with local values, including sexual behaviours and nudity. In fact, Pushkar's local culture frowns on all public displays of nudity and physical contact. The focus on the behaviour of foreigners comes to be a metaphor for the Pushkar community's own engagement with changing social mores and the shifting ideas of religion, family, and politics, here and in the local, regional, and national discourses of Indian heritage.

Chapter 9

Devotees, Families and Tourists: Pilgrims and Shrines in Rajasthan

John E. Cort

Religious shrines are among the many places tourists visit, for temples, mosques, cathedrals, and other religious sites are among the most significant creations of any culture.[1] Tourists come to a religious shrine to encounter history, to gaze at its architecture and sculpture, and to snap photographs, which they take away as mementos. The shrine may be of spiritual importance to a tourist, but just as likely it is not. On occasion, tourists will encounter people for whom the shrine is spiritually important. Some of these will be local inhabitants. Others have come from the surrounding region, perhaps a half-day's or a day's journey distant from their homes. Others will be pilgrims who have come from a considerable distance to visit the shrine (Gold 1988, 135).

In this essay, I explore some of the ways in which multiple visions cluster around the pilgrimage site of Osian, some forty-five kilometres north of Jodhpur city. Osian (also spelled Osiya) and its environs, with a 2001 population of around 20,000, is a bustling small town in an area that has seen significant economic growth in recent years. It is well-known to historians for a dozen temples dating from the late seventh through the twelfth centuries. The two most important temples have been in nearly continuous use since the mid-eighth century. The one dedicated to the Hindu goddess Sachchiya (also known as Sachchika) is fast becoming one of the most important pilgrimage temples in all of Rajasthan. The other is dedicated to the Jain Tirthankar ('congregation founder') or Jina ('spiritual conqueror') Mahavir, who according to Jain cosmology is the twenty-fourth and final enlightened and liberated teacher of this era. Other temples in Osian are in ruins, and have been so for hundreds of years, although some of them have seen periodic use and reuse.

---

1 The research was conducted in 1995–1999 under the auspices of a Senior Collaborative Grant from the J. Paul Getty Trust and, in Jaipur, in collaboration with the Institute for Rajasthan Studies. Lawrence A. Babb, an anthropologist and Michael W. Meister, an art historian and myself conducted the research. In addition to studying the site at Osian, we conducted research at Khed, near Balotra in Barmer District, and Dadhimati, east of Nagaur in the district of that name. We appreciate the enthusiastic support of the late Professor Rajendra Joshi of the Institute for Rajasthan Studies. Responsibility for any errors in presentation or interpretation lies with me alone. For more on this project, see Meister (ed.) (2000), and Babb, Joshi and Meister (eds.) (1998).

India has many temple complexes that have survived for hundreds of years as living entities. Others have fallen into disuse and then been recovered as religious sites. Yet others have been abandoned, have become archaeological sites, and have been managed as such by the Archaeological Survey of India or state-level archaeological departments. Governmental archaeological oversight can include the creation of tourist facilities, especially in Rajasthan where the state archaeological agency is under the department of tourism. Some archaeological sites have once again become the focus of religious veneration and shifted to the control of a religious board or trust. Religious sites are continuously renovated and recreated, as devotees mark a deity's increased presence with new and finer trappings, subsidiary shrines, and better facilities for visitors. At many sites, tourists mingle with worshippers (see chapter by Sanyal), and this may create interesting differences in the perception of sites.

My collaborators and I were interested in understanding why some temples survive as functioning entities for many centuries. Scholars often know why a temple was built. The sponsor may have left an inscription detailing his (or more rarely her) intentions, or there may be a narrative text telling the story of the temple. But these founding intentions rarely, if ever, account for a temple's survival for more than a generation or two. For this to happen, people must have an ongoing relationship (or relationships) with the deity (or deities) residing in the temple.

At Osian, tourists are aware of the Sachchiya and Jain temples, for these are the ones to which tourist guides and taxi drivers will take them. The tourists might notice the smaller, ruined temples on either side of the road as they enter Osian, but many guides omit these temples from their tours. Tourists also might be aware of a nearby camel camp that caters to them. What they are less likely to know is that Osian draws distinct religious constituencies with diverse social relationships to the deities present here.

One reason the temple complexes at Osian have survived is that there are multiple constituencies that patronize them, and as a result there are multiple, often overlapping, uses and visions of the temples. As will be seen, at Osian the practices of tourists and pilgrims overlap. At one temple, the pilgrim arrives for a specific religious purpose. At another, within the same complex, she or he is there for aesthetic enjoyment in company with the non-local tourist. One of the two main Osian temples discussed here is a shrine of the goddess Sachchiya, whose iconography indicates that she is a manifestation of the pan-Indian Hindu goddess Durga. She also receives attention from Jains, whose religious doctrine of salvation is distinct from that of Hindus (Babb 1996, Cort 2001, Dundas 2002). The second of the two temples featured in this chapter is the temple of a Jain enlightened teacher. While only Jains worship Mahavir, some Hindus worship other deities in the temple compound. In addition, this is the temple in Osian that tourists visit most frequently.

This blurring of religious boundaries is not a matter of great import to worshippers at these temple complexes. Deities may speak to individuals of any religious background, and individuals of any religion may come to the deity for help. In Rajasthan, the social and ritual subcultures of Hindus and Jains significantly overlap, as members of the two groups intermarry, interdine, and share many other aspects of life (see Cort 2001, Dundas 2002). This shared subculture is prominent in the case of devotion to Sachchiya, as devotion to her comprises part of a complex of ancestor veneration and family ritual that is broadly understood and participated in by members of all religious groups in this region of Rajasthan.

Although the bulk of our research focused on religious personnel, local devotees, and pilgrims at Osian, my collaborators and I were also aware of the attraction of the temples for tourists. We used a variety of methods in our research: mapping the temples; transcribing and translating inscriptions; reading relevant Hindi, Sanskrit, Gujarati, and English literature; conducting interviews with trustees, priests, and other employees; observing and documenting rituals; and engaging in conversation with pilgrims.

I begin this chapter with a consideration of the concept of the diverse constituencies of the Osian temple complexes. Next, I examine three dimensions of practice that, broadly constituted, encompass the temples' constituencies and their motivations, and also denote three modes of a deity's identity: as a family protector, as protector of place, and as a personally adored deity. Finally, I look briefly at Jain patterns of pilgrimage in western India, to see why some shrines are more popular than others. Each of these subjects could be the focus of an extended discussion, touching as they do on complex issues relating to religious belief and practice in western India. Space does not permit such a discussion; however, in this chapter I aim to identify the multiple interactions, beliefs and practices at a site shared by pilgrims and tourists.

Multiple Meanings, Multiple Intentions

Given the multiplicity of temples, deities, pilgrims, and intentions associated with any pilgrimage shrine, it can be seen as a locus of complex linkages and disjunctions. Multiple intentions mean that there are multiple relationships between humans and deities expressed in a single shrine. A pilgrimage shrine therefore does not have a single 'meaning.' Most temples are also homes to more than one deity, which further distinguishes the experience of one pilgrim from another.

In the temple, there is the main deity in the central sanctum, after whom the temple is usually named. There are other deities, often numbering in the dozens. They reside both on the central altar and subsidiary altars. Many shrines attract subsidiary temples. Some of these are newly built to share in the glory of the main temple. Others are older nearby temples that are pulled into the orbit of the sacred power of the shrine. A pilgrimage shrine thus is a sacred complex, an elaborate network of shrines and sub-shrines (Vidyarthi 1978; Vidyarthi, Saraswati and Jha 1979; Vidyarthi and Jha 1974).

A similar multiplicity characterizes those who visit the temple complex. Some visitors travel a great distance to arrive at the shrine; many go only once in a lifetime. Some live in the region, a day's bus trip away. Others live nearby and visit the temple daily. For the first of these visitors, experience of Osian's sacred character is out of the ordinary; for the latter, of something familiar. Individuals travelling from different far places will have different experiences, depending on their mode of travel, origin, and itinerary. Today, an increasing number of pilgrims come from overseas. As will be seen, a multiplicity of experience also characterizes those who live nearby.

Not all of these visitors' relationships with the temple complex (or with individual deities within the complex) are the same. Tourists' relationships with the deity probably are the least complex: they come to admire, to learn, perhaps to have a brief sense of encountering something sacred. Pilgrim expectations include diverse goals and motivations. Pilgrims come to a shrine that is holy for a special reason: it is the site of a special image or icon, a sacred relic, or where an important event occurred. The pilgrim comes to a pilgrimage shrine to partake of direct access to something that is holy. Many pilgrims have a special personal relationship with a deity who resides in that temple in the form of an image.

People go on pilgrimage for different reasons, sometimes more than one reason.[2] Pilgrims go to different circles of shrines at any one pilgrimage site, and have differing relationships with the deities there. Does a pilgrim have a relationship with one, a few, or all of these deities? Does a pilgrim come every time to fulfil a relationship with the same deity, or on different visits does a pilgrim interact with different deities? Are the pilgrims' intentions uniform, or do they vary? If the intentions are variable, what factors shape them? Do intentions also vary for these different groups of pilgrims, local, regional, and distant?

In discussions that my collaborators and I held with pilgrims, trustees, and temple priests, three key concepts emerged by which they explained the differences among deities at Osian. Some deities are *kul devata* (family lineage deities), specific to a particular social group, usually defined as an entire *jati* (caste group) or as a *gotra*, a subunit within a jati that is a patriclan (a group based on stipulated descent through the male line). As a kul devata or, usually, *kul devi* (family lineage goddess), the deity has a special role in the history and identity of the kin group. Members of the group worship the deity in the context of life-cycle rituals, especially marriage and birth. The family lineage deity protects members of the group and pays special attention to their needs; on occasion, the deity may appear in a dream to a member of the group to warn of danger, or to provide advice (Harlan 1992).

Some deities are *sthaniya devata* (place deities) who are specific to a place. They guard those who live there and who, by consuming the water and products of the soil, share in the special sacred characteristics associated with the place and its deity. Place deity names are often synonymous with the place, as in the Osiya Mother Goddess (*Osiya Mata*), the Bheru of Osiya (*Osiya ka Bheru*), and the Mahavir Who Adorns Osiya (*Osiya-Mandan Mahavir*). Most, if not all, people who reside in the

---

2   On pilgrimage in general, see Turner 1973, Turner and Turner 1978, and Stoddard and Morinis 1997. Llewellyn 1998 provides an overview of recent literature on Hindu pilgrimage. Gold 1988 remains the best single study of pilgrimage in Rajasthan.

place worship these deities on specific annual occasions as part of a relationship of mutual residence.

Some deities are *aradhya devata* (adored deities). A relationship of adoration (*aradhana*) provides special meaning and spiritual sustenance in the lives of their devotees. Individuals believe that they can initiate such a personal relationship. Alternatively, the deity appears to the individual in a dream or a vision and establishes a unique relationship of help and devotion. Worship of a personally adored deity can occur whenever the devotee feels a need or a calling to reconfirm the relationship. One might visit the temple of the personally adored deity to give thanks for a special boon given, for instance.

Attachments to Family Lineage Deities

Traditionally almost all Hindu and Jain families in western India had a relationship with a family lineage deity who was understood to be their protector or progenitor. In most cases this deity was a goddess. Some family lineage deities are specific to only one group, but most, such as Sachchiya, have multiple groups for whom they are the family lineage deity. In addition to lineage deities, specific families often also revere ancestral figures, such as deceased heroic ancestors (Harlan 2003). Often, in the local context, other groups, who do not claim them as lineage deities, also revere a lineage deity or a family's deceased heroic ancestral figure as a place guardian. In the local context, the category of lineage deity may shade over into that of place deity. Some of the rituals directed to lineage deities also may be performed in the context of revering a place deity.

Sachchiya is the family deity for several Hindu groups, including lineages of Jats, Rajputs, Bhojaks, Maheshvaris, and others. Of particular note in Osian is Sachchiya's role as kul devi for groups of the Jain Oswal (also transliterated Osval) caste. Inscriptional evidence indicates that Sachchiya has been the lineage goddess for some Oswal patriclans since at least 1315 A.D. (Handa 1984,7).

Oswals comprise one of the largest castes of Jains in western India. Jains from northern Rajasthan to southern Gujarat identify themselves as Oswals on the basis of beliefs in a shared descent from a common ancestor (Singh 1990, 128). Historically, Oswal Jains are one of the principal trading castes of western India (Babb 1996, 2004; Cort 2004). Like most other Jains, Oswals tend to be well-educated, urban professionals. Many have received an English-medium education, and are well travelled as a consequence of their educational and business commitments. Members of several Oswal patriclans from the Shekhawati region of northern Rajasthan recently have become the most important devotees of Sachchiya. Oswals from towns in southern Rajasthan, such as Sirohi, Balotra and Bhinmal, make up the second largest group of donors, according to the inscriptions at the Sachchiya temple complex. Oswal visitors at Osian range from pilgrims who have come from great distances, to those who live in nearby regions of Rajasthan, although there have been no Oswals resident in Osian itself for many centuries (Babb 1996, 153).

A second prominent group that claims Sachchiya as lineage goddess are the Bhati (also spelled Bhatti) Rajputs. They are the former rulers of Osian, on feudal estates granted to them by the Maharaja of Jodhpur (see chapter by Jhala). The founder of the Osian branch brought Sachchiya (his lineage goddess) from Jaisalmer to Osian when he was given the feudal estate of Osian. Bhati Rajputs who view Osian as their native place – even if they live far away – worship Sachchiya as their lineage goddess. They also worship her as their place goddess, if their families still reside in this area. In Osian, they are likely to be engaged in commerce, farming, or tourism-related entrepreneurship.

The Jats are a third important group that claims Sachchiya as their lineage goddess. Members of this caste group are widespread in rural areas of Rajasthan where their traditional identity is as farmers. Jats are likely to be among the local and regional pilgrims who revere Sachchiya as their lineage goddess. Other groups who view Sachchiya as their lineage goddess are also likely to be local, or from nearby.

As a lineage deity, Sachchiya receives specific rituals that emphasize the special relationship between a family and the deity, such as births and weddings. Both events involve the introduction of new members of the lineage group to Sachchiya. In the tonsure ritual, a family introduces its young sons to Sachchiya, and in 'giving *jat*' – a term that in Rajasthani and Hindi is etymologically unrelated to the caste name 'Jat' – the bride and groom seek her blessings. The tonsure ritual is carried out only in the context of worship of a lineage deity, but the ritual of giving jat may also be performed for lineage deities and for deities of place.

A corner of the Sachchiya temple compound is reserved for tonsuring. On busy days, there is a crowd of barbers in the area, and hair clippings are strewn about the compound floor. The specifics of the ritual vary from family to family, but there is a basic order common to all. The barber shaves all the hair on the child's head. The family makes cash payment to the barber, ranging from several rupees for poor peasants to several hundred rupees for wealthy businessmen. The family then offers sweets, coconuts, and flowers to the goddess, part of which is received back as *prasad* (offerings which have received the deity's blessing). The priest at the main altar places an auspicious sandalwood paste mark on the child's shaved head. The barber is responsible for disposing of the cut hair, although some peasants keep a small amount of it for offerings at other shrines.

In giving jat, a newlywed couple presents themselves to the goddess for her to witness the sacred transformation in the couple's status upon marriage. The bride and groom wear tinsel crowns to appear as a princess and prince. The groom wears a prominent turban, and the bride wears her wedding outfit. One end of the bride's sari or blouse is tied to the end of the groom's turban, as in the wedding ceremony.

A barber guides most couples through the rite. Some couples purchase 125 coconuts outside the temple to present as an offering, because one-and-a-quarter is an auspicious number, signifying open-endedness and therefore a continued flow of worldly well-being. As the party walks up the steps of the hill to the temple, one barber makes an auspicious red dot on each step, and another barber places a coconut on the dot. As soon as the couple has passed each step, a third barber

Figure 9.1   **Bride and groom (kneeling) accompanied by groom's relatives, 'giving jat' at the Bheru shrine attached to the Mahavira temple, Osian.** *Photo courtesy of John E. Cort. All rights reserved.*

grabs the coconut, places it in a burlap bag, and later resells the coconuts to the original vendor. Finally, the couple approaches the deity and makes their offering. The central act of worship consists of the sacred dynamic viewing, or *darshan*, of the deity. Hindus understand this act to be as much a case of the deity viewing the human worshipper as the humans viewing the deity (Eck 1998). Worshippers also may offer flowers, sweet foodstuffs, and incense, and perform a fire ritual, known as *arati,* with a small lamp in front of the deity.

In many cases, the family both gives jat and performs the tonsure rites in one visit. The couple gives jat to the goddess and then performs the tonsure of one or more young sons who are the fruit of the marriage. Oftentimes these life-cycle rites are performed in the context of a pilgrimage to Ramdevra, site of the tomb of a deified medieval Rajput who was the founder of an important syncretic Hindu-Muslim cult in western Rajasthan, for Ram Dev's shrine is only a few miles up the road from Osian (Binford and Camerini 1974; Khan 1997; and Kothari 1982, 17–18).

Attachments to Deities who Protect a Place and its People

For people who reside in and around Osian, Sachchiya is *their* goddess. In the words of some informants, she is the *sthaniya devi*, the 'place goddess', or Osiya Mata, 'The Mother Goddess of Osian.' Some locals visit Sachchiya daily. Most attend her on the occasions of the *Navratri* (Nine Nights) festivals that occur in the spring and fall. These festivals draw the largest number of participants during the year to any single event.

Pilgrims to Sachchiya circumambulate the main shrine, stopping briefly to bow to the three goddesses enshrined in the outer niches of the shrine: Shitala (a goddess concerned with the well-being of children and of diseases of children, such as chicken pox), Sachchiya, and Chamunda (a fierce form of Durga). Many also worship the images of Bheru and Ganesh located in niches on either side of the sanctum. Pilgrims next proceed to other deities in shrines in the vicinity of the main sanctum, particularly Ganesh, Shiva, Surya, and the twinned images of Lakshmi-Narayan.[3] Pilgrims who have come from afar to give jat to Sachchiya usually stop at this point. But for locals, Sachchiya is merely one of a circuit of deities to whom jat is given. Each patriclan and family has its own circuit of place-specific deities to whom jat is given. Sachchiya may or not be included as their lineage goddess. In addition to the lineage goddess, local couples give jat to the local place deities. This custom is highly family-specific.

Two Bhati Rajput informants told us different circuits of place deities to whom jat is given. One informant, for whom the family's royal Jaisalmer roots were important, said that in addition to giving jat to Sachchiya in Osian, his family also gives jat in Jaisalmer. In Osian, his family gives jat at the shrine of a deified heroic ancestor named Pratap Singh. According to this informant, Pratap Singh was a nineteenth-century Robin Hood, who robbed from the rich and gave to the poor, and was killed in an encounter with policemen from Jodhpur State (see also Harlan 2003, 158–63).

The second Rajput informant, head of Osian's other big landholding family and a member of the Sachchiya temple trust, said that in his family couples give jat at two other shrines besides that of Sachchiya. One of these is in a small garden near the Jain temple. Each one of three marble plaques depicts a sword-bearing hero riding a horse. These are memorial images to *bhomiya*s, deceased heroic ancestors. A sign outside the garden identifies the principal deity, our informant's ancestor, as Jhunjhar Singhji Dadosa ('heroic ancestor and honoured grandfather Singh').[4]

The other place deity shrine mentioned by this informant was that of the most important Bheru in Osian, Roivale Bheru or 'Desert Bheru.' A bheru is a masculine deity who guards the village (Harlan 2003, 16, 35). There is a strong relationship between a bheru and the goddess. Every goddess has a bheru who assists her, and almost every bheru is associated with a goddess (Gold 1988, Harlan 2003, 135–48

---

3   These deities are, in order: the elephant-headed god, who presides over beginnings and transitions; the pan-Indian ascetic and renunciatory deity; the sun deity; and Lakshmi, goddess of prosperity, paired with Narayan, another name of the pan-Indian deity Vishnu, lord of order.

4   See Gold 1988, 64–79, Harlan 1992, 197–99 and 2003, and Kothari 1982, 13. Etymologically the term *bhomiya* is closely related to *bhumi*, land, and denotes this local deity's special connection to the land he defended.

and 197–204). Thus, Osian's chief bheru is also sometimes called Sachchiya ka Bheru (Sachchiya's Bheru).

There are two shrines of this bheru in Osian. One is on the side of the Jain Mahavir temple, and the other is several miles north of town. Together, these two images make up the totality of the deity, for bheru images are frequently bilocational in Rajasthan. One aspect of this deity is worshipped in one place, its other aspect worshiped in a second location – usually in the form of a *Gora* (Light) Bheru and a *Kala* (Dark) Bheru. Osian's Light Bheru, located within the residential area, receives vegetarian offerings. The Dark Bheru located outside the inhabited area, receives meat and liquor offerings.

Rajputs, and some other higher-caste informants, go only to the image at the Mahavir temple[5]. This image of Roivale Bheru receives vegetarian offerings of flowers, coconut, incense, and vermillion paste, in line with the Jain ethical imperative of *ahimsa*, non-harm to any living being. People sometimes offer a lock of the boy's hair at the time of the tonsure ritual. The image outside of town of the Dark Bheru, in an unpretentious brick structure built fairly recently, receives offerings of goats and liquor. Several informants said that one should make half of one's offerings at each location. Since meat and liquor obviously cannot be offered within a Jain complex, this requirement is met by splitting one's monetary offerings in half.

The Bhojaks are another group with ties to multiple deities at Osian. They are the hereditary priests of both the Sachchiya and Mahavir temples. Bhojaks give jat to several deities at the time of marriage: Sachchiya, Roivale Bheru and Mundhiyar, another goddess whose image is located in the main sanctum of Sachchiya. Mundhiyar is the lineage goddess of the patriclan of the majority of Osian Bhojaks. Other Bhojak patriclans honour Pipla Mata in this way, whose modern image is found in an ancient temple near the Mahavir temple. Still others worship Bayosa Mata ('Revered Little Girl [sister] Mother'), a manifestation of the pan-Indian Seven Sisters goddess (Harlan 1992, 82–83 and Kothari 1982, 26–27), whose small shrine is a simple, recently constructed brick structure on a small hillock just outside Osian.

Bayosa Mata's shrine also houses two images of Bheru. In a small wall niche inside the shrine, is a Bheru stone. Bhojaks and other high and middle ranking caste groups give jat to Bayosa and to this bheru. Outside the shrine is another bheru stone, to which members of nonvegetarian castes offer liquor and goats. At Osian, two other male deities also receive jat from some Bhojaks: Guga or Goga, a snake deity (see Blackburn et al.1989, 224–27, Khan 1997, 232–33, Kothari 1982, 18, and Lapoint 1978); and a bhomiya, also called a Dadosa ('Honoured Grandfather'). Guga's shrine in Osian is one of the early temples important to archaeologists and art historians and labelled by them as 'Vishnu Temple Number 1', but in recent

---

5   There is also a second image of this bheru located immediately outside the temple, where, prior to legal reform, members of Scheduled Caste groups had to worship this deity, as they were not permitted inside the temple precincts. While a few individuals still worship the aniconic plain stone outside the temple as bheru, all may enter to worship the image inside the compound.

years reclaimed for this other deity. Inside this temple is a plaque of the dog-headed serpent deity.

The Dadosa is specific to the Bhojaks. His shrine is on the side of the hill on which the Sachchiya temple is located, in an area formerly inhabited by Bhojaks. There are two images here, which depict the Dadosa as a man holding a sword in his downturned right hand and a flower garland in his upturned left hand.

Whereas Jains, Rajputs, and Bhojaks rank high in the local hierarchy of castes, Nayaks, a fourth group that worships in Osian, are a Scheduled Caste of Rajasthan.[6] Previously they gave jat to Sachchiya at an old pillar outside the entrance to the temple, not to the main image, for they were forbidden to enter the temple. Many still give jat here, for the image retains sacred power. Nayaks also give jat at Roivale Bheru, at the Guga shrine, and at a nearby Nayak bhomiya.

These surveys of the circles of deities to whom members of these four caste groups give jat by no means exhaust the list of deities who reside in Osian. Depending on one's group, need, and inclination, other deities situated here include (but are not limited to) the goddess Shitala, traditionally the goddess of smallpox and of diseases of the skin (Gold 1994,46, 62–63); Gangaur, a form of Shiva's consort Parvati who is associated with marital happiness (Erdman 1985, 165–81); and the Nine Durgas, different forms of Durga venerated on each of her Nine Nights festivals (Coburn 1991 and Slusser 1999), located in a set of temples currently under construction on the hill surrounding the Sachchiya temple. Among the many old and only occasionally visited temples on the plain is one that has been reclaimed as a temple to the god Shiva. There is a temple of Lakshmi-Narayan, home to a medieval image, located on the main alley running between the Mahavir and Sachchiya temple complexes. On a nearby hill there is also a Jain shrine known as a *dadabari* (literally 'grandfather's garden') that contains footprint images of two medieval monks, but this appears to be visited only by the officiant of the Mahavir temple (Handa 1984, 199 and 224; Babb 1996 and 2000; Cort 2000).

Personal Attachments to Deities for Protection and Help

My collaborators and I were surprised to find that the most prominent pilgrims to the Sachchiya temple to receive the blessings of the goddess as an adored deity are Oswals from the Shekhawati region who belong to the Terapanthi Jain sect. Terapanthis generally do not perform the tonsure ritual, nor do many of them come to Sachchiya to give jat as one would to a lineage or a place deity. The Terapanthi sect within the Shvetambar division of Jainism is the smallest of the Jain sects, and it is made up almost entirely of Rajasthani Oswals.[7] Terapanthis reject the worship of Jina images

---

6   Rajasthani Nayaks differ from the middle-caste Nayaks of Gujarat, a caste of musicians and actors who intermarry with Gujarati Bhojaks.

7   Jainism divides into the major Shvetambar and Digambar sects. Shvetamber Jains further subdivide into the image-worshipping Murtipujaks and the iconoclastic Sthanakvasis and Terapanthis.

in temples and many other aspects of the ritual cultures of the Shvetambar Murtipujak Jains. The Murtipujaks ('Image Worshippers'), in contrast, venerate images as part of their religious ritual. Under the leadership of the late Acharya Tulsi (1913–1997), the Terapanthi sect has grown and been quite successful in adapting its ethics and metaphysics to the demands of modernity (Flügel 1995–96; Vallely 2002).

Over the past several decades, members of the Terapanthi sect have financed extensive construction at Sachchiya's temple complex. The executive president of the temple trust, which manages the property, is a Terapanthi Oswal with business interests in Jaipur and Calcutta. In an interview, he said, with little hyperbole, that contemporary financial patronage of Sachchiya is almost exclusively undertaken by Terapanthi Oswals. Many businessmen from this community have made Sachchiya a partner in their firms, so that she receives two, five or even ten percent of the firms' profits in recognition of her contribution to their success.

This same man said that his community's devotion to Sachchiya dates from only about 1970. While most Oswals venerate other lineage goddesses, two patriclans of Shekhawati Oswals claim Sachchiya as their lineage goddess. A series of miraculous cures occurred three decades ago and all were credited to Sachchiya. As word of these cures spread, devotion to Sachchiya expanded from these patriclans to others in the Oswal community.

How is it that members of this sect have taken so wholeheartedly to Sachchiya as a personally adored goddess, even though this seemingly contradicts their sect's teachings? Under the charismatic leadership of Acharya Tulsi and his long-time heir-designate Acharya Mahaprajna, many Terapanthi lay members have imbibed the basic ideology that engagement in Jain ritual is fruitless unless solely dedicated to liberation (*moksh*). Unlike other Jain sects, in which religious activities can both advance one toward liberation and increase one's worldly well-being (Cort 2001), Terapanthi ideology holds that any ritual action done with the slightest intention of improving one's worldly condition has no positive affect. Such actions might even harm one's pursuit of liberation.

Jains see Sachchiya and other non-liberated deities as active deities who respond directly to the petitions of the devotee. The Jina, on the other hand, is inactive and unresponsive. The many hymns Jains sing before images in temples express the goal of awakening in the devotee right faith in the Jain teachings. These teachings are symbolized by the image of the Jina, who for Jains is the only deity to be worshipped (*aradhana*) for progress along the path to liberation. A hymn dedicated to the Mahavir of Osian says that bowing to Mahavir 'will always purify your soul' and 'removes lust, anger, and ignorance from everyone.'[8]

---

8   'Hymn to Mahavir Who Adorns Osian' (Osiya Mandan Mahavir ka Stavan). This hymn is from book #687 in the collection of the Jnansundar Pustak Bhandar in Jodhpur. It has no cover or title page. It contains hymns for use in the Varddhman Jain Vidyalay, a Jain boarding school in Osian, and was published in the twenty-third year of the school, circa 1938 CE. The hymns are in standard Hindi, not the local Marwari, so I surmise that they were composed in the 1930s by a schoolmaster.

In Jain cosmology, the devotee's spiritual condition is improved as a result of a reflexive meditation upon the spiritual values embodied in the image of the Jina who, having transcended the earthly realm through liberation, is not present to receive the worshippers' petitions (Babb 1996, 174–95; Cort 2001, 93–98). The Jina has nothing to give. Worship awakens a Jain to right knowledge concerning how to act in the world, and as a result, she or he acts in a virtuous manner.

Several Terapanthis whom we interviewed about their devotion to Sachchiya quickly distinguished between religion (*dharm*), focused solely on liberation and involving rituals of meditation, asceticism, and veneration, and the engagement with powerful supernatural powers such as Sachchiya. Other deities mentioned in this context included Bheru; Ramdev; Salasar Balaji, a guardian deity in Shekhawati; and Karni Mata, a goddess whose shrine is near Bikaner. Informants also mentioned many local goddesses, including Oswal lineage goddesses, as able to act in this fashion.[9] One informant – whose adherence to the anti-temple position of the Terapanthi ideology was so strong that he did not visit the Mahavir temple – expressed this distinction in English: 'Mahavir is our religious deity, Sachchiya Mata is our family deity.'

The Terapanthi rejection of worship of Jina images, and the exiling of all rituals aimed at worldly well-being from a strictly defined Jain context, may have even helped focus Terapanthi attention upon Sachchiya. Another informant said that the Terapanthi monks used to preach against lay worship of goddesses and similar deities, but were losing devotees. Faced with the choice of worshipping a deity who can ensure wealth and health in return, or abandoning that deity, many Terapanthis chose to pursue tangible pragmatic goals in this life rather than intangible goals in a future life. In response, the mendicants have downplayed their anti-goddess rhetoric, and Terapanthis can now participate in the worship of Sachchiya wholeheartedly (Tulsi 1995, 19).

Terapanthi Oswals are conspicuous during the two annual Navratris, nine-night celebrations at the Sachchiya temple complex. At each Navratri, a different family arranges to pay for the observances, in particular the lengthy fire-sacrifice on the eighth night. For many years these families have been exclusively Terapanthi Oswals, instead of prominent Hindu families from the region.[10] So many families

---

9   The devotion evident from Terapanthi laity to their *acharyas* (revered teacher/scholar), both living and deceased, expressed both in pilgrimage and monetary donation, indicates that in spite of this ideology people feel that devotion to the acharyas helps ensure worldly well-being. Some Terapanthis on pilgrimage tours around Rajasthan mentioned Sachchiya and the 'non-Jain' deities in the same tone as their visits to the *samadhi sthals* (cremation sites) of the late Acharya Tulsi and Acharya Bhikhanji (eighteenth-century founder of the Terapanth), and the living presence of the current Acharya Mahaprajna. This is an area of Terapanthi culture that needs to be researched, as recent work on Terapanthis has focused almost exclusively upon the mendicants and the normative ideology.

10   The pattern of vegetarian groups such as the Jain merchant castes increasingly becoming prominent in shrine management over meat-eating groups, including Rajputs, is very common all over Rajasthan. See also Babb 2004:220–37.

are clamouring for the right to sponsor the observation that the temple trust is being forced to consider how to deal with this demand in an equitable manner.

Members of the sponsoring family gather in Osian from their dispersed residences in Jaipur, Delhi and elsewhere throughout India for the entire nine nights. They reserve most of the block of rooms in the pilgrim guesthouse on the hill. Every morning and evening they attend the *arati* (offering of light) to the goddess. When I observed Navratri in April 1998, a group of Oswal young men followed the daily arati by half-an-hour of vigorous singing of devotional hymns to the goddess. In these songs they asked for help and succour in their lives. There is much here that is generic to temple experience and the worship of the goddess throughout India, albeit manifested here with a distinctly mercantile flavour. The songs describe Sachchiya as 'Mother of the World' and 'Queen of the Three Worlds', who grants her devotees mercy and good fortune. They also sing, 'Dear Mother of Osian, I give twenty million rupees, the rest I deposit with you.'

Sometimes the assembled Oswal women, whose expensive silk saris and heavy gold jewellery stand out from the dress of the local peasant women, joined in the singing. There were also occasional instances of Oswal women becoming possessed, but in a more restrained fashion, compared with possession in non-Jain settings in India.

The highlight of the Navratri festival was the eighth night's grand fire sacrifice in the middle of the temple's main pavilion. Aided by a number of local priests, a married couple, who had paid for the nine days' observance, performed the sacrifice. While there is no clear evidence, we have assumed that fifty and more years ago Osian's Bhati Rajput rulers presided over the sacrifice on the eighth night. Formerly, this observance evidently involved the sacrifice of goats, and on occasion, also of a buffalo.

All this has changed with the rise of the Jain Oswals to prominence at the Sachchiya temple, although there had earlier also been pressure from resident Maheshvari merchants, the most important commercial caste group in the region, to end public animal sacrifice (which was declared illegal by the government of Rajasthan some two decades ago). Today's main sacrifice now is strictly vegetarian, although everyone admitted that there may well be privately conducted animal sacrifices to Sachchiya outside the temple complex, and so beyond the control of the temple trustees. This was underscored at the conclusion of the sacrifice, when the priests and patrons made sure that all the ingredients were offered into the fire in a final inferno, all the while loudly proclaiming '*purn ahuti, purn ahuti*', ('the sacrifice is complete') i.e., there was no additional secret offering (of animals) elsewhere.

Pilgrims and Tourists at Osian and other Jain Shrines in Western India

Osian's Mahavir Temple, unlike the others described above, draws perhaps as many tourists as pilgrims. It is a convenient stopping place for Jains on pilgrimage tours of Rajsathan. Osian's location, between the major transportation hub of Jodhpur, and Jaisalmer, with its famous Jain temples, makes this a convenient place to stop. At the

Mahavir temple, Murtipujak Jains are the biggest subgroup of Jains. The Murtipujak sect is the largest of Jain sects, and its religious belief and practice centre on temples and their Jina images.

Figure 9.2   Ranakpur temple complex is a popular tourist destination, as well as pilgrimage site of Jains, located approximately two hours drive from Udaipur. *Photo courtesy of Maxine Weisgrau.*

Jain pilgrims to the Mahavir temple may have a less clearly defined goal than at other Jain sites, such as the temples at Mount Abu and Ranakpur in southern Rajasthan with their spectacular carvings, or the five Jain temples inside the fort at Jaisalmer. Kesariyaji and Nakora, two sacred sites on Rajasthan's Jain pilgrimage itinerary, are practically unknown to tourists. Kesariyaji, in southern Rajasthan near Udaipur (and not too distant from Ranakpur) is the site of an image of the Jina Adinath, described by one pilgrim guidebook (*Tīrth Darśan* 1980:I.186) as 'beautiful, wonder-working, and fulfilling of devotees' desires.' Nakora, located in Barmer district, is the most popular Jain pilgrimage destination in Rajasthan. The devotional focus here is the wonder-working protector deity, Nakora Bheru, not the Jina image in the temple.

The Multiple Visions of Pilgrims and Tourists

One day my colleagues and I were discussing with an officiant at the Sachchiya temple the circles of deities to whom Osian residents give jat. He turned to a local man who was listening to our conversation and asked him where his family gave jat.

The man explained that he was by origin a Sikhval Brahman from Merta (a town east of Jodhpur), and his lineage goddess was Brahmani. But since he now was settled in Osian, his family gave jat according to the local traditions, and so gave to Sachchiya, Kesariya Kanwar (Guga) and Roivale Bheru. We see in this example how familial and geographical identities are intertwined.

There is also a connection between the categories of place deity and adored deity. People from afar for whom Sachchiya occupies a special place in their devotional universe will refer to her by her place-specific name, Osiya Mata. The deity's efficacy counts, too; if the Osian Mahavir were a wonder-working image, one would find his shrines elsewhere, as in the case of wonder-working Jinas such as Shankheshvar Parshvanath. His main temple is in a small village in northern Gujarat, but replication images and temples of Shankheshvar Parshvanath are found throughout western India (Cort 1988).

In India *who* one is, is very much a matter of *where* one is, not simply one's ancestors' identities (Cort 2004; Daniel 1984). Where (and therefore who) one is involves elements of both geographical and social – including kinship – location. All Hindus in Osian bear a relationship with Sachchiya, the goddess of the town, and Roivale Bheru, Sachchiya's own Bheru. The centrality of these two deities is underscored by their alternate names of Osiya Mata and Osiya ka Bheru. Each caste group in the area also has relationships with deified heroic ancestors, lineage goddesses, and other deities who are specific to that caste or even smaller social units such as patriclan and family, and who are tied up with Osian as a place.

Those who come to Osian with a religious purpose enact this purpose with the temples and deities with whom they have a relationship. At other temples here, they may visit as tourists. Tourists mingle with the devotees and pilgrims. Tourists' interests generate different patterns of travel, and result in differing levels of popularity for specific destinations. Thus tourists may outnumber pilgrims to the Jain Mahavir temple at Osian; but pilgrims clearly outnumber tourists at the Sachchiya temple complex.

I started this research by asking why Hindus and Jains in Rajasthan go on pilgrimage to Osian, and therefore what is going on at its temple complexes. The answers to these questions quickly lead to the complexities of Hindu and Jain theologies, for the answers vary according to the contextualizing factors of kinship, geography, and spiritual orientation. Multiple visions frame individuals' experiences. Rather than emphasizing fixed categories, such as lineage, place, adoration, and aesthetics, our research suggested that for Jain and Hindu pilgrims to Osian, these categories easily slide into each other. Tourists, who visit the temple complex briefly, become part of this intersection of multiple intentions, identities, and practice. Indeed, the willingness of a temple complex to tolerate the visits of tourists may rest precisely upon its capacity to absorb these multiplicities.

References

Babb, L.A. (1996), *Absent Lord: Ascetics and Kings in a Jain Ritual Culture* (Berkeley: University of California Press).

—— (2000), 'Time and Temples: On Social and Metrical Antiquity', in M. Meister, (ed.) (2000) 193–222.

—— (2004), *Alchemies of Violence: Myths of Identity and the Life of Trade in Western India* (New Delhi: Sage Publications).

Babb, L.A., V. Joshi, and M.W. Meister (eds.) (2002), *Multiple Histories: Culture and Society in the Study of Rajasthan* (Jaipur: Rawat Publications).

Binford, M.R. and M. Camerini (directors) (1974), *An Indian Pilgrimage, Ramdevra* [Documentary film] (Madison: Centre for South Asian Studies, University of Wisconsin).

Blackburn, Stuart H., P.J. Claus, J.B. Flueckiger, and S.S. Wadley (eds.) (1989), *Oral Epics in India*. (Berkeley: University of California Press).

Coburn, T.B. (1991) *Encountering the Goddess: A Translation of the Devī-Māhātmya and a Study of Its Interpretation* (Albany: State University of New York Press).

Cort, J.E. (1988), 'Pilgrimage to Shankheshvar Pārshvanāth', *Centre for the Study of World Religions Bulletin* 14:1, 63–72.

—— (2000), 'Patronage, Authority, Proprietary Rights, History: Communities and Pilgrimage Temples in Western India', in M. Meister, (ed.) (2000) 165–91.

—— (2001), *Jains in the World: Religious Values and Ideology in India* (New York: Oxford University Press).

—— (2004), 'Jains, Caste and Hierarchy in North Gujarat', in D. Gupta (ed.) *Caste in Question: Identity or Hierarchy?* (New Delhi: Sage Publications, 73–112).

Daniel, E.V. (1984), *Fluid Signs: Being a Person the Tamil Way* (Berkeley: University of California Press).

Dundas, P. (2002), *The Jains*, 2nd Edition. (London: Routledge).

Eck, D.L. (1998), *Darśan: Seeing the Divine Image in India,* 3rd Edition. (New York: Columbia University Press).

Erdman, J.L. (1985), *Patrons and Performers in Rajasthan: The Subtle Tradition* (Delhi: Chanakya).

Flügel, P. (1995–96), 'The Ritual Circle of the Terāpanth Śvetāmbara Jains', *Bulletin d'Études Indiennes* 13, 117–76.

Gold, A.G. (1988), *Fruitful Journeys: The Ways of Rajasthani Pilgrims* (Berkeley: University of California Press).

—— (1994), 'Sexuality, Fertility, and Erotic Imagination in Rajasthani Women's Songs', in Raheja and Gold (eds) (1994).

Handa, D. (1984), *Osian: History, Archaeology, Art and Architecture* (Delhi: Sundeep Prakashan).

Harlan, L. (1992), *Religion and Rajput Women: The Ethic of Protection in Contemporary Narratives* (Berkeley: University of California Press).

—— (2003), *The Goddesses' Henchmen: Gender in Indian Hero Worship*. (New York: Oxford University Press).

Khan, D. (1997), *Conversions and Shifting Identities: Ramdev Pir and the Ismailis in Rajasthan* (New Delhi: Manohar).

Kothari, K. (1982), 'The Shrine: An Expression of Social Needs', trans. Uma Anand, *Gods of the Byways: Wayside Shrines of Rajasthan, Madhya Pradesh and Gujarat* (Oxford: Museum of Modern Art, 5–31).

Lapoint, E.C. (1978), 'The Epic of Guga: A North Indian Oral Tradition', in S. Vatuk (ed.) *American Studies in the Anthropology of India* (New Delhi: Manohar, 281–308).

Llewellyn, J. E. (1998), 'The Centre Out There: A Review Article of Recent Books on Hindu Pilgrimage', *International Journal of Hindu Studies* 2, 249–65.

Meister, M.W. (1998), 'Sweetmeats or Corpses? Community, Conversion, and Sacred Places', in J.E. Cort (ed.), *Open Boundaries: Jain Communities and Cultures in Indian History* (Albany: State University of New York Press, 111–138).

—— (ed.) (2000), *Ethnography and Personhood: Notes from the Field* (Jaipur: Rawat Publications).

Raheja, G.G. and A.G. Gold (1994), *Listen to the Heron's Words: Reimagining Gender and Kinship in North India* (Berkeley: University of California Press).

Singh, H. (1990), *The Castes of Marwar*, 2nd Edition (Jodhpur: Books Treasure).

Slusser, M. (1999) 'Illustrated Folios from a *Devi Mahatmya* Manuscript', in Vidya Dehejia (ed.), *Devi: The Great Goddess: Female Divinity in South Asian Art* (Washington: Arthur M. Sackler Gallery, Smithsonian Institution, in association with Mapin Publishing, Ahmedabad, and Prestel Verlag, Munich, 226–229).

Stoddard, R.H. and A. Morinis (eds.) (1997), *Sacred Places, Sacred Spaces: The Geography of Pilgrimages* (Baton Rouge: Geoscience Publications, Department of Geography and Anthropology, Louisiana State University).

Tīrth Darśan (1980), 2 vols. (Madras: Śrī Mahāvīr Jain Kalyān Sangh).

Tulsī, Ācārya (1995), *Terāpanth aur Mūrtipūjā*. 8th printing. (Churu: Ādarś Sāhitya Sangh Prakāśan).

Turner, V. (1973), 'The Centre Out There: Pilgrims' Goal', *History of Religions* 12, 191–230.

Turner, V. and E. Turner (1978), *Image and Pilgrimage in Christian Culture: Anthropological Perspectives* (New York: Columbia University Press).

Vallely, A. (2002), *Guardians of the Transcendent: An Ethnography of a Jain Ascetic Community* (Toronto: University of Toronto Press).

Vidyarthi, L.P. (1978), *The Sacred Complex in Hindu Gaya*. 2nd Edition. (Delhi: Concept).

Vidyarthi, L.P., B.N. Saraswati, and M. Jha (1979), *The Sacred Complex of Kashi: A Microcosm of Indian Civilization* (Delhi: Concept).

Vidyarthi, L.P., and M. Jha (eds.) (1974), *Symposium on the Sacred Complex in India* (Ranchi: Council on Social and Cultural Research, Bihar).

Chapter 10

Tourists, Pilgrims and Saints: The Shrine of Mu'in al-Din Chisti of Ajmer

Usha Sanyal

If Mu'in al-Din moved to Ajmer as a new Mecca, the inner Mecca for Chishtis remains Ajmer, ... [this is so] for all – both Chishti and non-Chishti, Muslim and non-Muslim – who identify with the devotional legacy of this ancient and still vibrant brotherhood.– Carl Ernst and Bruce Lawrence, *Sufi Martyrs of Love*, 144

The city of Ajmer, which lies two hundred and thirty miles southwest of New Delhi, is known to pious Muslims as Ajmer Sharif ('Ajmer the Exalted') as if it were a person of high rank. Residents comment on the city's natural beauty and historical importance, located as it is in a valley in central Rajasthan, surrounded by hills. Above it is an eight-hundred-foot mountain topped by the historic fort Taragarh ('Star Fort'). Ajmer was a plum in the Mughal Empire, headquarters of the imperial province of that name, and later a prized possession of the British Raj, for it commanded the marches southward to the Deccan and the lucrative trade routes to the Indian Ocean and central India.

But what makes Ajmer special for Muslims – and a large number of Hindus – is neither its physical landscape nor its role in Indian history but the shrine of Mu'in al-Din Chisti, the thirteenth-century Sufi saint known to devotees as Gharib Nawaz ('one who helps the poor') or simply as Khwaja Sahib ('Lord', 'Master'). Mu'in al-Din founded the Chisti Sufi order in India, one of the largest in the subcontinent. Over the centuries, the shrine where he is buried has attracted both Muslims and Hindus in increasing numbers. Today it is the leading Muslim holy site in India. In 2001, for example, the shrine attracted between 1 and 1.5 million tourists of all religions, one-third of them during the shrine's major festival, the *'Urs* or death anniversary commemoration of the saint (India. Parliament. Rajyasabha. Joint Committee on the Functioning of Waqf Boards [IPRJC] 2002, 6). Overall attendance figures are likely only to rise, given the expansion of tourism infrastructure such as a projected airport in Ajmer, and ongoing improvements along the national highway that links Ajmer with Jaipur. In addition, the shrine's management is planning improved facilities for its guests (IPRJC 2002, 13).

Figure 10.1   Exterior view of Dargah with a group of assembled *khuddam* (religious attendants) and others bearing offerings. *Photo courtesy of Catherine B. Asher. All rights reserved*

This chapter examines the use of the Internet in bringing the shrine of Mu'in al-Din Chisti to diverse audiences.[1] Although the attention given to the *dargah* ('saint's tomb complex') on the Internet is slight, compared with that given to religious places and practices associated with Hinduism, the Dargah is beginning to have a presence on the Web. The Dargah is promoted on the Internet to both an Indian and an international audience which has little knowledge of its religious significance. Overseas interest in the shrine varies from pure 'tourism' to a deep religious interest. Some people take religious mentors or Sufi *pirs* (saints) in South Asia even though they live in a Western country. Others visit Sufi shrines in South Asia as part of a religious pilgrimage. Unlike the curious but uninformed Western tourist, they have some cultural knowledge of the shrine and of Sufism more generally, though being foreign-born and bred, they too may be visiting South Asia for the first time and experience it in some ways as 'Other.'

How the shrine markets itself on the Internet (and elsewhere) to its diverse audience will be crucial to its future expansion. It is situated in a cultural space dominated until independence by Hindu rulers and a largely Hindu population. Pushkar Lake, one of Hinduism's holiest spots, lies less than ten miles (14 km) away. Recent national politics in India and in Rajasthan especially have been marked by the rise of the Bharatiya Janata Party (BJP), with its saffron colours and overt Hindu messages and slogans. As of this writing in 2005, Rajasthan has a BJP government, even after the BJP had lost to the Congress Party at the national level in 2004. Given this background, the shrine faces substantial questions: how can it sustain its ecumenical characteristics, its ability to reach out to both Muslims *and* Hindus, which has been its hallmark for centuries? On the other hand, it also faces a different threat, namely, the need to negotiate the distance between its unique character in a world of globalizing Muslim identities that, inspired and funded by the Saudi and other states' narrow interpretations and visions of Islam, regard Sufi faith and practice as heterodox. Were the shrine to present itself as a place that was strictly 'Islamic', where non-Muslims were unwelcome, it would almost certainly suffer a loss in popularity among the many Hindus who come here. Thus it has to be multivocal, speaking to different people in different ways, satisfying many constituencies, and holding diverse interests in balance.

The paper starts with a review of the historical and cultural context of Mu'in al-Din Chisti, including the ritual calendar of the shrine. I examine several historical descriptions of the shrine over time to show how different authors have presented it to their perceived peer groups over history, and finally, I examine the presentation of the Dargah on Internet websites, first those devoted to selling tourism services, and second those aimed at visitors whose orientation is religious. The data for this paper are drawn from a variety of English and Urdu-language sources, including newspaper accounts, court records, and of course, websites.

---

1   I would like to thank Carol Henderson and Rupa Bose for their comments and suggestions for revision of this article in its earlier incarnations.

Mu'in al-Din and the Chisti Order

The life of Mu'in al-Din Chisti having been much embellished by legend, the historical facts are somewhat sketchy. He lived in the town of Chisti, in the Sijistan region of central Afghanistan (hence his name Mu'in al-Din Sijzi [Chisti]), in the late twelfth century, though he may have been born elsewhere. Having come under the influence of a Sufi master (*shaykh*) in his youth, Mu'in al-Din Chishti sold his possessions and 'went to Balkh and Samarkand [in Central Asia] to be educated' (Currie 1989, 54). Although scholars differ on when Mu'in al-Din Chisti settled in India, he appears to have been established in Ajmer (then known as Ajayameru) by the first decade of the thirteenth century.

Mu'in al-Din founded the Chisti order in India, which eventually became one of the four major Sufi orders in the country (the Qadiris, Naqshbandis, and Suhrawardis being the other three). His teachings, and those of the early Chisti Sufis, according to Currie, were the following:

> Obedience of the murid [disciple] to the murshid [master].
> Renunciation of the concerns of the material world.
> Independence from the state.
> Approval of *sama'* [literally, 'to hear', specifically to listen to religious singing ensembles].
> Strenuous personal routine of prayers and devotions.
> Dependence on either cultivation of waste-land, or unsolicited offerings.
> Disapproval of displays of miraculous powers.
> Service to others in the form of a) teaching and guidance; b) distribution of surplus food and wealth.
> Tolerance and respect for other religions. (Currie 1989, 65)

Some of these teachings were difficult to observe in practice. This was most notably the case with Mu'in al-Din's ideal of keeping his distance from the political powers of the realm and not accepting any land grants from them. This ideal was restated in the memorable words of a famous later Chisti master, Nizam al-Din Awliya (d. 1325) of Delhi, who said, 'My room has two doors; if the sultan comes through one door, I will leave by the other' (Robinson 1982, 39). The literature is replete with similar stories about other Sufis. For instance, Farid al-Din (d. 1265) of Pakistani Punjab, who is also one of the founding Chisti Sufis, is said to have 'refused land grants' and to have 'routinely [given] away all money and other gifts brought to his lodge' (Ernst and Lawrence 2002, 67). These acts, however, made the Chistis very popular among the people, which in turn made kings eager to cultivate their friendship. The Mughal emperor Akbar (d. 1605) and his successors lavished gifts on Mu'in al-Din's shrine, endowing the site with buildings, equipment, embellishments, and land income. Even after they had accepted such gifts, however, the Chistis continued to lay claim to a moral power superior to the worldly power of the rulers.

What made the Chistis so popular among the people, aside from their disdain for worldly wealth and power, were their teachings and spirituality. At their best, they lived simply, communed with God through daily prayers and meditation, attracted disciples, and helped solve the problems of those who came to them, regardless of religion. Since the sixteenth century, they have also had *langar* (a public feeding for the poor) every Thursday evening.

Figure 10.2   Pilgrims and tourists entering the shrine, which is a popular and welcoming destination for both foreign and domestic travellers of all religious backgrounds to Ajmer. *Photo courtesy of Rakesh Gupta. All rights reserved.*

Over time, the Chistis became known for certain ritual practices that distinguished them from other Sufis. The most important of these is the *sama'*, (an assembly of devotional singing for male devotees). The purpose of the singing is to aid the mystic in his concentration (*dhikr*) on God and the saint (Ernst and Lawrence 2002, 35). The result, several hours into the sama', may be a state of trance for the participant-singer, who experiences a transcendent sense of connectedness with the divine.

Not all Muslims approve of sama'. There are both Sufi and non-Sufi critics of the practice, who argue that the unitiated mystic may falsely believe he has attained, or come close to attaining, union with God while in the trance state. Sufi masters regard that this as given to the very few, if at all, and only after years of rigorous discipline and self-control. Morcover, the very goal of union with God is unacceptable to some, as it obliterates the distinction between God and man, the creator and the created. In Sufi parlance, the desire for union with God is viewed as the supreme form of spiritual 'drunkenness', which many reject in favour of strict 'sobriety.' The latter is pursued by means of close adherence to the precepts of the faith, principally through prayer, fasting, making the pilgrimage to Mecca, giving alms, and of course through impeccable moral behaviour within the framework of Shari'a (Islamic law).

Major Rituals

In the course of the year, Muslim shrines throughout the subcontinent observe a series of devotional practices. Since each Sufi shrine has a different ritual calendar, devotees may engage in a series of pilgrimages to different shrines through the year if they so choose. The major ritual event in any shrine is the *'Urs*, literally 'marriage [with God]', the death anniversary of the Sufi saint buried there. Since, over time, a shrine bears the grave not just of the original founder of the site but of several of his close successors as well, the shrine may observe several such anniversaries in a given year.

Large shrines such as Mu'in al-Din's Dargah at Ajmer are constantly full of people whose relationship to the shrine and to the Sufi master may be understood in terms of varying degrees of spiritual closeness (*qurbat*) to them (Ewing 1980). The majority of visitors come for a specific purpose such as asking for the saint's help in begetting a son, passing an exam, getting through some other difficulty in life, or maybe returning to give thanks and make a monetary donation. These visitors, spiritually speaking, are far removed from the true heart of the shrine as they have only a sporadic relationship with it. A second group, smaller than the first, is made up of people who have become disciples of one of the Sufis associated with the shrine or maybe even of the current Diwan (head of the shrine) in a simple ceremony called *bai'at*. At this ceremony, the initiate swears allegiance to the Sufi master and promises to carry out his religious duties faithfully (Eaton 1982, 54; Ernst and Lawrence 2002, 24). At some Chisti shrines, the initiation is marked by a handshake, the shaving of the initiate's head, and the presentation to him of a cloak. Boys as young as twelve are initiated at some shrines (Eaton 1982, 54). Whatever the age at which they enter into the relationship, the tie is lifelong, and the level of obedience to which they commit themselves is total.

Many aspects of the ritual activities at the shrine, whether they be formal events such as the installation of a new Diwan, or purely religious ones such as a sama', strongly resemble royal practices. Thus the symbolism of the turban, as Eaton notes, is markedly regal. 'A proper successor to Baba Farid's [a Chisti saint buried in Pakistani Punjab] shrine had to be 'crowned' with a turban representing the saint's own turban' (Eaton 1982, 57). Such associations are reinforced in other ways as well, as in the clothes worn by the Diwan during a sama'. They are patterned on the attire of a Mughal king. And the entourage that follows behind him when he arrives at the musical session resembles the courtiers who accompanied a royal person (Moini 1989, 72).

A Brief History of the Dargah, Sixteenth through the Twentieth Centuries

As noted earlier, the Dargah was patronized by Emperor Akbar and succeeding Mughal emperors. In 1567 Akbar made a dramatic display of his reverence for the saint by walking the entire distance from Agra to Ajmer on foot after winning a tough battle against the independent Rajput ruler of Mewar, south of Ajmer. He ascribed his success to the intervention of the saint. He walked the two hundred and thirty miles between his capital and Ajmer again a few years later after his first son (Salim, later Emperor Jahangir) was born, once again ascribing this happy event to the saint's intervention on his behalf. He ordered the building of the Akbari Mosque, which still stands, and most importantly, gifted one of the two large cauldrons used for the public feeding of pilgrims. This practice continues to this day.

Further construction and gifts continued under the next two emperors, including the gift of a second cauldron. Emperor Shah Jahan gave land grants to the Diwan and his helpers (the *khuddam*) for the maintenance of the complex and its ongoing expenses (Tirmizi 1989, 51–52). Shah Jahan's daughter Jahanara was a genuine devotee of the saint, praying at his tomb during his 'Urs in 1643 and describing herself as a disciple (*faqira*). She also wrote a biography of him (Ernst and Lawrence 2002, 87–89).

Meanwhile, the British East India Company was beginning to send trading ships to Indian ports and to seek the emperor's permission to engage in trade. As the Emperor Jahangir (r. 1605–1627) prepared for war against Mewar's ruler Amar Singh I, he received the first English emissary, Sir Thomas Roe, in Ajmer on 10 January, 1616. As the Mughal empire fragmented over the course of the eighteenth century, control over Ajmer switched between rival claimants. It was the Maratha ruler Daulat Rao Scindia (r. 1794–1827) who ceded Ajmer to the East India Company by treaty on 25 June, 1818. From then until 1947, Ajmer remained a British possession amidst a number of independent princely states in Rajputana, as pre-independence Rajasthan was known.

After East India Company rule in India ended in 1858 and the British Crown assumed direct control, the Deputy Commissioner decided between rival claimants to the position of chief custodian of the shrine (*sajjada nishin*) and the Religious Endowments Act of 1863 regulated the affairs of the shrine. This act devolved the powers of shrine management, including its trust properties, onto local committees rather than through the government itself, and established the right of the Trustees or interested persons to seek satisfaction in the civil courts in case of a dispute, according to the Religious Endowments Act, 1863 (IPRJC 2002, 4). After independence, the family which had been in charge of managing the shrine since 1912 migrated to Pakistan, setting off a dispute over the succession. The matter ended up in the Supreme Court, and led in 1955 to the passing of a new law, the Dargah Khwaja Sahib Act, which applied specifically to the Ajmer shrine (IPRJC 2002, 6; Ernst and Lawrence 2002, 102). Under the new law, the Dargah Committee had the authority to appoint a new Diwan, and its decisions were open to judicial review.

The Dargah's income declined with independence, as many Muslims migrated to Pakistan. Land reforms intended to benefit the peasantry reduced the shrine's traditional financial base (Baldick 1995, 280; IPRJC 2002, 9). The situation began to improve in the 1970s as a result of remittances from the Gulf, and again in the 1990s when the rapid growth of the Indian middle-class as a result of economic reforms brought new funds to the Dargah. Nevertheless, according to Ernst and Lawrence, the BJP's political ascendancy in the state has been detrimental to the shrine's interests, as that government chose to divert funds intended for infrastructural improvements to the area around the shrine to the neighbouring Hindu site of Pushkar (Ernst and Lawrence 2002, 103).

Today the Dargah Endowment's properties include the Dargah itself, nearby shops, apartments, several smaller shrines, a farm, the Dargah Guest House, and several additional religious trust properties (IPRJC 2002, 8–9). The Dargah Committee is empowered to solicit contributions and raise funds for the Dargah Endowment. In addition, there is an independent committee, namely, the Khadims' Committee, consisting of the *khuddam* or *khadims* (the hereditary religious functionaries of the shrine, who, as noted earlier, conduct pilgrims through the Dargah complex and assist them in their devotions. The two committees dispute each other's jurisdictional claims, as the khuddam want control over the monies they collect from pilgrims, rather than passing this income on to the Dargah Committee, while the latter believes it has oversight over these funds and over the khuddam as well (IPRJC 2002. 9–11).

Social Construction of the Shrine over Time

I turn now to a consideration of how the shrine has been seen and written about in three very different kinds of historical writing. They range from a seventeenth-century Muslim biographical dictionary, *Siyar al-Aqtab* ('Lives of the World-Axes'), to nineteenth-century British travel accounts, to an Urdu-language newspaper account by a devotee of Mu'in al-Din writing in the early twentieth-century. Each person's purpose in writing was different, as was of course the historical context in which he wrote. These factors are mirrored in their accounts.

The seventeenth-century source, *Siyar al-Aqtab*, was written by one Ilah Diya Chisti who lived during Emperor Shah Jahan's reign (r. 1627–58) and about whom little is known. He completed the work in 1647, or about four hundred years after the death of the saint. It contains twenty-seven Chisti biographies (Ernst and Lawrence 2002, 224), one of which is that of Mu'in al-Din. The saint was also the subject of two earlier biographies, or more properly, hagiographies, that is, biographies that give idealized portraits.

According to Currie (1989), who has studied the legends of Mu'in al-Din in great detail, the purpose of the author of the *Siyar al-Aqtab* was to show that Mu'in al-Din exemplified the early Chisti teachings (listed above) in every way. By comparing the different accounts, Currie is able to see the construction of the legend of the saint evolving over time, with each subsequent account creating ever greater, more fanciful details, of his powers. Thus the *Siyar al-Aqtab* is not an 'historical' document, though historical facts are embedded in it. Rather, its purpose was to show that Mu'in al-Din had done what the Chisti Sufis taught, namely, he had obeyed his master to the letter, had renounced personal wealth, was independent of the state, was immersed in prayer and close to God, was kind and generous to others, and so on.

There were some difficulties, however, because one of the early Chisti Sufis' ideals was to minimize the display of miraculous powers, which over time had given way to the reverse, namely, a profusion of miracles ascribed to the saint. This propensity, Ernst writes, was the result of competition with Hindu yogis, who claimed to be able to levitate, exercise breath control, and survive on very little food, among other things (Ernst 2005, 22). The *Siyar al-Aqtab* purported to show that the claims of the yogis were false, while the powers of Mu'in al-Din, although modestly hidden beneath the surface for the most part, were inspired by the one true God and could be invoked when called for by the situation.

Turning now to eighteenth- and nineteenth-century British travel accounts of Mu'in al-Din's shrine, we see that James Tod, author of the comprehensive *Annals and Antiquities of Rajast'han*, stopped at Ajmer in 1819 on his return visit from the court of Maharaja Man Singh of Jodhpur (see chapter by Freitag), but his description of the town does not mention the Dargah, or the saint. Tod only noted one small shrine near Ana Sagar Lake, where one of the saint's followers stayed, what Tod called the 'Khwaja Kootub' (Tod 1914, 613), is today identified as Chilla Qutab Shah, the shrine of disciple Khwaja Qutbuddin Bakhtiar Kaki (d.1237) (Dhoundiyal 1966, 714). Bishop Reginald Heber visited Ajmer on February 7, 1825, but could not visit the shrine due to a sandstorm. He was clearly aware of its importance, however, and recorded his Hindu servants' eagerness to visit it (Heber 1829, 26). In 1828, another contemporary British observer, Walter Hamilton, noted in the *East-India Gazetteer*, that

> [t]he principal object of attraction [in Ajmer] is the tomb of Khoja Moyen ud Deen, a renowned Mahomedan saint, to whose tomb the great and wise emperor Acber [Akbar] made a pilgrimage from Agra (230 miles) barefoot, in order to procure male progeny, in which he succeeded. Crowds of pilgrims still frequent the saint's tomb (Hamilton 1828, 28).

Finally, I discuss a third kind of source, namely, an early twentieth-century Urdu-language newspaper account from Rampur state. In June 1915, Muhammad Fazl-e Hasan Sabiri Chisti, follower of the Sabiri line of Chistis, and editor of the Urdu newspaper *Dabdaba-e Sikandari* ('Alexander's [Awesome] Majesty') in the then-independent Muslim princely state of Rampur, about three hundred miles northeast of Ajmer, wrote an article. This described his visit to the Dargah during the annual 'Urs for Mu'in al-Din Chisti (Fazl-e-Hasan Sabiri, 1915). Not only did he describe the events of the 'Urs (which I will not summarize here, as I have done so above), but he also described what he considered a miracle performed by the saint and commented bitterly on what he saw as corrupt (*be-shar'*) practices at the shrine.

This kind of writing – newspaper editorials, articles, and news reporting – was entirely different from both the hagiographical and the travel writing noted so far. It arose in the context of the spread of print technology among Indians starting in the 1880s, going beyond the narrow group of Christian missionaries who hitherto held a monopoly over this technology, using it to publish Bibles in different Indian languages for the purposes of proselytization. Beginning in the 1880s, however, Muslim religious scholars (the *'ulama*) began to own and operate their own presses. Publications of all sorts (pamphlets, newspapers, *fatwas* [juridical opinions], and so on) began to appear in urban and rural towns all over the country, often offering competing interpretations of the same events.

The intellectual context for Fazl-e Hasan's 1915 account of the 'Urs at Mu'in al-Din's Dargah was his (and his newspaper's) interest in the Muslim reform movements among the north Indian 'ulama and reformist Sufi orders. Starting in the 1880s, a number of Muslims founded educational institutions that became focal points of Islamic reform. Notably, these included the Dar al-'Ulum at Deoband in western Uttar Pradesh, the Anglo-Muhammadan Oriental College in Aligarh (later renamed Aligarh Muslim University), and the seminary of the Nadwat al-'Ulama in Lucknow. Although 'reform' was differently understood by the different groups, it included in all cases an emphasis on the study of the Qur'an and *hadith* (traditions of the Prophet), on the life of the Prophet as a model for emulation by individual Muslim men and women, a renewed commitment to observe the daily prayers, the Ramadan fast, and to be observant Muslims in general, and a commitment to be guided by the Shar'ia (see Metcalf 1982 for specifics on the many movements involved). Debate with regard to Sufism centred on its ritual practices – 'Urs and sama', for example – with some religious scholars arguing that these practices were completely impermissible, and other scholars arguing that these distinctive Sufi practices were intended to honour the Prophet and the saints, and were therefore permissible as long as these acts did not cross the bounds of the Shar'ia.

In light of these debates, Fazl-e Hasan's comments about the miracle that he thought Mu'in al-Din had performed during his visit to the Dargah interesting. It was a rather pragmatic miracle, related to making the hot, tired visitor (for the 'Urs took place in June that year) cool and comfortable. Although Ajmer was punishingly hot at the time,

....a few days before the *'Urs* was to begin ... a cold wind blew , and it got so cold that one couldn't sleep without a blanket. Water stored in no matter what kind of vessel would become cold. The stones, which were too hot during the day for one to walk on them, became so pleasant that the pilgrims could never have imagined that they had come to the [Dargah] in the hot weather. The sky was just as clear as before. No one could say that the sky was overcast with clouds; nor was there any rain which suddenly made it cool. ... Travelling on the train, some Hindus had told the writer about [Mu'in al-Din's] miracles. But they were astonished by this spectacle ... . Praise be to God. God's people's miracles are so clear that they even make others read their *kalima* [attestation of faith] (*Dabdaba-e Sikandari*, vol. 51, no. 29, 7 June 1915 [translation by the author]).

Fazl-e Hasan implied in this passage that by this simple, highly effective miracle Mu'in al-Din converted the Hindus he had met on the train to Islam. But unlike the *Siyar al-Aqtab*, in which Mu'in al-Din performed a series of fanciful miracles to convert first the Hindu yogi and then the Hindu king to Islam, in this instance the same effect was achieved without any display of force.

Later in his account, Fazl-e Hasan was critical of what he saw as a number of impermissible (*be-shar*) actions being performed at different parts of the shrine. One of these was the pursuit of commercial activity in hallowed ground, on top of graves:

> When shops are set up on top of graves, and their business is related to food and drink, it follows that the fires [of hell] will never [cease to] burn. Those who are buried in this spot are the sons and brothers of the shaykh's family. (*Dabdaba-e Sikandari*, vol. 51, no. 29, 7 June 1915).

Other objections included the alleged consumption of marijuana and alcohol by a group of self-proclaimed *jogis* (ascetics), and their sounding of a loud gong during morning and evening prayers. What did the Dargah need of 'silver balustrades or gold inlay work?' Fazl-e Hasan asked, and why didn't the Organizing Committee do something to punish the offenders? Fazl-e Hasan said he felt obliged to bring these matters to the attention of the newspaper-reading public in the hope that this adverse publicity would force the Organizing Committee to respond to his complaints.

It is interesting that Fazl-e Hasan singled yogis out for criticism. As we have seen, conflict between Mu'in al-Din and a yogi was a prominent theme in the *Siyar al-Aqtab*, written over two hundred and fifty years before Fazl-e Hasan's newspaper article, and competition between yogis and Sufis in general had a long history. On the other hand, there is also a very modern note to Fazl-e Hasan's comment that he hoped that the publicity generated by his article would force the Dargah authorities to act so as to do away with what to him were a number of unseemly activities at the shrine.

The Dargah in Cyberspace

The newest technology in the marketing of the Dargah is the Internet. The majority of websites on the Dargah fall into three categories: websites for and/or by tourists, which promote the Dargah as an important historical site which tourists should visit; websites aimed at religious travellers or pilgrims; and religious or philosophical sites that mention the Dargah in a religious context. Tourism websites promote and reflect on the Dargah as an important historical and cultural site. Pilgrimage websites attend to the religious character of the site, while religious or philosophical websites are primarily interested in sharing their religious beliefs and practices. All three categories overlap, as many tour companies offer both sightseeing tours and pilgrimages and the religious sites frequently include contact information for potential guests.

The travel-oriented websites greatly outnumber those that attempt to record or analyse the philosophy of the Chisti order. These have an essentially secular approach to the shrine, while noting its religious character. Thus, for instance, the Government of Rajasthan website 'RajDarpan' specifically calls the Dargah 'India's most important pilgrimage centre for people from all faiths' (Rajasthan. Government, 2006), a designation repeated in other government-sponsored links and websites:

> Today, Ajmer is a popular pilgrimage centre for the Hindus as well as Muslims. Especially famous is the Dargah Sharif – tomb of the Sufi saint Khwaja Moin-ud-din Chisti. (Rajasthan Government 2006).

The website acknowledges the religious significance of the shrine to Muslims, while emphasizing its general appeal. The website highlights the Dargah's historical association with the Mughal emperors and mentions their contributions to the shrine. The description of the Dargah's architectural features, particularly the use of marble and gold and the two huge cauldrons used to prepare food for pilgrims, underscores the royal.

Another website, http://pinkcity.net (a Rajasthan portal offered by a commercial Internet provider) takes a similar approach, noting the sacredness of the site as 'one of the holiest of Muslim shrines in the country.' It goes on to name prominent royal donors, such as Emperors Akbar, Humayun, Jahangir, and Shah Jahan (pinkcity.net 2006)

The websites dedicated to religious travel – such as Pilgrimage India (2006) – do not differ significantly in their treatment of the Dargah. A little more information about the saint may be provided, including a biographical sketch and a few paragraphs about his philosophy and achievements. These websites often tell the story of how, in anticipation of his death, Mu'in al-Din asked not to be disturbed for six days before he died. They describe the 'Urs in considerable detail, as this is an event they expect the pilgrim will surely want to attend. However, the focus of the websites is to provide a potential traveller with a contact point for the provider.

By contrast, the religious and philosophical websites provide information on the Sufi context of the shrine and on the religious rituals and ceremonies. I examined three websites of this sort, namely, dargahajmer.com, gharibnawaz.com, and sufiajmer.com. Dargahajmer.com, a website set up by Gaddinashin Haji S.M Hameed Chishty, probably a *khadim*, appears very consciously directed toward the non-Muslim outsider (Hameed Chishty 2006a, b, c). Its message is inclusive. Indeed, the phrase 'Love towards all malice towards none' appears at the top of each webpage. Explictly addressing itself to the non-Muslim reader, the text reads:

> One of the strangest facts in today's world is that Islam, a religion which in many ways is almost identical to Christianity and Judaism, should be so poorly understood in Europe and America. Since there are millions of Moslems in the world, and since they control many strategic areas of the earth it is essential that we understand them better. (Hameed Chishty 2006b)

This website repeats stories featured in the *Siyar al-Aqtab*. It says that Mu'in al-Din, like other great 'Sufi saints and Hindu seers in the East', was able to perform miracles, though he employed them sparingly:

> Miracles … are displayed only when there is a great emergency to justify them. In fact they are used as a 'last remedy' when all other common sense persuasion failed to convince the devil in man … in order to maintain a harmonious equilibrium among mankind in the 'Divine Scheme of God', so essential for the happiness of His creation on earth (Hameed Chishty 2006c).

The text then goes on to relate how Mu'in al-Din overcame a crowd of hostile Brahman priests at Anasagar Lake by throwing 'some dust upon them which forced them not only to shrink back but [also] caused the loss of their senses and vitality.' When Prithviraj Chauhan, (c. 1168–1192) the Hindu ruler of this region of North India heard of this,

> …he got furious in spite of his mother's warning to control his temper. She reminded him calmly of her 12-year-old prophecy about the entry of a fakir in his kingdom and warned him to treat the dervish with restraint if he wanted to preserve his kingdom.

Instead of heeding his mother's advice, Prithviraj called upon Ajaipal, his *guru* (spiritual counsellor) and right-hand man, to help him oust Mu'in al-Din and his followers from the shore of the lake. While on his way to the site, Prithviraj was filled with thoughts of hurting the saint. But 'as soon as the evil thought occurred, he lost his vision and could not move forward. But when he recollected his mother's pacifying warning to treat the fakir reverently his heart suddenly softened and he regained his eyesight' (Hameed Chishty 2006).

This sequence of events occurred seven times on his way to Anasagar. Unfortunately, Prithviraj Chauhan (a heroic figure in Rajasthan) ultimately would lose his kingdom to the Muslim invader Muhammad Ghuri, an event soon succeeded by the founding of Muslim rule in northern India (Thapar 1966, 235–236). As for Ajaipal, he and his army were defeated by Mu'in al-Din and his followers in a series of magical encounters, at the end of which Ajaipal embraced Islam, became a devotee of Mu'in al-Din, and was given a new name, Abdulla Bayabani. This event was followed by the conversion of the rest of the local population.

As noted, this story is broadly based on the *Siyar al-Aqtab*. Despite differences in detail (of which there are many), the overall idea, in which the hero vanquishes the evil villain and all comes out well at the end, is the same. The fact that miracles are described as a means of last resort points both to the Chisti disapproval of miracles and to the intended audience, which is envisaged as a modern Western one, skeptical of anything that cannot be explained by 'modern science and logic.' Moreover, despite the conflict between the Hindu Ajaipal and his army on the one hand and the Muslim saint on the other, Mu'in al-Din's victory is portrayed as that of an innocent, peace-loving, inclusive saint armed with nothing but the truth against 'the redoubtable master of the evil science of his day [magic].' The dargahajmer website does not doubt that good Hindus do occasionally appear, such as Prithviraj's mother and unspecified 'Hindu seers in the East.' Although religious conflict is at the heart of this story, it is presented as the conflict between a self-evidently good man against a self-evidently bad one, not as competition between two religious worldviews.

The second website, http://gharibnawaz.com is maintained by a khadim, Moullim Syed Mohammed Hadi Moini (Syed Moini 2006). This website also sounds the theme of religious unity and inclusion, but talks equally about visitation to the shrine as a means of gaining psychological well-being in an age of stress and dysfunction. A letter from the khadim reads in part:

> The Holy Shrine of this Saint is visited by people of different caste[s], creed[s] and colour[s] who visit here to fulfill [their] wishes ... and nobody ever returns empty-handed ... because of this the number of people visiting this holy shrine is increasing day by day.... This is [a] great miracle [in an] age where every house ... is surrounded with less ease and more anxiety and perplexity, pain and [grievous] misunderstanding between husband & wife, hatred between parents and children, jealousy and malice among relatives, disorder between neighbours. There is no sincerity in social life. No respect for elders in children, ... there is trade without prosperity, property without satisfaction, and all these [have] made ... life miserable (Syed Moini 2006).

Syed Moini writes that the solution to these ills lies in following the message of Gharib Nawaz and, if possible, visiting his shrine. He believes that this will 'give you new Strength, Power, Courage to conquer both the worlds.' He also encourages readers to keep in touch with him so he can 'give you a helping hand in [the] future.' In keeping with this practical message of wanting to help no matter where a person may be, the site has a form in which the petitioner can state his or her personal problem and to which a response will be given by one of the khuddam. The gharibnawaz site has several informational headings, each more specific than the first (Syed Moini 2006). Under 'Islam', 'Sufism, and 'Gharibnawaz', the first three, the reader is given a general education on the subjects mentioned. Then follows a heading about the khuddam ('About Us'), which traces their history to the first person to have served Mu'in al-Din in the thirteenth century, and a heading about 'Offerings.' This one talks about the two enormous cauldrons of food cooked twice daily to feed the poor, and the on-line contributions which one may make if one so wishes ('if you are interested in earning the *sawab-e-azam* [heavenly reward] by feeding the poor people and devotees, contact me').

Other ways of contributing to the shrine's recurrent expenses are also mentioned, including contributions toward a velvet cloth to cover the tomb (a prestigious gift), flowers, and sandalwood, or toward the housing of pilgrims. Monetary offerings are also welcomed when Fatiha prayers are offered on the sixth of every month, at the end of Ramadan, during the annual 'Urs, or at any other time. In return, the khuddam include the contributors in their prayers.

These websites emphasize the rituals and ceremonies that would interest the religious participant rather than the sightseer or the seeker of favours. The website sufiajmer.org thus includes a comprehensive list of daily ceremonies (for example, listing the morning opening, first offerings of flowers, and evening candle lighting). *Langar*, or the distribution of food, sama', and the recitation of the holy Qur'an in the mosque located within the Dargah are all mentioned. The site also includes photos of the 2005 'Urs (Sufi Ajmer 2006).

Personal Narratives on the Web

In addition to the websites mentioned above, the Internet can also be accessed for personal narratives, weblogs or blogs, posted by tourists, pilgrims, and religious seekers generally. These narratives range from cursory notes about Ajmer, complete with photos ('me and my mum in front of the Dargah'), to more complex musings about the nature of the shrine, the visit the person has just completed, and the nature of the encounter. These first-person accounts offer another kind of voice, in that they are not commercial and are not trying to 'sell' a religious 'product.' I end this chapter with a journal posted on the web by a young Muslim man who has grown up in the West, about his visit to Mu'in al-Din's shrine. His name is Noufal Ibrahim. He visited Ajmer in April 2004, travelling by train with two other companions from Bangalore. The train ride to Jaipur took two days, by the end of which the young men were hot and tired. They had to take a bus for the last lap of the journey. I quote from the online journal[2]:

> Got into a Shobaraj Hotel. Not a Taj [a luxury hotel chain] but not bad for 550 Rs. a day [approximately US $10.00]. The city of Ajmer is really ancient and quite beautiful. More than once, I felt like a character in an Indiana Jones movie.

> We travelled from the bus stand to the hotel by a horse drawn cart which was an experience in itself. I'm finally going to get a shower and clean off two and a half days' worth grime off me.

> …11.15 p.m. Finally, we visited the shrine of the great Sheikh. Wonderfully constructed. A descendant of the Sheikh showed us how to get to the shrine and told us about the place and about who constructed the various buildings surrounding the actual shrine.

> The pomp, show, and overall commercialisation of the whole place was quite *appalling* [italics in original]. I must confess that there was no 'enlightenment.' I did spend a good amount of time reciting there. All of the remaining 4 of my 5 daily prayers were at the Durgah and I felt satisfied and happy with my efforts there. We hope to finish visiting all the other places in Ajmer early and leave by the coming Monday. [This was written on Saturday.] (Ibrahim 2004)

---

2   Since 2004 when this chapter was in preparation this blog has been removed from the Internet. The concerns expressed by the blog author are typical of comments in current tourist blogs and mirrors some of the remarks by the Indian Government Parliamentary Committee cited elsewhere in this chapter.

Apparently disappointed by what Ibrahim described as the 'number of swindlings we've been through', the friends decided to leave on an earlier train than the one on which they had originally booked themselves. He complained about delayed schedules too:

> [11 April 2004, 5.30 p.m.] Right now, I'm at a place where a private bus was supposed to leave for Jaipur 1.5 hours ago. ... The people here thanks to their slow, unhurried and monotonous lifestyle have an interesting disregard for other people's time. Being a couple of hours late is hardly a problem for anyone native to this place and aliens like us find that quite unacceptable.

His final thoughts about the trip were mixed, positive in some respects but negative in others:

> Everyone in Ajmer, regardless of whether they're Hindus, Muslims, or Sikhs, have pictures of the Ajmer Sheikh's Durgah in their shops. A sight for sore eyes in these times of religious intolerance in India. This is probably a testament to the Sheikh's teachings [about] love and equality.

> During the whole trip, I see why the Prophet Muhamad's (PBUH [short for 'Peace Be Upon Him']) son-in-law, Imam Ali (R) extolled knowledge by saying that it protects you and contrasted it to [the] wealthy, saying that you have to protect it. Knowledge of the country and the language would have *really* protected us.

> One thing that pains me a lot is the overt commercialisation of the shrine. People of all faiths and education flock to the place and a lot of people who claim to be descendants of the Sheikh fleece people. 'Come here, let me pray for you.' 'If you say no, I'm going to curse you.' 'If you say yes and don't pay, I'm going to curse you.'

Ibrahim's complaint about the commercialization of the shrine is not, of course, a recent phenomenon. Earlier I noted the complaint made by Fazl-e Hasan Sabiri, the Urdu editor of the *Dabdaba-e Sikandari*, in 1915 about the setting up of shops on hallowed ground, their purpose being to make a profit. Yet the history of religious pilgrimage has been associated with commerce since the very beginnings of Islam, notably at the Ka'ba during the hajj season. Closer to home, right next door to Mu'in al-Din's shrine, there is a vibrant annual cattle fair at Pushkar, the site of Brahma's temple.

To return to the present: despite his indictment, Ibrahim ends his web journal by saying, 'The trip was a success, I think. The Sheikh whom we visited is the ruler of the Indian spiritual kingdom (and is often referred to [as] Sultan al-Hind in prayers) as far as Sufi ideology is concerned and I feel a lot closer to my task of achieving the state of enlightened bliss and love of God which I had so longed for.' So perhaps Noufal was able to feel the influence of the saint's loving spirit at the Ajmer shrine despite the trials he and his friends endured there.

Conclusion

This chapter has come full circle, from describing the Mu'in al-Din of history and legend, to the 1915 account of a reform-minded Muslim newspaper editor to the shrine, to the 2005 visit to the shrine by a young, foreign-born Muslim visitor who describes himself as an 'alien' in India who feels like a character in an Indiana Jones movie. The earliest of these texts, the seventeenth-century *Siyar al-Aqtab*, set out to create the perfect Chisti saint and to refute the claims made by Hindu ascetics about their extra-human powers in order to establish the superiority of 'Islam' over 'Hinduism.' Therefore it constructed a miracle-wielding, world-renouncing, but simultaneously world-conquering hero (to borrow Tambiah's [1976] phrase) who converted Hindus of all classes – both the masses and the rulers – to Chisti Sufism. In modified form, this image has endured to the present and has been incorporated into Internet sites promoting the Dargah.

The 1915 newspaper account is quite different. While it does not renounce belief in miracles, its miracle is a very simple, mundane one: making the intolerable heat of an Ajmer summer not only tolerable, but cool and pleasant. Fazl-e Hasan's world was shaped by British colonialism, although Rampur State was a small self-governing Muslim state. The newspaper for which he wrote was a symbol of the age: it reached a large Urdu-speaking and -reading public far beyond the confines of Rampur, and spoke to fellow Muslims all over British India. In this context, Muslims – among them Fazl-e Hasan – were re-evaluating their religious and cultural traditions and trying to bring about change from within in what was a difficult, tentative, and sometimes contentious process.

Ibrahim's account, written in our own time, speaks to a generation born to transplanted, immigrant South Asian parents in Europe and North America who are trying to understand their 'roots.' This too is a difficult negotiation, especially for those who are making the journey for the first time as young adults, for their parents' world is alien to them. Noufal is both attracted and repelled by the activities at the Dargah. We do not know enough about his background or of his previous contact with South Asian Islam, to know whether he will try to learn more about his parents' world and become more comfortable with it, or not.[3]

The websites examined in this paper arise from a similar context, namely, the expatriate South Asian Muslim community in Europe and North America on the one hand and the Western tourist trying to tap into a nostalgic sense of India's 'exotic heritage' on the other . While the commercial, tourist-oriented sites tend to create a homogenized image of Rajasthan as a world of palaces, kings, and saints, with an emphasis on its royal history, the religious ones are more detailed, targeting both the Western seeker as well as the South Asian Muslim immigrant. Nevertheless, they too keep the prospective pilgrim at arm's length, explaining the activities and their significance through the lens of a custodian, one of the shrine's *khuddam*. Judging

---

3 Noufal Ibrahim has asked that access to his journal be made available to all who wish to have it.

from Noufal Ibrahim's journal, it is hard to forge a sense of personal connection in the age of instant access.

Since the early 1990s, India has been in the throes of unprecedented social and economic change, including an embrace of Internet technology. The commercialization of the Ajmer shrine, including its self-conscious marketing on different websites by the *khuddam*, is part of this phenomenon. If tourism to the shrine may leave some visitors feeling vaguely dissatisfied, the longer-term influence of the saint on his devotees, no matter what their religion, has obviously endured. At the heart of the Sufi quest at Mu'in al-Din's shrine, as at others, is the personal connection forged between the individual seeker and his chosen master. Today, with so many more people trying to make this connection than before, the task is that much more daunting and complex.

References

Baldick, J. (1995), 'Chishtiyah', in John L. Esposito (ed.), *The Oxford Encyclopedia of the Modern Islamic World*, vol. 1 (New York: Oxford University Press).

Currie, P. M. (1989), *The Shrine and Cult of Mu'in al-din Chishti of Ajmer* (Delhi: Oxford University Press).

Dhoundiyal, B.N. (1966), *Rajasthan District Gazetteers: Ajmer* (Jaipur: Government Central Press).

Eaton, R.M. (1982), 'Court of Man, Court of God: Local Perceptions of the Shrine of Baba Farid, Pakpattan, Punjab', in *Contributions to Asian Studies*, vol. 17 (Leiden: E. J. Brill).

Ernst, C.W. (2005), 'Situating Sufism and Yoga', in *Journal of the Royal Asiatic Society*, Series 3, 15:1, 15–43.

Ernst, C.W. and B.B. Lawrence (2002), *Sufi Martyrs of Love: The Chishti Order in South Asia and Beyond* (New York: Palgrave Macmillan).

Ewing, K.P. (1980), 'The *Pir* or Sufi Saint in Pakistani Islam', PhD. dissertation, University of Chicago.

Fazl-e Hasan S. M. (1915), *Dabdaba-e Sikandari*, 51:29, 7 June (Rampur State, United Provinces).

Hameed Chisty, H.S.M. (2006a), 'home page' of website *Hazart Khawaja Moihuddin Hasan Chisty (R.A.)* http://www.dargahajmer.com/. Accessed 26 August 2006.

—— (2006b), 'Subject of Islam', *Hazart Khawaja Moihuddin Hasan Chisty (R.A.)* http://www.dargahajmer.com/i_subject.htm. Accessed 28 August, 2006.

—— (2006c), 'Arrival', *Hazart Khawaja Moihuddin Hasan Chisty (R.A.)* http://www.dargahajmer.com/g_arrival.htm. Accessed 28 August 2006.

Hamilton, W. (1828), *East India Gazetteer*, 2 vols. 2nd Edition (London: William H. Hamilton & Co).

Heber, Reginald (1829), *Narrative of a Journey through the Upper Provinces of India, from Calcutta to Bombay, 1824–25* (Philadelphia: Carey, Lea & Carey).

Metcalf, B. (1982), *Islamic Revival in British India: Deoband 1860–1900* (Princeton: Princeton University Press).

Moini, S.L.H. (1989), 'Rituals and Customary Practices at the Dargah of Ajmer', in C.W. Troll, (ed.) *Muslim Shrines in India* (Delhi: Oxford University Press).

Pilgrimage India (2006), 'Ajmer Sharif', http://www.pilgrimage-india.com/muslin-pilgrimage/ajmer-sharif.html. Accessed 28 August 2006.

Pinkcity.net (2006), 'Ajmer-Pushkar: Dargah', www.pinkcity.net/rajasthan/ajmer_pushkar/durgah.htm. (Jaipur: Data Infosys Limited). Accessed 28 August 2006.

Rajasthan. Government (2006), 'Tourism: Ajmer', http://www.rajasthan.gov.in/Ajmer.shtm. Accessed 28 August, 2006.

Robinson, F. (1982), *Atlas of the Islamic World since 1500* (New York: Facts on File).

Saheb, Ajmer [IPRJC] (2002), 'Report on Durgah Khwaja Saheb, Ajmer, Presented to the Rajya Sabha 20 December 2002 and Laid on the Table of the Lok Sabha, 20 December 2002', (New Delhi: Rajya Sabha Secretariat), http://www.rajyasabha.gov.in/book2/reports/wakf/6threport.htm. Accessed 28 August 2006.

Siddiqui, I.H. (1989), 'The Early Chishti Dargahs', in C.W. Troll, (ed.) *Muslim Shrines in India* (Delhi: Oxford University Press).

SufiAjmer.org (2006), 'Homepage' of website dedicated to Hazrat Khwaja Minuddin Hasan Chishti. www.sufiajmer.org/html/home. Accessed 28 August 2006.

Syed Moini, S.M. Hadi (2006), 'Hazrat Mohuddin Hasan Chishty (R.A.) Messenger of Peace and Love', www.gharibnawaz.com/a_message. Accessed 28 August, 2006.

Tambiah, S.J. (1976), *World Conquerer and World Renouncer: A Study of Buddhism and Polity in Thailand Against a Historical Background* (Cambridge: Cambridge University Press).

Thapar, Romila (1966) *A History of India. Vol 1.* (London: Penguin Books).

Tirmizi, S. A. I., 'Mughal Documents relating to the Dargah of Khwaja Mu'inuddin Chishti', in C.W. Troll (ed.) (1989), *Muslim Shrines in India* (Delhi: Oxford University Press).

Tod, J. (1914), *Annals and Antiquities of Rajast'han,* vol. I, reprint of 1829 edition (London: George Routledge & Sons).

Chapter 11

Hindu Nationalism, Community Rhetoric and the Impact of Tourism: The 'Divine Dilemma' of Pushkar

Christina A. Joseph[1]

Introduction

For centuries, pilgrims have travelled to pay their respects to the sacred pilgrimage centre of Pushkar, in central Rajasthan. These visitors honour the sacred lake by performing religious rites and life cycle rituals on its shores. Pushkar, today a population centre of some 13,000 located approximately six miles from Ajmer, claims the only temple dedicated to the god Brahma, the creator of the Hindu pantheon. Pushkar is also host to a celebrated annual camel fair. This well publicized fair has attracted the attention of Western media, travel writers and Internet bloggers, who have discovered Pushkar's charms and made it an attraction for tourists worldwide.

This chapter focuses on how Pushkar's Brahman priests, the religious service providers referred to locally as *pandas*, regard this influx of non-Indian tourists. They refer to them by the English term 'foreign', by which they mean persons not of Indian descent, while all persons of Indian descent – both Indian nationals and non-resident Indians (NRIs) who are citizens of countries such as the United Kingdom or the United States – are not considered 'foreign.' The presence of these 'foreign' tourists – and for the purposes of this presentation I adopt this usage – in Pushkar makes for startling and incongruous contrasts.

Filmmaker Heeraz Marfatia, who grew up in neighbouring Ajmer and shot a short film in Pushkar, *Birju*, says 'Pushkar was my biggest inspiration. I saw it morph into its current shape. It is hard to pin the place down – it is a holy place where a Salvador Dali boutique and the only Lord Brahma temple coexist. The whole town is vegetarian and has a variety of cafés like the Pink Floyd Café. Here, traditional Hindus live with marijuana worshipping foreigners....' (Fernandes 2002). Another Indian visitor compared Pushkar with the Muslim pilgrimage site in Ajmer by saying, 'After visiting the Dargah, Pushkar was like hippie-land' (Anonymous, 2006). Such

1   This chapter is based in part on my dissertation research. Fieldwork was made possible through a grant from the American Institute of Indian Studies.

juxtapositions raise significant questions about the impact of tourism on local culture and the local responses to this dramatic change.

This essay examines the various and at times conflicting rhetorical strategies of resistance deployed by Pushkar's various Brahmans, even while mediating tourism to make it palatable as a livelihood – what a recent article in *India Today* refers to as the 'divine dilemma' of Pushkar (Parihar 2005, 50). I argue that the relationship between tourism and culture is a complex and nuanced one in that the Brahmans mediate, even while they resist it. A matrix of culturally derived rhetorical strategies, which constitute 'mediated resistance', transforms ambivalent relationships into culturally acceptable forms to this elite religious community.

The term 'strategies of mediated resistance' involves the use of effective rhetoric by different actors in the various host communities. Here, rhetoric is defined as the 'mobilization of signs for the articulation of identities, ideologies, consciousnesses, communities, publics, and cultures' (Deluca 1999, 17). This definition of rhetoric recognizes it as discourse that constitutes the social order, and not just an instrumental tool limited to formal politics and legal proceedings.

The significance of these strategies can only be fully appreciated in terms of the wider context of the Hindu fundamentalist movement, which in the 1980s shifted 'Hinduness' from the political margins to national centre stage. This chapter in part discusses Hindutva activists' role in organizing opposition to foreign tourism in Pushkar. I also briefly describe ongoing local responses to the changing tourism environment. The aim of the national Hindutva political movement, whose most important organizations collectively have been termed the Sangh Parivar, is to establish a Hindu nation-state and to delegitimize communities and citizens that fall outside the movement's exclusionary ideology, crystallized in the concept of Hindutva (Mukta 2000, 442).

This research is based on a year and a half of ethnographic fieldwork in the town of Pushkar from late 1987 to the end of 1988, with follow-up research conducted in 1990 and 1996. Interviews and surveys supplemented my participant observation. Archival research at the Ajmer District Collectorate, the national archives in Delhi and the Rajasthan state archives at Bikaner augmented the fieldwork. The data has been updated through regular correspondence with a key informant in Pushkar and use of Internet resources through 2006 (See Joseph 1994; Joseph and Kavoori 2001).

Strategies of Mediated Resistance in Pushkar

Throughout Pushkar, tourism has influenced life styles. Older Brahman men have changed their work habits to stay competitive. The Brahman women of Pushkar, rarely part of the public domain, are now even more sequestered. Elders continually admonish young children for talking to tourists and begging for candy, money and photographs. Analysis of these and other responses requires a local frame of understanding, vocabulary, meaning, and intention.

Classic tourism literature makes a case for a severe power asymmetry between tourists and host communities, because the latter bear the burden of adjustment economically, socially and culturally (Nash 1977, 1981; Greenwood 1977; Smith 1977; de Kadt 1979). This position has been reiterated by other scholars studying the impact of tourism at various sites (Eastman 1995; Eliot 1983; Erisman 1983; Palmer 1994; Pearce 1982) and from different perspectives (Bryden 1973; Freitag 1994; Hunter 1997; Lanfant 1980). Many of these studies approach host community mediation (i.e., the adjustments the community makes) primarily from the tourist's perspective. While tourism does in fact impose a one-sided power asymmetry in interaction situations between hosts and guests, neither is merely a passive subject acted upon by others.

MacCannell (1973) and Kemper's (1978) seminal research about the staging of authenticity for tourists by their hosts while allocating some aspects of their culture to 'back regions', makes a case for the agency of hosts. More recent work has focused on the complexity of local mediation of tourism (Teo and Yeoh 1997, Teo and Huang 1995; Van den Berghe 1995; Pitchford 1995), examining host perceptions (King, Pizam and Milman 1993) and possible benefits selectively among local peoples (Wilson 1997).

In Pushkar, three variations of rhetoric – exclusionary, religious, and political – constitute the most significant strategies of mediated resistance. The first, exclusionary rhetoric, draws on social frictions that is particularly divisive in Pushkar: the division of residents along an insider/outsider axis. The self-designated 'insiders' are the long-term Brahman residents, while the 'outsiders' are largely Hindu Rajasthani Rajputs. Some of these moved here to work in the travel industry or to oversee the government's administrative apparatus, while others have converted inherited family residences in Pushkar into tourist facilities. The 'insiders' say that these particular 'outsiders' – epitomize all the negative qualities symptomatic of people living in *kalyuga* (the current degraded era of disintegration and moral decline), and hence blame them for all the problems stemming from tourism. The term kalyuga derives from the Sanskritic Hindu cosmic chronology that constructs time as cyclical and devolving. The cosmos passes through many eons, each of which is made up of several ages. Kali Yuga or kalyuga, is the last age of the current eon, an 'era of culminating devolution' (Gold 1999, 167); an age of 'discord and disintegration where evil triumphs' (Eliade 1961, 132). The priests invoke the coherent narrative of kalyuga to explain any deviance from traditional modes of social conduct and behaviour.

Brahman hotel and guesthouse owners claim that the outsiders have contributed to the decline of Pushkar's sanctity, and target those outsiders who occupy administrative positions as the embodiment of the ill state of government. The Brahman insiders allege that these outsiders, particularly the Rajputs, whose traditional practices allow meat and alcohol consumption, transgress the Brahmans' prohibition on the consumption of food and drink in this sacred Hindu site.

Consequently, the insiders subject the outsiders to hostility and exclusionary rhetoric. This rhetoric is not aimed at tourists, despite similar transgressions, as they are completely outside the Hindu frame of reference. Even while exacerbating tensions and conflicts between the two local groups, exclusionary rhetoric has ironically served to mediate the relationship between tourism and culture by framing outsiders alone the cause of local problems.

The second, or religious, rhetoric surfaces in discussions of the town's desacralization. While the Brahmans specifically orient their exclusionary rhetoric to Indian outsiders, the religious rhetoric operates more broadly in local discourse. Similarly anchored by ideas of kalyuga, at some time or the other, everyone in Pushkar uses religious rhetoric against tourism and tourists. The Brahmans who cater to tourists and own hotels are often the very ones who are the most critical of the tourists' lack of respect for the town's sanctity. Religious rhetoric helps the Brahmans resolve their ambivalence towards tourist behaviour. Public notices all over the *Ghats* (the steps leading down to the lake on which pilgrims gather) proscribing certain behaviours are symptomatic of this tension. These notices read in part:

> Tourists are kindly requested to leave their shoes at least 30 feet away from the Ghats. In Pushkar, holding hands or kissing in public is not permitted. Ladies are kindly requested to wear proper clothes, which cover themselves sufficiently, so as not to offend. Alcohol and drugs are not permitted in Pushkar. These rules reflect aspects of the Hindu religion and tourists must understand that breaches of these rules cause offence and are against the law.

Each of these statements reflects problematic aspects of behaviour for a traditional religious community. The reference to shoes being kept at a distance allows for the use of cultural rhetoric to maintain a sense of control over the sacred space of Pushkar; the reference to holding hands and kissing signals the gender politics of a patriarchal community like Pushkar. The reference to 'ladies' and 'proper' clothes is an explicit attempt to control Western femininity and sexuality through local dress and behaviour (see chapter by Weisgrau). Overall, this rhetoric, as seen in these signs and their reiteration in day-to-day conversation, allows for a resistance to certain aspects of tourist behaviour without addressing the economic and sociological complicity of the host community itself.

The third, or political, rhetoric has the same ingredients as the cultural rhetoric, except that it holds the state government directly responsible for the ills of tourism. The rhetoric of the local political parties and activist groups, tirades against tourists, heightens during crises (some real, others manufactured). Political rhetoric is especially powerful, for in Pushkar there is a high degree of public participation in various events and meetings convened by the political parties.

Political rhetoric revolves around trumpeting the virtues of the sacred spaces of Pushkar as a pilgrimage site, criticizing tourism, absolving the locals (whether insider or outsider) of all blame and condemning the government for lack of appropriate action. The politicians in Pushkar periodically use tourism as political capital by attacking some of the 'outsiders' as well as the small communities of Pushkar's long-term foreign residents.

Strategies of mediated resistance, whether exclusionary, religious, or political reflect the complex composition of Pushkar's population, its shifting political economy, and its centuries-long history as a pilgrimage site across India. These diverse claims by different groups reflect both contemporary and historical framings of religion, pilgrimage, and tourism.

Figure 11.1   **Numerous prominent signs posted on the ritual bathing ghats in Hindi, English, German, French, Italian and Hebrew remind visitors to observe Pushkar's rules of conduct.** *Photo courtesy of Eric and Renata Jean. All rights reserved.*

Sacred Spaces and Social Relations

Pushkar is, first and foremost, a pilgrimage town for Indians. Its sacred character is constituted by the interplay of various historical, mythological, ritual, and sociological aspects (see Ensink 1974) interpreted through its spaces and sacred geography (Opperman 1993, Joseph 1994).

The sacred order of the town extends beyond temples and the lake to include the numerous sites around Pushkar that are mythologically related to gods and holy men. The geography of the town is the first dimension of sacredness encountered by the pilgrims who acknowledge its sacred boundary by praising Lord Brahma aloud. Locally available maps depict the town as a *mandala* (a ritual diagram) in which the central square represents the elliptical lake that lies at the heart of the town. On the lake's periphery are the ghats where *puja* (worship), the most important religious activity for pilgrims, takes place. Temples, the bustling narrow streets of the main market, lined on both sides by shops and restaurants, and the relatively quieter residential neighbourhoods encircle and overlook the lake.

The ritual and sociological dimensions of Pushkar are inextricably connected. The ghat*s* are the site for most of the ritual puja that gives economic sustenance to this pilgrimage town. Puja can consist merely of a brief prayer celebrating the sacredness of the pilgrimage, or it can commemorate life cycle events, especially – here – rituals for the dead (see chapter by Cort). Proceeds from puja and other religious activities form the livelihood of the Brahman priests. Pushkar is at the centre of an extensive priest-client network, whereby pilgrims from a certain region and caste come to a specific priests, who maintain their family genealogical records. These records, in some cases, go back three to four hundred years.

The priests cater to all the needs of their clients from the pragmatic, such as food and lodging, to ritual, for which they receive payments in cash or kind. Priests also take pilgrims to other religious sites. In their litany of praise, priests claim that the town has five hundred temples. These play an important part in the sacred constitution of the town. Daily ritual activities including both individual puja and collective prayer three times a day as well as the celebration of annual festivals.

The population of Pushkar divides among many social groups. Brahman informants claim that over half of Pushkar's population belongs to their group. This is not remarkable, given that Pushkar is a pilgrimage site. My informants claim that there are two thousand specialized priests in Pushkar, of which eight hundred belong to the Pushkar Priests Association (Parihar 2005, 50).

The Brahmans are an important force within the community and belong predominantly to the Parasar Brahman subcaste. They claim that they have inhabited the western *Badi Basti* ('big neighbourhood') section of the town since its mythological origin. Other Brahmans in town live in the neighbourhood of *Choti Basti* ('little neighbourhood') and belong to several subcastes. The two neighbourhoods have been feuding for decades over rights to land and pilgrims, but numerical, economic and political power rests firmly with the Parasars.

A small percentage of Pushkar's residents are Jains, Sikhs and Muslims. Jains are largely involved in commerce and have one temple. Muslims, about fifty families in all, have strong ties to the Dargah Committee that controls the shrine of the Sufi saint Mu'n al-Din Chisti of Ajmer (see chapter by Sanyal). Their spiritual centre in Pushkar is the Shahi mosque located among the temples at Gaughat and is attributed to the seventeenth century Mughal ruler Aurangzeb. There are two other mosques in Pushkar. Although restrictions have been intermittently imposed on Muslim religious processions in Pushkar, on the whole, Muslims report peaceful coexistence with their Hindu neighbours.

Scheduled Caste[2] populations (2,918 according to the 2001 census, about one fifth of the town population) generally live on the periphery of the town and have separate cremation grounds as well as temples. Pushkar Brahmans distinguish between the *acchi* (good) Scheduled Castes and the *sabse neech* (lowest) Scheduled Castes. The acchi castes are allowed to enter temples – in fact, state law mandates that any Hindu can enter any Hindu temple (see chapter by Cort). Some Scheduled Castes, such as the Regars, have a Parasar Brahman as their temple priest.

The Changing Order

The rising popularity of Indian spirituality among Westerners in the latter half of the twentieth century promoted interest in religious places such as Pushkar. The first wave of Western spiritual seekers arrived by the early 1970s; they were few in number and interaction with the locals was minimal.

Today the development of mass tourism has made ubiquitous the non-Indian tourist presence in Pushkar. The only source on statistics for tourists is the Rajasthan Tourism Office in Ajmer, Rajasthan. The numbers are unreliable as they depend on hotels to report stays and often do not include smaller hotels that operate under the radar of official reporting procedures. Further, the official category of non-domestic (what they term 'foreign') tourists is based on the nationality of the passport, and thus includes the NRIs, whom the locals emphatically regard as 'Indians.' Approximately 70,000 to 80,000 non-domestic tourists visit the town every year (Newindpress.com September 12, 2005).

The transition to mass tourism was facilitated by the national government's strategic promotion of domestic and international tourism to tap its revenue potential; an increasingly common strategy globally and one enthusiastically adopted by resource poor Rajasthan (Watson 1994, de Kadt 1979; Zamora 1978). This has resulted in an increase of 54 percent in non-domestic tourist arrivals in 2005, compared with 2004, displacing Kerala as the foreign tourist's most favourite travel destination in India (Khaleej Times 21 April 2006).

The Rajasthan government capitalizes on the state's religious and cultural festivals and fairs. In Pushkar, the focus is on the annual religious *cum* cattle fair, marketed internationally as an 'exotic' cultural event. The week-long fair in November/December draws thousands of tourists annually. In 2004 the fair attracted over 10,000 non-domestic tourists for the first time (Mahan 2004) and 12,000 in 2005 (Rao 2005).

The traditional landscape of temples and shrines is increasingly interspersed with hotels, guesthouses, restaurants, and shops that cater almost exclusively to tourists.

---

2 Scheduled Castes are those designated by the government of India on the schedule, or list, of previously 'untouchable' and other disadvantaged caste groups eligible for special benefits in education and employment.

There are 100 registered hotels and 54 restaurants in the two-kilometer periphery around the lake. Many priests offer accommodation in their houses overlooking the lake (Parihar 2005). The changing economic and sociological scene reflects a dual process of cultural commoditization, particularly with respect to food, dress, and interpersonal behaviour. Of crucial significance here is the reconstitution of the traditional sacred order to meet the requirements of tourists' presence. This is most apparent in tourist participation in rituals associated with temples and ghats.

The performance of Puja for foreign tourists has become commonplace. Priests extort large sums of money from them under the guise of religious donations. The impetus to engage non-Hindu tourists in ritual is anchored in the local knowledge that these earnings are at least four times what would be given by a pilgrim. Changing the function of puja from a sacred rite into an exclusively commercial enterprise has made the tourist as much a part of the ghats and the town's sacred order as the Hindu pilgrim.

Puja, as a touristic performance, has undergone a transformation in that it has become shorter and is conducted in the tourist's language with a few Sanskrit religious *slokas* (verses) thrown in for effect. The ritual concludes with bestowal of the 'Pushkar passport', a red string tied around the wrist that denotes completion of the puja ritual. Priests can now tell which foreigners should no longer be pursued.

Puja is also at the centre of another tourism activity, namely photography. Officially, town regulations prohibit photography on the ghats in order to preserve their sanctity and to ensure privacy for the pilgrim bathers. Enforcement of these regulations is informal and depends on whether the tourist agrees or refuses to participate in Puja. Priests invoke the authority of the public notices to bar tourists who refuse to do puja from taking photographs. Priests will, however, encourage their tourist clients to ignore the warnings and use their cameras.

Cultural commoditization is evident both in the casual performance of traditional ceremonies such as puja and in the use of temples and ghats as sites for touristic consumption, particularly through photography (see chapter by Karatchova). While a few temples in Pushkar have a policy of not allowing foreigners into their premises, most others welcome them and encourage their activities. The sight of tourists lounging and smoking inside temples testifies to this cultural commoditization, as do changes in the traditional roles of priests. Many have sold the rights to their traditional Indian clientele to other priests and forsaken the calling of the priesthood for other commercial ventures in the tourism trade.

Pushkar's bazaars and markets strongly reflect a shift from items catering to Indian pilgrims to those catering to foreign tastes. This process is seen in similar situations elsewhere (Bentor 1993; Cohen 1993; Graburn 1977; Schadler 1979). Examples of goods adapted to Western tastes range from utilitarian items, like embroidered saddlebags reincarnated as cushion covers, to luxury items produced locally specifically for the tourism market, such as carpets. Tourist demand for toilet paper has led to the incongruous sight of paper rolls festooned over the fronts of shops and restaurants. Streets are lined with western wear; hotels have regular yoga sessions and local youths run Indian music classes for foreign tourists (Parihar 2005, 50).

Figure 11.2 Pushkar attracts large numbers of foreign tourists; local entrepreneurs, such as these women, decorate a European tourist's hands with *mehendi*. *Photo courtesy of Rakesh Gupta. All rights reserved.*

The local repertoire of 'bland' food produced specifically for the foreign tourist includes pancakes, brown bread, spaghetti, macaroni, salad, fruit juice, and pizza. Many restaurants feature menu items from Germany, Italy, Israel and France. The presence of these foods, along with cheap accommodations, make Pushkar a significant inclusion in travel guides that cater to the casual backpacker type of tourist (Todhunter 2002).

Acceptance of Western dress codes among the young males of Pushkar (as in all parts of India) is high and a large number of them wear jeans, shirts, and caps either bought from tourists or presented to them. Most worrying to the local community is the alleged introduction of drugs by foreign tourists and their presence as a marketable commodity.

Sexual encounters with female tourists, rumoured to be frequent, are a common topic of discussion among the young men of Pushkar (see chapter by Weisgrau). *India Today* quotes a priest in Pushkar as saying, 'The youth here find the openness in foreign girls too tempting.' Every year, affairs between local youth and foreigners become public knowledge, some even ending in marriage (Parihar 2005, 50).

Kalyuga and Political Rhetoric

The discourse of kalyuga, as used by the priests, legitimizes the change in the traditional occupational structure, as evinced by Brahmans deserting their calling as priests to pursue business: kalyuga leaves the Brahmans no option but to do what they have to in order to survive. This forced acceptance of commerce and business links to two additional rhetorical claims: pilgrims' lack of devotion, and the presence of tourists in a holy place. Priests say that today's pilgrims lack the faith of their ancestors (Alley 1998, 315)

By assigning causality to an external condition (the nature of the age), the priests eschew personal responsibility for catering to tourists. In addition, the practices associated with the tourist presence, from skimpy attire and promiscuous behaviour to drug and alcohol abuse, are considered attributes that flourish in an age of little respect for morality or tradition. Interestingly enough, non-priests use the same argument against the priests for falling under the spell of the 'money grabbing ethos of *kalyuga*' (Alley 1998, 322).

Priests (along with most people in India) evoke the term 'government' as a gloss for local politicians and the state authorities, especially the civil service bureaucracy. The 'government' is perceived as external, unfeeling, insensitive, and corrupt. It is blamed for many local problems, such as shortages of electricity and water, the lack of jobs, inflation, the low standard of living, and low wages. In addition, people blame the government for the dilapidated state of the ghats and temples, the open sewers that flow into Pushkar Lake, the deforestation of the surrounding hills, and the sedimentation of the lake.

Priests accuse contemporary politicians and state authorities of violating the concepts of *ramrajya* or the mythical and just reign of the god Rama which represents the highest standards for government and morality in public life. The national government is especially indicted for its role in promoting Pushkar as a tourism destination and the ensuing problems with drugs, public promiscuity, and local inflation. Public work sponsored by the local government is invariably criticized as only benefiting tourism, and not the needs of the residents.

These cultural constructs of kalyuga and government constitute particular strategies of mediated resistance which combines religious, exclusionary, and political rhetoric. This is especially evident in the workings of local activist groups, which I will explore in the balance of this section The *Pushkar Bachao Samiti*, or Save Pushkar Committee, is one example reflecting national Hindutva rhetoric. This short-lived movement – at least in Pushkar – had a brief success. Two other examples are the Pushkar Priests Association and the local government's responses to tourist scandals.

As a Hindu pilgrimage town, in the 1980s Pushkar merited the attention of two VHP affiliated volunteers, a husband and wife team who organized the now-disbanded Save Pushkar Committee. The VHP (Vishwa Hindu Parishad of the World Hindu Council) forged links among Hindu religious leaders, politicians, bureaucrats, police and business groups throughout India (Fox 1990, 60; McKean 1996, 32; Mukta 2000, 443). The VHP mobilized populist support through various Hindu unity events and campaigns. Its success came from its ability to establish an almost ecclesiastical structure (Jaffrelot 2005, 319) that consisted of an organizational grid of volunteers at the state, provincial, district and local levels with almost 20,000 local units (Bhatt 2001, 183). These local units propagated the message of Hindutava and warned against anything that might contaminate or erode it (Hansen 1999, 154, 162). VHP activities notoriously contributed to the highly publicized destruction of the Muslim mosque, the Babri Masjid, in Ayodhya in December 1992.

VHP rhetoric represented the visits of foreigners as attempts to recolonize India by defiling and desecrating its sacred places. In Pushkar one of the group's most important goals was the removal of hotels and guesthouses from the ghats. They painted their slogan all over the town on whitewashed walls: 'Hotel *hatao*, Pushkar *bachao*' (Remove Hotels, Save Pushkar). The rhetoric at Save Pushkar Committee rallies invoked both religious nationalism and anti-foreign sentiment.

According to the chairperson of the Save Pushkar Committee, the British divided India up in the past. Now there is a conspiracy by 'foreign' tourists, aided by the government, to capture the *Tirthas* (holy pilgrimage sites) and destroy Hindu culture by settling there, bringing in drugs and ruining local youth. A Save Pushkar Committee's stridently anti-foreigner broadside stated this position:

> For the past couple of years, foreign tourists have been settling down in Pushkar and even buying houses. Hotels catering to them have opened on the ghats where they openly consume meat and alcohol. The bones are thrown into the lake. They can be seen roaming around town half naked behaving in an immodest fashion. Due to their influence the younger generation has taken to drugs and has become characterless. They are wasting their youth in debauchery. What will happen to this belief centre of millions, the leading *tirtha* of Pushkar? We demand an answer from the government.

This statement reflects the embedded nature of the relationship between religion and tourism. The Save Pushkar Committee linked the Tirtha's desacralization to the purported activities of tourists, and these activities' impact on the local youth. The Committee argued that the government was both the site of responsibility and remedy for this situation, which its actions have helped to shape. The Committee demanded that the government create a plan of action that would include local accountability. In this argument, the government itself appropriates the symbols of colonialism in order to market itself to foreigners, and in doing so becomes enmeshed in an exploitive neocolonial situation (Turner and Ash 1976, 193, Picard 1997).

In retrospect – for VHP efforts peaked in 1992 and the Committee was defunct by 1999 – the attempts of VHP activists to stir up hostility towards foreigners can be seen as part of the concerted plans of Hindu nationalists to motivate and expand their volunteer network. The campaign against tourists gained traction as it reflected the local anxieties about social change. Anti-foreigner activities were not framed in the anti-Christian terms seen elsewhere in India in the late 1990s (Bhatt 2001, 198), but as a movement that opposed colonialism. This xenophobic discourse is consistent with the anti-colonial nationalism propagated by V.D. Savarkar (1883– 1966), the founder of the concept of Hindutva; and the 1980's rejection of 'western consumerism' construed as an 'invasion' by the propagators of Hindutva (Hansen 1999, 12). Although the Save Pushkar Committee did not survive, in more recent times a series of scandals have once again exacerbated anti-foreigner sentiments in Pushkar. In 2004, at a dinner sponsored by the state Tourism Development Corporation for Israeli tourists[3] outside Pushkar's municipal limits, two women attending the festivities allegedly took off all their clothes. The resulting scandal forced the transfer of the Ajmer District Collector (the chief executive of the government bureaucracy for the district), who was present at the time (Parihar 2005, 50). In 2005, an Israeli couple was arrested and fined Rs. 500 (approximately $11) by the Judicial Magistrate Court at Pushkar for 'hurting Hindu sentiments' by kissing each other in public. Evidently the couple was carried away with sentiment after attending a Hindu wedding ceremony, according to the complaint filed by the Pushkar Priests Association (Outlook India, 20 September, 2005). A Finnish female tourist was arrested and charged with Section 416 of Indecent Representation of Women (Prevention) Act and Section 294 of Indian Penal Code 'for exhibiting obscenity in a public place.' She allegedly walked naked through Pushkar after bathing in the sacred lake (Outlook India, 25 October, 2005).

A Parasar priest referred to the above incidents collectively as 'cultural pollution' (Indo-Asian News Service, 23 October, 2005). According to the President of the Pushkar Priests Association, the group representing most of the Parasar Brahman Priests 'Foreigners are spoiling this place. Either everyone should sit together to check the foreigners' behaviour or we will throw them out' (Parihar 2005, 50).

An organizer for the Pushkar Priests Association added that he resented that Hindu customs were being reduced to entertainment for tourists. Thus, in October 2005, the Pushkar Priests Association organized a protest march against the municipal committee's proposal to expand their promotion of Pushkar as a tourist centre, saying that tourism was destroying its religious aura (Parihar 2005, 50).

These actions seem to be producing results: in 2005, the Sub-Divisional Magistrate issued twenty pages of guidelines in English, French and German asking pilgrims and foreign tourists not to indulge in 'any kind of vulgarity, including smooching and hugging, in the holy town' (*Outlook India*, 19 November, 2005). Giant billboards caution, 'No vulgarity, no kissing and no hugging at Ghats. Dress up decently in public spaces…' (*Deccan Herald*, 16 April, 2006).

In April 2006, a Pushkar Clean Operation was launched. This seeks to remove twenty-six hotels and restaurants from the ghats, in keeping with the Pushkar

---

3   According to tourism statistics, Israeli passport holders account for 10–15 percent of non-domestic tourist arrivals in Pushkar.

Municipal Committee ordinance banning these enterprises from within 100 meters of the lake (Zee News, 25 April, 2006). From all accounts the recent protests are home-grown, with local priests as the main organizers. As some government-sponsored tourist facilities are at the lake shore, this, however, may prove difficult to accomplish.

Conclusion

Mediated resistance plays a central role in Pushkar's discourse of tourism and cultural change. The opposition to tourism has taken on many of the attributes of political theatre. The different strategies of mediated resistance deflect direct confrontations with tourists and in the process act as a channel for grievances against tourism and the bewailing of a lost tradition. This allows an expression of sorrow and condemnation, and assuages any local sense of guilt or personal responsibility. It permits participants to return to then return to their homes and businesses secure with a sense of duty done to their town and religion. Public participation in these multiple rhetorics of tourism also circumvents the need for any action against the tourism industry. It makes the disjunction between tourism and local culture palatable and functions to create conditions for the acceptance of cultural change.

The case of Pushkar raises important questions for tourism policymakers. Are local/national religious sites inherently antithetical to international tourism? This is becoming an increasingly widespread question, as the world grows interconnected by processes of globalization, capitalism, and cultural homogenization (Clifford 1992). For example, in Uluru (Ayers Rock) in Australia aboriginal 'traditional owners', the Anangu, who hold the site sacred, are trying to restrict its use by tourists with strategies like the recent 'no-climbing please' campaign even though they reap significant financial rewards from tourism (Digance 2003).

Nearly forty years of negotiating the foreign presence in Pushkar has not resolved the conflict between sacred and secular activities. The current articulation of discontent reiterates the 'divine dilemma' of Pushkar: how to impose cultural checks on foreign tourists while profiting from them materially. This dilemma is far from being resolved to the satisfaction of its self-appointed defenders.

References

Alley, K. (1998), 'Idioms of Degeneracy: Assessing Ganga's Purity and Pollution', in L. Nelson (ed.) *Purifying the Earthly Body of God: Religion and Ecology in Hindu India* (Albany: State University of New York Press, 297–330).

Anonymous, 'Personal Communication', 15 January 2006.

Bhatt, C. (2001), *Hindu Nationalism: Origins, Ideologies and Modern Myths* (New York: Berg).

Bentor, Y. (1993), 'Tibetan Tourist Thangkas in the Kathmandu Valley', *Annals of Tourism Research* 20, 107–137.

Bryden, J. (1973), *Tourism and Development: A Case Study of the Commonwealth Caribbean* (Cambridge: Cambridge University Press).

Clifford, J. (1992), 'Travelling Cultures', in C. Nelson and P. Treichler (eds.) (1992), *Cultural Studies* (London: Routledge, 96–116).

Cohen, E. (1993), 'The Heterogenization of a Tourist Art', *Annals of Tourism Research* 20, 138–163.

Deluca, K. (1999), *Image Politics: The New Rhetoric of Environmental Activism* (New York: Guilford Press).

Digance, J. (2003), 'Pilgrimage at Contested Sites', *Annals of Tourism Research* 30, 143–159.

Eastman, C. (1995), 'Tourism in Kenya and the Marginalization of Swahili', *Annals of Tourism Research* 22, 172–185.

Eliade, M. (1961), *The Sacred and the Profane: The Nature of Religion* (New York: Harper & Row).

Eliot, J. (1983), 'Politics, Power and Tourism in Thailand', *Annals of Tourism Research* 10, 377–393.

Ensink, J. (1974), 'Problems of the Study of Pilgrimage in India', *Indologica Taurinensia* 2, 57–79.

Erisman, M. (1983), 'Tourism and Cultural Dependency in the West Indies', *Annals of Tourism Research* 10, 337–361.

Fox, R. (1990), 'Hindu Nationalism in the Making, or the Rise of the Hindian', in R. Fox, (ed) *Nationalist Ideologies and the Production of National Culture* (Washington, DC: American Anthropological Association, 63–80).

Freitag, T. (1994), 'Enclave Tourism Development: For Whom the Benefits Roll', *Annals of Tourism Research* 21, 538–554.

Gold, A. (1999), 'Sin and Rain: Moral Ecology in Rural North India', in L. Nelson (ed.) *Purifying the Earthly Body of God: Religion and Ecology in Hindu India* (Albany: State University of New York Press, 165–196).

Graburn, N. (1977), *Ethnic and Tourist Arts: Cultural Expressions from the Fourth World* (Berkeley: University of California Press).

Greenwood, D. (1977), 'Culture by the Pound: An Anthropological Perspective on Tourism as Cultural Commodization', in V. Smith (ed.) (1977), *Hosts and Guests: The Anthropology of Tourism* (Philadelphia: University of Pennsylvania Press, 129–138).

Hansen, T.B. (1999), *The Saffron Wave: Democracy and Hindu Nationalism in Modern India* (Princeton, New Jersey: Princeton University Press).

Hunter, C. (1997), 'Sustainable Tourism as an Adaptive Paradigm', *Annals of Tourism Research* 24, 850–867.

Jaffrelot, C. (2005), 'The Vishva Hindu Parishad: Structure and Strategies', in C. Jaffrelot, (ed.) (2005), *The Sangh Parivar: A Reader* (New Delhi: Oxford University Press, 318–334)

Joseph, C. (1994), 'Temples, Tourists and the Politics of Exclusion: The Articulation of Sacred Space at the Hindu Pilgrimage Centre of Pushkar, India', Ph.D. dissertation, Department of Anthropology, University of Rochester.

Joseph, C. and Kavoori, A. (2001), 'Mediated Resistance: Tourism and the Host Community', *Annals of Tourism Research* 28, 998–1009.

de Kadt, E. (ed.) (1979), *Tourism: Passport to Development?: Perspectives on the Social and Cultural Effects of Tourism in Developing Countries* (Oxford University Press: New York).

Kemper, R. (1978), 'Tourism and Regional Development in Taos, New Mexico', in Zamora, Sutlive, and Altshuler, (eds.), 89–104.

King, B., Pizam, A. and Milman, A. (1993), 'Social Impacts of Tourism: Host Perceptions', *Annals of Tourism Research* 20, 650–655.

Lanfant, M.-F. (1980), 'Tourism in the Process of Internationalization', *International Social Science Journal* 32, 1–3.

MacCannell, D. (1973), 'Staged Authenticity: Arrangements of Social Space in Tourist Settings', *American Journal of Sociology* 79, 589–603.

McKean, L. (1996), *Divine Enterprise: Gurus and the Hindu Nationalist Movement* (Chicago: University of Chicago Press).

Mukta, P. (2000), 'The Public Face of Hindu Nationalism', *Ethnic and Racial Studies* 23:3, 442–466.

Nash, D. (1977), 'Tourism as a Form of Imperialism', in V. Smith (ed.) *Hosts and Guests: The Anthropology of Tourism* (Philadelphia: University of Pennsylvania Press, 33–47).

—— (1981), 'Tourism as an Anthropological Subject', *Current Anthropology* 22, 461–481.

Opperman, M. (1993), 'Tourism Space in Developing Countries', *Annals of Tourism Research* 20, 535–556.

Palmer, C. (1994), 'Tourism and Colonialism: The Experience of the Bahamas', *Annals of Tourism Research* 21, 792–811.

Parihar, R. (2005), 'Westernised Ghats', *India Today*, 7 November, 50.

Pearce, P. (1982), *The Sociology Psychology of Tourist Behaviour* (New York: Pergamon Press).

Picard, M. (1997), 'Cultural Tourism, Nation-Building, and Regional Culture: The Making of Balinese Identity', in M. Picard and R. Wood (eds.) (1997), *Tourism, Ethnicity, and the State in Asian and Pacific Societies* (Honolulu: University of Hawaii Press, 181–214).

Picard, M. and Wood, R. (eds.) (1997), *Tourism, Ethnicity, and the State in Asian and Pacific Societies* (Honolulu: University of Hawaii Press).

Pitchford, S. (1995), 'Ethnic Tourism and Nationalism in Wales', *Annals of Tourism Research* 22, 35–52.

Schadler, K.-F. (1979), 'African Arts and Crafts in a World of Changing Values', in E. de Kadt (ed.) (1979), *Tourism: Passport to Development?: Perspectives on the Social and Cultural Effects of Tourism in Developing Countries* (Oxford University Press: New York, 146–156).

Smith, V. (ed.) (1977), *Hosts and Guests: The Anthropology of Tourism* (Philadelphia: University of Pennsylvania Press).

Teo, P. and Huang, S. (1995), 'Tourism and Heritage Conservation in Singapore', *Annals of Tourism Research* 22, 589–615.

Teo, P. and Yeoh, B. (1997), 'Remaking Local Heritage for Tourism', *Annals of Tourism Research* 24, 192–213.

Turner, L. and Ash, J. (1976), *The Golden Hordes* (London: Constable).

van den Berghe, P. (1995), 'Marketing Mayas: Ethnic Tourism Promotion in Mexico', *Annals of Tourism Research* 22, 568–588.

Watson, G.L. and Kopachevsky, J. (1994), 'Interpretations of Tourism as Commodity', *Annals of Tourism Research* 21, 649–660.

Wilson, D. (1997), 'Paradoxes of Tourism in Goa', *Annals of Tourism Research* 24, 52–75.

Zamora, M., Sutlive, V. and Altshuler, N. (eds.) (1978), *Tourism and Economic Change: Studies in Third World Societies* (Williamsburg: College of William and Mary Press).

Internet Documents

Deccan Herald (2006), 'In Search of Nirvana', April 16. http://www.deccanherald. com/deccanherald/apr162006/finearts1435252006413.asp

Fernandes, V. (2002), 'The Sundance Kid', February 4. http://www.rediff.com/ entertai/2002/feb/04birju.htm

Indo-Asian News Service (2005), 'Storm in Pushkar after Tourist Bathes Naked, 'October 23.http://www.latestcinema.com/tourism/Pushkar-tourist.html

Khaleej Times (2006), 'Is Tourist Destination being Dented?' 21 April. http:// www.khaleejtimes.com/DisplayArticle.asp?xfile=data/subcontinent/2006/April/ subcontinent_April796.xml&section=subcontinent&col=

Mahan, R. (2004), 'Record Turnout of Tourists at Pushkar',November 22. http:// ndtv.com/morenews/showmorestory.asp?id=64008

Newindpress (2005), 'Israeli Lovebirds Anger Priests in Pushkar', September 12. http://www.nuke.humanrightskerala.com/index.php?name=News&file=article&s id=6727

Outlook India, (2005), 'Israeli Couple Fined for Kissing in Pushkar Ghat', September 20. http://www.outlookindia.com/pti_news.asp?id=323964

Outlook India (2005), 'Finnish Woman, Held for Streaking, Asked Not to Leave Pushkar', October 25. http://www.outlookindia.com/pti_news.asp?id=331033

Outlook India (2005), 'Maintain Sanctity of Pushkar City: Foreigners Told', November 19. http://www.outlookindia.com/pti_news.asp?id=336194

Rao, H.S. (2005), '200,000 People Expected for This Year's Pushkar Fair', http:// www.outlookindia.com/pti_news.asp?id=327846

Todhunter, C. (2002), Pancake Overload from Chasing Rainbows in Chennai: The Madras Diaries, November. http://www.bootsnall.com/articles/04-11/pancake-overload-chennai-india.html

Zee News (2006), 'Pushkar to get a Makeover', April 25. http://www.zeenews.com/znnew/articles.asp?aid=290848&sid=REG

Part 4
Conclusions

Chapter 12

Composing the Raj Rhapsodies

Carol E. Henderson and Maxine Weisgrau

The processes of engagement in tourism produce diverse and sometimes confounding perspectives. These are informed by history, power relations, and contingency. All the case studies in this book have explored three intertwined themes: the production of images and discourse about tourism in Rajasthan; the processes of mediation of tourism; and the ramifying impacts of globalization.

Macrolevel processes in the production of a tourism economy or economic sector focused on the delivery of tourism products and services pull together expectation and history. We see in this a simplification of images of India in tourist discourse that profoundly contrasts with the multiple dimensions evident in local discourses about tourism and its linkages to political and social life.

The marketing of India, in the middle of the twentieth century, emphasized urban exotic locations such as the Taj Mahal, Delhi's Red Fort complex, and the great temples of south India. Rural locations were largely symbolized by Kashmir, but on European terms, touted as 'the Switzerland of India.' Kashmir also was depicted as repository of the most traditional cultural heritage often symbolized through its readily consumed crafts and textile production. As its infrastructure was beginning to expand to accommodate mass tourism, the political conflict here – along with several much-publicized kidnappings of tourists – caused both domestic and foreign travel to Kashmir to plummet.

New destinations within India have picked up the touristic imprimatur of 'rural' and 'traditional.' Rajasthan in particular provided new spaces that could effectively convey the images of a 'traditional' and 'old' India seamlessly embedded in rural life that provided a counterpoint to the urban destinations. These destinations, by the end of the twentieth century, were surrounded by high-rise office complexes, hotels, multi-lane highways, new suburbs, and industrial complexes, along with their accompanying congestion, noise and air pollution.

Rajasthan's reinvention of itself as a tourism destination drew on the production of travel narratives by elite British colonial guests of the princely rulers in the nineteenth century. This body of discourse established many of the images of Rajasthan that remain today as staples of tourism marketing. Although the tigers are nearly gone, the palaces remain to draw the tourists' gaze. Although princely rule has ended, the former royals enact hospitality, modelled on that of the old days. New guests today experience the attractions of 'Raj rhapsodies.' Here the tourism construction of Rajput history seduces. Outside the tourist's bubble of experience, however, these

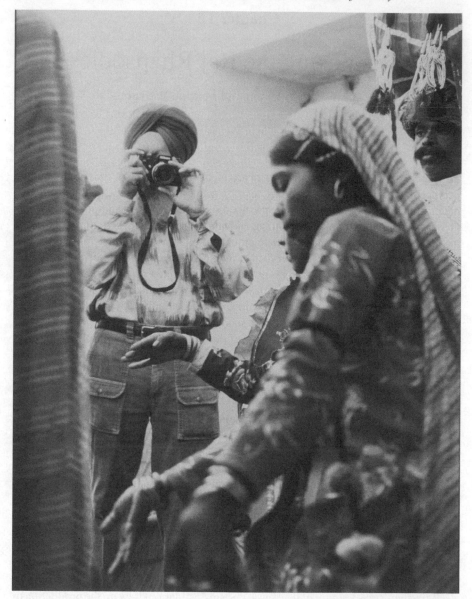

Figure 12.1   **Indian urbanites enthusiastically consume Rajasthan tourism spectacles alongside their European and American counterparts. These Kabelia dances were photographed at a *mela*, celebrating the anniversary of a Rajasthan-based company that uses traditional hand arts techniques to produce high-end clothing and textiles widely available in India and exported globally.**
Photo courtesy of Carol E. Henderson. All rights reserved

meanings are complex, layered with diverse understandings, and reflect ongoing transformative processes in the multiple societies and cultures of India.

There is a profoundly ironic aspect to the content of tourism discourse and tourism promotion for India, couched as it is in the language of the timeless, spiritual, colourful, and exotic that draws steadily increasing numbers of foreign tourists (projected by the Government of India's Ministry of Tourism to rise by over 16% in 2006 over 2005). The counter-narrative, well known to multinational corporations and business developers, and increasingly familiar to American and European consumers, is India's rapidly-expanding industrial economy. This today is rapidly providing an expanding and highly skilled, technologically sophisticated workforce servicing European and American corporations both in India and abroad.

This disjuncture between the simplified and apolitical tourism discourses that abounds in India in general and in Rajasthan in particular, contrasted with the local complexities of political, social, and economic conflicts embedded in tourism as contested forms of social capital, is a theme reiterated throughout this collection of essays. To account for this disjuncture, we refer in part to the idea of tourism as 'a highly mediated activity' (Chambers 2000, 30), and reiterate some of the many forms and processes of mediation referenced in the various articles in this collection.

Figure 12.2   A group of Rajasthani musicians, accompanying Indian dancers, on a government-sponsored exchange tour of the former Soviet Union in the mid-1980s. Today's touring groups are often sponsored by performance entrepreneurs in European and American venues. *Photo courtesy of Kuldeep Kothari. All rights reserved.*

On the geopolitical level, one of the major mediators of tourism experience to any destination is the global media. The way in which world events are portrayed, and the amount of space devoted to particular stories and events, profoundly impacts tourist decision-making. One example is the recent widespread coverage in the international media of a purported outbreak of plague in India; much less reported was the subsequent news that it was not plague at all, but an epidemic of flu, locally contained and quickly resolved.

Where a tourist goes within India, what he or she sees and doesn't see, is highly mediated by the transportation infrastructure. Air routes linking New Delhi, Jaipur, Udaipur, and Jodhpur historically created this route of mass tourism. Other destinations in India have fallen off the mass tourism radar screen because of the lack of the airline access. This means that for example Mount Abu, a former hill station (touted locally as 'the Kashmir of Rajasthan' because of its beautiful hills and lakes) that contains some of the most beautiful Jain temples in India, is rarely visited by foreign tourists today, even though it was a highly popular destination for British travellers in the nineteenth-century. Contemporary Raj Rhapsodies are rewritten to exclude in some cases colonial history, even that related to travel and tourism.

During her residence in Udaipur district, Weisgrau struggled with the poor roads, dangerously overcrowded and obsolete buses that travelled from Udaipur city to the villages of Gogunda Tehsil less than 50 kilometres (35 miles) away. These journeys via public transportation inevitably took over two hours. In contrast, the buses to tourist-oriented destinations were sleek, air conditioned, well maintained and operated on schedule. And tourists can always find local cars and drivers that will make these trips in comfort. The price for one round trip by private car to, for example, the temples at Ranakpur from Udaipur, far exceeds the monthly income of rural agriculturalists.

Another mediation, largely invisible to tourists, is the considerable investment in sanitation and water treatment by major hotels and by the government generally in regions surrounding tourist centres. In contrast to this concentration of state financed infrastructure, the small towns and villages becoming small towns, conspicuously and well known to municipal development planners, are still lacking in access to clean water and waste management. This situation, in a state whose intimacy with droughts and famines has been recorded historically since the Mughal period, if not earlier, further underscores the urgent necessities of water infrastructure development.

A related level of mediation is the distribution of benefits resulting from tourism to urban centres. The struggle over these benefits within destinations is documented in several chapters of this collection. Rural populations living on the outskirts of these urban centres have virtually no access to these benefits. Tourism discourse regards these individuals as costumed atmosphere producing 'extras' in this tourist drama on a par with the camels, sand dunes and thatched roof huts.

In India, one of the most influential of tourism mediators is the local tour guide, very often attached to groups of tourists by virtue of his or her connection with travel and hotel entrepreneurs. Freelance tour guides (in Rajasthan, generally men) are also a part of the scene at many of the sites described in this volume. Unlike other countries that train and license tour guides, there is no national or even statewide training and licensing of these mediators in India. In Rajasthan, these issues are at best a matter of local and often site specific discussion. On-site narratives therefore may reflect an idiosyncratic understanding of the destination, often constructed to appeal to the presumed interests of a particular constituency visiting the site. These narratives may be class- or caste-specific and may reflect local stereotypes of the presumed national origin of the tourist. The narratives may also reflect hegemonic visions of Indian history that draw in part on Orientalist or colonial historical narratives that have become entwined with local understandings of history.

Taking into account these forms of mediation provides an important counterpoint to the claims of tourists for why they travel to India. Inevitably these claims resonate with the nineteenth-century vision of the Grand Tour as part of an (upper class then, but now increasingly accessible to the middle classes of Europe and America) educational experience, to learn and understand the world and its people. What is learned, and how this process of understanding is mediated, therefore is a critical part of analysing the tourism encounter.

All the chapters in this volume touch on issues related to globalization. The earliest European travellers to Rajasthan detailed in this volume were part of the vanguard of processes implicated in the colonialist and imperialist project in South Asia. Colonial writers' focus on the imagined isolation of Rajasthan's princely states from the processes of modernity is contradicted by the historical evidence of famines, the spread of commodity production of crops such as wool, cotton and opium (in south Rajasthan), and the spread of peasant cultivation systems among former horticultural and pastoral groups. Remittance economies expanded with the recruitment of men into military units such as the Jodhpur Legion, which served in locations as far-flung as France in World War I. In other words, although the various princely states of Rajasthan looked like, and could be easily depicted as isolated, quaint and traditional, multitudinous processes of global interpenetration were afoot.

Recent travel and tourism in Rajasthan reflects the intensification of globalization. The financial networks for supporting tourism development today more than in the past reflects the role of international finance. Development planning focuses on physical infrastructure compatible with international expectations. Rajasthan's tourism increasingly is a vehicle for business and commercial travel. Rajasthanis involved in tourism at all levels, from high-level corporate executives to illiterate puppet masters, are more and more likely to have travelled abroad and to have experienced tourism encounters elsewhere.

Defining a tourist is becoming a complicated business as diverse identities and statuses cross-cut, proliferate, and interpenetrate with one another. Given the popularity of Rajasthan as a destination for scholars and college students in study abroad programs, as well as business and development related travellers, we see that being a tourist is a shifting and contingent state of mind. One can be a tourist, and one can be many other things at the same time. Similarly, destinations have multiple identities; each of these constituents stakes out a particular version of Rajasthan to explore, and to exploit. These multiple identities and the idioms in which they are couched are the contemporary manifestations of the on-going and never-ending composition of the powerful 'rhapsodies' of tourism in Rajasthan.

Reference

Chambers, E. (2000), *Native Tours: The Anthropology of Travel and Tourism* (Prospect Heights, Ill.: Waveland Press).

Index